CONTENTS

CONGREGATION

COMMUNITY

CULTURE

Babylonian Talmud, Ta'anit 23a

INTRODUCTION

"The rich have ancestors. The poor have grandparents."

In 2011, our shul began a year-long celebration of its centennial year. From September of that year, until December of 2012, we organized a series of events to recognize Newton's oldest synagogue and to celebrate our community's role in Newton's history. I planned to write a small commemorative booklet about the synagogue's history to serve as a souvenir of its centennial. When I began to work on the booklet, I realized there was almost no source of information about the founding of the congregation, its early years, its membership, its activities. If I did not try to compile the historical record, in a few short years the synagogue might simply be an old building, an historic building with no history.

My goal is to provide a written history where none existed. As a granddaughter of one of the founders of the synagogue, I have known many of the founding families as well as local community members. If the synagogue's historical record, along with its members' memories, is not written down, in time all will be forgotten and lost. I want this book to give life to people who are long dead. Their contributions might have been small and local, but they were essential to the life and health of the community. It's not just the rich and famous who are deserving of recognition and remembrance.

Today there are over twenty synagogues in Newton and every one of them has been built on the shoulders of the Adams Street Shul and its pioneering families who built and maintained the shul and enabled it to continue to serve the community for over one hundred and five years.

Beryl Gilfix
September 2017, Newton MA

ACKNOWLEDGEMENTS

This book turned out to require more extensive research than I had anticipated to locate all available resources regarding the synagogue and the community. I have done my best to seek out and to interview every family I could locate. Descendants of some of the families cannot be located. If anyone has information and/or photographs to contribute, please contact me (AdamsStreetFirstHundredYears@gmail.com) so that your information can be included in future editions.

I thank every person who shared their memories and photographs and enabled this book to reflect the community which built the synagogue and the Jewish community in Newton. Thank you to Sandra Berman for her efforts in editing this book. Thank you to Jean Schribman Birnbaum for sharing her invaluable research and interviews with Philip Bram, Louis Fried, Isaac Gilfix, Philip Gilfix, Nate Goodman, the Greenwald sisters, Rose Gilfix Schribman and Ike Silverman. Thank you to Diane Lurie Berg for her contributions regarding the Hungarian community in Newton. Thank you to Zhanna Cantor for her recording of several interviews, including those with Saul Aronow, Norma Fried Lurie and Diane Lurie Berg, Bert Grand, Mark Needleman, Eric Roiter, and Harry Standel. Thank you to Carol Clingan and Jewish Genealogical Society of Greater Boston for making her monumental work listing every synagogue in MA available to me. Thank you to Brenda Gilfix Foner for information on Gilfix family geography in Ukraine. Thank you to Jonathan Frieze for locating the memoir by his cousin Minnie Baker Gerson. Thank you to Steven Gilfix for photographs. Thank you to attorney Jeremy Poock for hours of work reading old mortgages and deeds. Thank you to Eric Roiter for sharing his aunt Sylvia Cohen Spitzer's memoir with me. Thank you to Dr. Gerald N. Shapiro for his invaluable suggestions about the organization of the book. Thank you to Historic Newton, previously known as the Jackson Homestead, for sharing their archives and resources. The interviews they conducted with Newton Jewish residents in the 1980's included interviews with Elliot Gilfix, the Greenwald sisters, Betty and Barbara Hoffman, Rose and Lewis Silverman and Jane Shriberg.

THE CITY OF NEWTON

An exploration of the history of Newton's Jewish community and the Adams Street Shul begins with the City of Newton itself. Newton drew people who worked in Boston and returned at the end of the day, using the railroad which reached the city in 1834. The commuter rail continues to run along the same Washington Street route that ran from Boston to Worcester in its earliest days. (The word "commuter" derived from the fact that riders who used the railroad frequently paid a reduced or "commuted" fare). In the early twentieth century, a trolley line went down Watertown Street, Nonantum's main street, into Newton Corner and then into Boston.

Even as late as 1885 the town still had a country atmosphere, with open space and farms, but also opportunities for employment for new immigrants as well. In the late 19th century Nonantum was still mostly farmland. Try to imagine Crafts Street and California Street as "picturesque country lanes!"

The city census of 1885 recorded the population of Newton at 19,759. There were a total of 190 black residents in Newton, most of whom did not live in Nonantum but lived in West Newton near their church, Myrtle Baptist Church. There were 31 churches but no synagogue. There were five Italians and one Chinese male. The census also counted 114 French Canadians, two people from Poland and one from Russia. There were 5,400 foreign born residents, (mostly from the British Isles) and 14,265 native born residents. The population grew to about 28,000 in 1895, to 33,587 in 1900, to 40,000 in 1910, to 53,000 in 1930 and today is about 85,000. [1]

NONANTUM, WHERE IT ALL BEGAN

Nonantum is one of Newton's thirteen villages. The word Nonantum means "blessing" or "prayer" in the Algonquian language [2] . The village of Nonantum was originally the site of the settlement of the Nonantum "Praying Indians," a group belonging to the Massachusetts tribe of the Algonquian nation. The villages of Praying Indians were established to separate newly Christianized Indians from their non-Christian relatives as well as separating them from white settlers. Reverend John Eliot, called the Apostle to the Indians, preached to the Indians in Newton in the seventeenth century and translated the Bible into the Algonquian language. This community, established by Eliot in 1647, moved to Natick in 1651.

Nonantum is the village in Newton with the most distinct character. It has its own rich history, varied religious and ethnic groups, housing patterns, social activities, economic opportunities and personal stories. Nonantum has been and remains the gateway neighborhood for new immigrants to our city. It has been and remains the most densely populated village, with a population today of about 4000. Its nickname, "the Lake," derives from Silver Lake which was located on Watertown Street. The Lake existed until the late 1930s when it was mostly filled in except for a small marshy body at the back of a large parking lot. It was a favorite recreation spot for the community, providing swimming and ice skating for the residents. Nonantum was also an important location of industry in Newton, using the water power of the Charles River.

Nonantum was the soil in which the Jewish community was planted. It flourished and continued to grow and change with the village itself. The village was as much a part of our synagogue's history as the brick and mortar building and the membership. To understand the Jewish community of Newton today, you need to know what that location meant to its development.

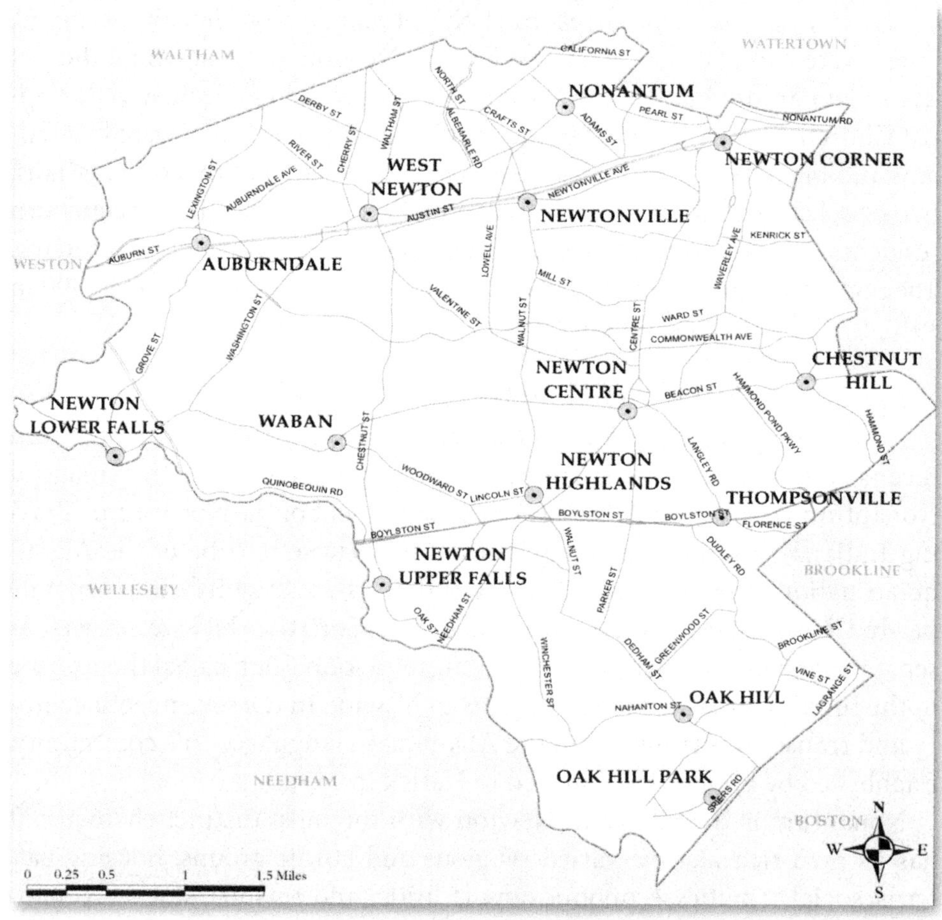

Map of Newton's villages

A community may share geography, socio-economic facts, ethnic and religious facts. Boundaries can define and create community but the boundaries are not necessarily physical. [3] A larger community may contain smaller units within it. This community is made up of subgroups which met in the marketplace, on the streets and playgrounds and in the public schools. It was and is the diversity of The Lake that made it a safe haven for the immigrants who moved here. It has been and is home to different religions and ethnic groups. In 1889 the major population groups in Nonantum were French Canadian, Irish and English. At that time, the Italians and Jews did not even rate a mention. Nonantum was the most populated village in Newton with a population of about 3000. The Irish residents were more established and built housing on streets like Quirk Court and Maguire Court. At that time, many of the immigrant residents were single men who came to Newton to work in the mills or as laborers who planned to return to Europe when they had saved some money.

The mills, some of which can still be seen on Bridge Street and Pleasant Street in Watertown, used the water power supplied by the Charles River. The mills and factories provided jobs for the new immigrants who settled in the small four room houses that lined the unpaved streets of Nonantum. These houses are a unique style of architecture that is rarely found elsewhere in the city. The houses had two rooms on the first floor, a kitchen and a room that served as living room and dining room. Upstairs were two bedrooms.

Local institutions and businesses grew up to serve successive waves of immigrants. The first wave of non-English immigrants were the Irish, who founded Our Lady Help of Christians Church in 1873; then the French, who founded Lafayette Hall around the turn of the twentieth century, which became St. Jean L'Evangeliste Church in 1911; then the Italians and finally the Jewish immigrants who arrived around the turn of the century and whose synagogue opened in 1912. They were separate groups who lived literally side by side but who worshiped separately and shopped in stores owned by people of their own ethnicity. Over time, these stores and institutions changed as new immigrants arrived. In 1901, there were forty churches in Newton but no synagogue.

The French Canadians and the Irish did not socialize. The Irish did not mingle with the other ethnic groups at that time, partly because many other immigrants did not speak English. At that time, the trolley ran down Watertown Street. The French and Irish lived literally on the opposite sides of the tracks, the French on Dalby Street and that side of Watertown Street, and the Irish off Adams Street and West Street on the other side of Watertown Street.

The French Canadians played an important role in Nonantum for many years. For nearly one hundred years, Dalby Street was the focus of French Canadian life in Newton. Lafayette Hall served as a community center for the neighbors who clustered on Dalby Street, Chapel Street and Faxon Street. The Jewish community used to rent Lafayette Hall for religious services on the High Holy Days when they did not have a building of their own. In 1911, the French community created St. Jean L'Evangeliste and Lafayette Hall was now a church as well as a community center. There were more than 200 French speaking families in the church at the time. In 1960, this group built a new church on Watertown Street and until 1967 services were conducted in French and Latin. The community ran a French speaking parochial school at 251 Watertown Street until 1982. The congregation was absorbed into Our Lady's in 1997 and the church was torn down and replaced with condominiums.

There was a certain amount of animosity between the Irish and the Italians. The two groups competed for the same unskilled or semi-skilled work. There was a language barrier. There was a certain amount of religious friction as well. The Italians considered that the Irish form of worship was much too formal and restrained, unlike the more spirited services they were accustomed to. In those early years, the Catholic church was dominated by Irish priests. At Our Lady Help of Christians Church, the Irish parishioners worshiped in the main sanctuary with the Italians literally downstairs in the basement. That changed in 1932 when the Boston Archdiocese sent Father James Fahey to the parish. Father Fahey spoke Italian, having spent five years in Rome as a student. He gave sermons in Italian and heard confessions in Italian. It was said that he spoke "better" Italian than many of the local Italian population, who spoke a dialect of Italian.

The Jewish community began arriving in the middle 1890's. There were about forty families in the early years. There was no unique Jewish neighborhood, as there was as yet no synagogue. It is possible that the impetus in the Jewish community for building a synagogue was when Lafayette Hall became a church and was no longer available to them for services on major holidays. A private home on Dalby Street also served as a synagogue for a few years.

By World War II, the Jewish and French Canadian families were no longer dominant in Nonantum.

The community had several schools. The grades each school served were recalled by residents who had attended those schools. The Adams School was located on the corner of Watertown Street and Bridge Street and included kindergarten through the second grade. The Elliot School was a wooden building on Pearl Street. It housed grades one through four. The Lincoln School was located on Thornton Street and served grades one through six. The Lincoln and Elliot Schools were later merged into a new brick building located geographically between the two schools. Horace Mann, located on Watertown Street as well, held third through eighth grades. The Stearns School on Jasset Street was a wooden building located on land given to the city by the Stearns family for a school and served kindergarten through sixth grade.

From about the 1920's until the middle 1990's the residents in the Lake were predominantly Italian. But earlier, the numbers tell a different story. In the city census of 1885, there are only five Italians listed in Newton and in 1895 only 134 Italians. The population of Italians increased slowly and steadily but it was a long time before they became a major presence. The first Italian business was listed in Newton in 1895. It was called Biscotti's Confectionery on Watertown Street. In 1905, there were only 150-200 Italians in Nonantum. Out of a population of about 4000 in 1910 in Nonantum, there were only 300 Italians, but 524 French speakers and 158 Jews. In 1920 there were about 700 Italians. In 1970 the city census showed that 64 % of the population of Nonantum was Italian. The heavily Italian population and the presence of a widely spoken Italian dialect was completely different from the rest of the city and many non-residents considered the neighborhood, with its immigrants, small houses and small house lots, to be a "slum." By 1990, the Italian population was only 39%. The Italian population of today's Nonantum is approximately 25-30% and shrinking, due primarily to the high cost of housing.

The Language of the Lake

This article was published in the Boston Globe September 13, 2001

By Erica Noonan, Globe Staff

NEWTON — It's a sunny morning in the heart of The Lake, and Anthony "Fat" Pellegrini is standing on Watertown Street, ready for business. He's armed with hand-written fundraising lists and an old cigar box, and ready to remind pals and passersby – largely one and the same – of their civic responsibilities.

These folks don't actually need any reminding; they have already pulled wads of bills from their pockets for Fat, who will use the cash to buy flowers for the wake of a local woman at Magni Funeral Home and fruit baskets for several hospitalized locals.

Most people here see Fat as the unofficial mayor of this village, nicknamed for now-vanished Silver Lake. Fat is one of the few who still remember the old Bottle Alley, named for its Prohibition-era misdeeds, the stables that once housed draft horses, and his own youth spent running numbers between barrooms along this same sidewalk.

"Hey, mush!" he calls out to greet his fellow Lake old-timers, in a special lingo used by generations of Nonantum natives, many of whom, like the 76-year-old Fat, can trace their heritage to the turn of the century when their ancestors emigrated from San Donato, Italy, to Newton.

The mark of a true, old-school Lake resident is talent for the so-called Lake language - a collection of words and phrases believed to have roots in Romany, a language spoken by Gypsy immigrants from Europe, and brought back to the Lake early this century by local youths who worked for a time with traveling carnivals.

The Romany words mixed with Italian, English, and other street slang of the 1930s and '40s to produce a lively mix that is one of the strongest links to the Lake's proud and rough-and-tumble past.

Language experts say it is not uncommon for mini-dialects to crop up in tightknit communities like Nonantum, which has held tight to its cultural identity, while other villages in Newton changed and diversified.

"Language varies by a number of factors, including region, geography, and social factors, and educational levels, and it thrives under certain kinds of isolation," said Joe Pickett, executive editor of Houghton Mifflin's American Heritage Dictionary. "People have always used language to assert their identity."

Street Speak

You don't have to be a lifelong Laker or of Italian descent to speak the lingo, Fat says, but it doesn't hurt. It's an expressive, no-nonsense language of the street, spoken mostly among close male friends to communicate camaraderie, or to say things that could not be said openly or politely - warnings of a stranger in the neighborhood, an approaching police officer, or a beautiful woman coming down the street. Meaning comes not just from the word, but tone of voice, body language, facial expression, and social status of speaker and listener.

Like teenagers in all cultures, the young men of the Lake embraced a language that allowed them to talk to one another privately in words outsiders could not understand, said Allan Metcalf, author of "How We Talk: American Regional English Today."

"People use words because they find them useful. If you dress in a way that is streetwise and tough, you have a verbal image as well as a physical image," he said. "You want to be one of the guys, you dress like one of the guys and talk like one of the guys."

"Quister jival [Quis-tah jiv-il]," explained Fat. "That means `pretty girl.' " Lake lingo also has other phrases that comment specifically on a woman's physique.

Mush, pronounced moosh, means guy. Sometimes friend, sometimes foe, depending on tone of voice. A divia mush [di-vy-ah moosh] is a crazy guy, while a quister mush is a good, stand-up guy.

Lake language - which is phonetic with no official spellings - is most often mixed with English words to make its meaning clear. For example, "How can you oy [eat] that inga [junk, crap]?" or "This mush is divia" [this guy is crazy] or "That mush has some overshay" [he lies, tells untruths, pronounced ovah-shay].

The lingo comes in particularly handy when a speaker wants to warn a companion about impending trouble, according to a guide written by retired Newton Police Sergeant Charles Kennedy, a Lake native.

Kennedy was on patrol with another local-born officer when his partner barked, "Sarge, mush has a coramunga in his cover!" or, loosely translated, "That guy is carrying a gun!" (Kennedy later confiscated a .45 revolver from the interloper.)

Many of the words seem to have clear roots Italian and Romany.

Such words as "jivial," or young girl, bears a resemblance to "gioventa," the Italian word for young person. "Divia," Lake language for crazy, could come from the Italian word "divila," meaning devilish. "Chabby," which means young boy among Lakers, could be descended from "chavvie," the Romany word for boy. Likewise, the word "chor'd," which means stolen, bears a striking resemblance to "choro," the Romany word for thief. Other Lake words bear no obvious resemblance to either language, leaving unanswered questions about where they come from.

Locals don't care so much about where Lake lingo comes from, they are much more interested in how it has helped bond Lake residents together long after they have left the neighborhood.

Legends abound of Lakers who reconnected with old friends and neighbors after catching a word or phrase of the language as far away as Asia.

"If you hear it, you know that someone is from the area," said Robert Pupa, a Lake native now living in Hudson. Pupa recalled once getting annoyed with a coworker, and muttering "Cuya moi" [pronounced coo-ya moy, meaning shut up, or go to hell] under his breath.

"The guy turns to me and says, `I didn't know you were from The Lake.' We were best friends after that," said Pupa. "It's a language from no place else."

Local talk show host Jackie Morrissey said that one of the most famous stories is of a young infantryman from the Lake, Joseph Rousseau, who was serving with the Marine Corps in Korea. Rousseau lay badly injured on a train returning from battle at the Chosin Reservoir, when he heard an MP in a nearby car yelling in frustration, "All you divias sit down! Sit down you divias!"

"He was lying there, dying, and all of a sudden he hears Spike Aikens shouting and coming through the car, and Joe realized it was someone from home. Joe started to yell out Lake talk and Spike came over. Joe said it gave him the will to live. He said he'd given up a little bit."

But most of the time, the language is just for kibbitizing among the guys.

"You talk the Lake language and only people from there can understand you," said state Auditor Joe DeNucci, who grew up in the Lake during the 1950s, and now lives in West Newton. "An awful lot of what it means is how you say it and how you use it. You improvise a lot, mixing it with carnival talk and bebop."

"Mush is the earie," said DeNucci. "That means, 'The guy is listening.'"

End of an Era

As they watch The Lake enter the 21st century, Pellegrini and his friends readily admit that they have at least one foot planted in another era.

Most of them are children of non-English-speaking Italian immigrants, survivors of the Great Depression and veterans of World War II who came of age long before the world had heard of personal computers, equal opportunity, or political correctness.

They are amazed by skyrocketing real estate prices and infuriated by assumptions that Newton is a city full of wealthy yuppies. They lament how many young people leave The Lake because they cannot afford to buy a home.

Pellegrini worries the Lake lingo and the neighborhood's iron-clad ethos - that people stick together and help each other out in need - will die when he and his friends do.

For now, though, it appears at least the Lake language is alive and well. Fat's granddaughter, 11-year-old Siobhan Anderson, said she even uses some of the Lake words with her pals from Lincoln-Eliot Elementary School. Siobhan said she knows the new kids she will encounter at Bigelow Middle School may not be down with the lingo. "They'll be, like, `What?,' " she said. "Sometimes you have to explain."

The population of Nonantum was relatively stable, but with the dominant ethnic group changing over time. Irish and French residents in the neighborhood were replaced by Italians and there was an influx of Jewish immigrants. The pattern of Irish and Italian men coming to the United States by themselves and without their families held true until the start of World War I and World War II. When travel resumed after the wars, the men had acclimated to America and were less likely to return to Europe to stay, although they often returned to Europe for brides.

The heart of the Greater Boston Jewish community in the early 20th century was located in the North End, and then in the West End and South End. Newton's Jewish housewives would take the streetcar which ran down Watertown Street to those areas of Boston to buy kosher meat and kosher bread which was baked in a bakery that used no lard. Jewish owned shops in Nonantum sold fresh fruit and vegetables and packaged goods as well. Local Jewish businesses ran delivery services which brought goods and purchases from Boston to Newton on Saturday nights after the Sabbath was over.

From about 1895 to the middle 1930's, almost the entire length of the business district of Watertown Street, from Bridge Street to Faxon Court, was composed of Jewish businesses. The oldest of these businesses, Swartz Hardware, was established on Watertown Street in 1890 and is one of the oldest businesses in Newton. Another business which survived into the 21st century is Fox Pharmacy, which was established by a Jewish pharmacist. The Nonantum Spa was a small Italian restaurant that served the local population, owned and operated by the Jewish Pass family. Where Antoine's Pastry is located today was the home of Fried's Department Store, which advertised itself as Newton's oldest department store. There was Perry's Department Store, Perlmutter's Department Store and the Nonantum Furniture Company, which sold everything from baby strollers to chairs and tables. The phrase "department store" was a label used by the shop owners to indicate to the public how modern they were. They were not really department stores, as they did not sell everything but mostly what was called "dry goods," clothing and household linens. These were the larger businesses; there were Jewish shoemakers, grocers and tailors as well.

In 1900, there were three Chinese laundries on Watertown Street. In 1911, there were 17 Chinese laundries in Newton and two of them were located on Watertown Street. In the years before home washing machines, people would make every effort to send large items, like sheets and towels, to a Chinese laundry. Doing these items at home by hand was extremely difficult and even working class families would sacrifice to use the services of a Chinese laundry. The Asian population of Newton was historically rather small. Chinese laundrymen were not married as immigration by Chinese women was illegal until 1965. That population has grown. In 1990, there were 416 Asians in Newton and in 2002, there were 10,000 (including South Asians), about 10% of the population.

In 1905, Watertown Street had Italian food stores, Jewish dry goods stores, a Chinese laundry, an Irish barber shop and French dry goods stores. Negrotti's fruit store was at 321 Watertown Street. Mr. Negrotti's grandson, John Negrotti, is the proprietor of Silver Lake Liquors on Watertown Street today, carrying on a family tradition of business on Watertown Street for over one hundred years. Samuel Bram, the blacksmith, had a shop on Watertown Street. Many of the Jewish businesses at this time were tailors and shoemakers or shoe repairers. Off Watertown Street, on West Street, there were six Jewish junk dealers and a Jewish tailor. The French community was served by three grocers. Vachon the barber shared space with Mme Doucette, a milliner. Flaherty's billiard parlor was located at 357 Watertown Street. Billiards parlors, also called pool parlors or pool halls, were considered low class and some people considered them to be sinful places filled with beer drinking men, hanging around when they should have been working. But they served as informal social clubs for the working men of the community, who may have preferred the atmosphere at the pool hall to the church. Homes were small and crowded, and workmen often had single rooms in rooming houses with no space for entertaining or socializing.

The Italian community, no longer the completely dominant group they were forty years ago, continues to sponsor a variety of programs and institutions. This includes the Italian tri-colored stripe down the middle of Adams Street as well as tri-colored fire hydrants. The St. Mary of Carmen Society sponsors a major street fair every summer in the neighborhood and a public Christmas program in December. For many years, the neighborhood held its own Memorial Day Parade in competition with the official city parade.

One site of historic importance was the Stearns School, on Jasset Street, off Faxon Street. The Stearns School, built in 1908, was of tremendous value to the immigrant community, first as an educational force. It also housed the local branch of the library and was the first school-sponsored community center in the United States, providing evening classes in English and in citizenship and health care as well as summer recreation programs, which were very important in a crowded community like the Lake. Old timers remembered swimming and fishing in the Charles River.

Anthony "Fat" Pellegrini

No discussion of Nonantum would be complete without a mention of Anthony "Fat" Pellegrini, the unofficial mayor of Nonantum until his death in 2004. Fat raised money to provide charitable and social services for the community, including an annual children's Christmas party and the senior citizens cookout. He was responsible for the alternate Memorial Day Parade in Nonantum. He made sure that the city established and maintained appropriate memorials to Newton's war dead.

He was also involved in the synagogue, meeting regularly with Elmer Lippin, the long time caretaker of the synagogue, to discuss items of mutual interest. Fat considered himself an honorary member of the synagogue and was invited to serve on a committee to maintain the building. The synagogue benefited from the symbolic and material good will from the community. Fat donated money to the synagogue and mobilized local Catholic contractors and landscapers to donate their services to the synagogue and also called on the neighborhood to protect the building against vandalism and anti-Semitism. Community activists took great pride in the protection that they provided and in Mr. Lippin's public appreciation of their support.

CONGREGATION

ONE COMMUNITY, TWO CONGREGATIONS

The years 1909 to 1912 were years of growing determination in Newton's small Jewish community to secure a permanent home for the increasing numbers of Jewish families moving into Nonantum. Earlier, religious services were conducted in the homes of members of the community and space was rented in local facilities for the High Holy Days. Among the spaces they rented were Lafayette Hall on Dalby Street and a Masonic building on Washington Street in Newtonville. Despite the fact that the community was very small, numbering fewer than one hundred families, two separate groups (Keneses Israel Anshe Sephard and Congregation Agudas Achim Anshei Sfard) petitioned the Massachusetts Secretary of State's Office for charters to establish Orthodox synagogues.

At the start of this project, this author did not know of any congregation besides the Adams Street Shul. Except for a brief mention in a local history booklet, the existence of any other congregation had been forgotten. I have reconstructed the history of this early congregation from deeds and mortgages located in the Middlesex County Registry of Deeds.

The earlier congregation was called Keneses Israel Anshe Sfard. One member of the community, Louis Fried, told an interviewer some details about the congregation. "We didn't belong [to the Adams Street Shul]; we had two shuls at the time. The Sephards were the Russians, and we were the Ashkenazis, like the German Jews." The Russian born peddlers were more religiously observant than the Hungarians whose stores were open on the Sabbath. (The peddlers often chose that profession because it allowed them to refrain from working on the Sabbath). We do not know why that congregation, founded by the leading business owners of the Jewish community, failed, and why the congregation founded by the junk dealers was a success.

The elaborate official names of the two congregations were rarely used (Keneses Israel Anshe Sephard and Congregation Agudas Achim Anshei Sfard). In the immigrant communities, "street-centric" synagogue nomenclature resulted in the congregations being referred to by their street addresses, thus "the Dalby Street Shul" and the "Adams Street Shul." The Hasidic religious influence was very strong in both congregations and both used Anshe/anshei Sfard in naming their congregations.

"The references to Anshe/Anshei Sfard in the names of both synagogues do not refer to Sephardic Jews or Spain, but rather to the style of prayer used by Hasidic Jews who were attracted to the mysticism of Sephardic Jews. As a result, the prayer books used by Hasidim came to be known as nusach sephard (Sephardic version) while the prayer text of real Sephardim (from

Spain and North Africa) is commonly referred to as nusach sephardi (prayer version of Sephardic Jews). The prayer book used by most American congregations is referred to as "nusach Ashkenaz."[5]

KENESES ISRAEL ANSHE SEPHARD

On April 14, 1909, a congregation was incorporated under the name Keneses Israel Anshe Sephard. The spelling of the name had several variations. Keneses, Kenases, Koeneses, Conaseo are all variations on the Hebrew word "Knesset," which means gathering or assembly. (The K in Knesset is pronounced, not silent). They never used the English term "congregation" in their name.

When they incorporated in 1909, Keneses Isarael Anshe Sephard did not own land or a building. The only records that remain from Keneses Israel Anshe Sfard are deeds and mortgages. Morris Fried's name, first in the list of incorporators of the synagogue, and his involvement in every real estate transaction on behalf of the synagogue, indicates that he was the leader of that group from its inception to its demise.

The incorporating address at 308 Watertown Street was the office of Reuben Forknall, a local non-Jewish insurance agent and justice of the peace. Born in England, Forknall provided the immigrants of Nonantum with some legal assistance. Forknall also signed several deeds written by the congregation between 1909 and 1920.

All of the incorporators of this congregation owned their own businesses, which were located on the main shopping street, Watertown Street. The Perlmutters, Frieds and Perrys were of Hungarian origin. They were Morris Fried, William Perlmutter, Maurice Perlmutter, Reuben Slesinger, Morris Pactovis, Abe Goodman (the lone non-Hungarian), Sam Swartz, Herman Perlmutter and Charles James. Fried had a dry goods store, the Perlmutters had a men's clothing store, Slesinger and Pactovis were listed as "boots and shoes" in the city directory, which might mean they repaired and/or sold boots and shoes. Goodman was a shoemaker. The Newton city directory had no listing for Sam Swartz or Charles James. They might have lived in the adjacent community of Watertown. By the end of 1909, Pactovis was no longer listed in the directory and Herman Perlmutter had moved to Charlestown.

Respondent Ruth Pass recalled that the congregation used to meet in her house at 329 or 331 Watertown Street, on the corner of Chapel Street. She also remembered that they met in Lafayette Hall and then in the house at 97 Dalby Street.

In May 1910, the trustees of Koeneses Israel Anshe Sephard purchased a plot of land for the benefit of their planned synagogue. The land was purchased "in consideration of the sum of one dollar and other valuable considerations." Every deed regarding the synagogues contains that phrase, making it impossible to know how much money changed hands for any transaction. The land in this case was located on Watertown Street in a block of four lots bounded by Watertown Street, Hawthorne Street and Barrieau Court. The purchasers of the land, Reuben Slesinger, Julius Pass and Abraham Shrier, described themselves as being "trustees of a religious corporation organized under the laws of the Commonwealth of Massachusetts." The employment patterns of the purchasers was in contrast to the incorporators. Two of the three trustees were not original incorporators of that congregation and Pass and Shrier were junk dealers.

In May 1911 Morris Fried purchased a four room house at 97 Dalby Street. Acting on behalf of Kenases Israel Anshe Sevard, he applied for a building permit to add a room, 15 feet by 16 feet. The addition, described in the permit as a "church," was located at the back of the building, and it would function as the synagogue. The property was sold in 1914 and purchased in 1917 by the family of Samuel Swartz.

In April 1920, trustees Pass, Slesinger and Shrier wrote a deed "to perfect and confirm the legal title of land called Lot #40," the piece of land on Watertown Street that had originally been intended for a synagogue. The purpose of the transaction was to confirm that the synagogue had sold the land to Morris Fried, who may have used his own money to acquire the property on Watertown Street and that is why the land was deeded over to him.

All the relevant deeds, mortgages, etc., related to this congregation can be found in the Appendix.

CONGREGATION AGUDAS ACHIM ANSHEI SFARD

On July 6, 1911, Congregation Agudas Achim Anshei Sfard applied for a charter, which was approved on July 16. The official charter was granted on October 6, 1911 by the Commonwealth of Massachusetts. The incorporators were Benjamin Gilfix, president, and Jacob Swartz, Treasurer. The other incorporators were Joseph Mielman, Clerk, Joseph Roiter, Jacob Kligman, Morris Gilfix and Hyman Mielman. The official address of the congregation was Benjamin Gilfix's home at 93 West Street. Of the seven incorporators of the Adams Street Shul, six were junk dealers. The seventh, Jacob Swartz, owned a hardware store on the main street. This charter is the foundation document of the synagogue which survives and functions as a synagogue to this day.

The Jewish immigrants in Newton were not simple pious Jews, praying and struggling to make a living, paying little attention to the world around them. In Newton they included many whom we would today call real estate speculators, trading pieces of land back and forth "for one dollar and other considerations," both for the synagogues and for their own benefit. They understood the real estate laws and had formal deeds drawn up and recorded, using Jewish and non-Jewish notaries public and justices of the peace to witness their transactions. Many of them owned businesses in the neighborhood. Being a junk peddler tells us nothing about the education or business skills of the individuals, but it tells us about the choices they made in choosing a way to earn a living.

Koneses Israel Anshe Sephard ultimately dissolved when Agudas Achim Anshe Sfard was built in 1912. Donations to the Adams Street building fund came from families like Pass, Shrier and Canter, previously trustees of the earlier synagogue, and now to be found in the donor lists of Agudas Achim Anshei Sfard.

FOUNDING FATHERS

Here are portraits of four of the seven incorporators of the Adams Street Shul. If you have photos of the missing members of the group, please notify the author so their photos can be included in subsequent editions of the book.

Benjamin Gilfix *Morris Gilfix* *Joseph Roiter* *Jacob Swartz*
Missing: Joseph Mielman, Hyman Mielman, Jacob Kligman

Notes on the original fundraising letter

When people wanted to raise money for a synagogue, they wrote a prospectus to describe their plans. At that time, the fundraisers would also indicate that their endeavor had the support of local religious leaders.

On the following pages is the founding document for the Adams Street Synagogue. We do not know who composed this document but the language suggests a well-educated, Americanized member of the community, perhaps Charles Gilfix, Harvard College Class of 1913.

The fundraising letter is written in English, which is surprising since all the members of the congregation would have been fluent in Yiddish. This use of English indicates that the fundraisers were appealing to an audience beyond the confines of the immediate neighborhood and hoped perhaps to appeal to non-Jews as well. (There are in fact donations from non-Jews). Approval of the fundraising effort by two local prominent rabbis was included in English and appended to the fundraising letter, for the benefit of those who could not read Yiddish. The note states that Rabbi Friederman also wrote a letter of support which has not survived.

There are several interesting things to note about the document.

The use of the word "Hebrews." This was a term favored by those philo-Semitic Yankees who thought it more "genteel" than the word "Jew," which at that time was often used pejoratively. And it associated the Jews with the Bible, which was thought to honor the descendents of the Bible. It was never used by Jews to describe themselves.

"That their children receive the same religious training that their fathers had received in better circumstances and perhaps more congenial surroundings." Czarist Russia could never have been considered "more congenial surroundings" than Newton, Massachusetts.

"Philosophy teaches us...." The use of the word philosophy" is foreign to Jewish thought at this time. Members of the community would have used the word "religion."

Use of the word "temple." The use of the word "temple" to describe a Jewish house of worship at that time was used only by Reform Jewish congregations.

The "unity of God" and "the hallowed dominion of the brotherhood of Man." These are phrases which are entirely foreign to the religious members of the community, but would likely have been acquired in public school or university.

A copy of the original document is located in the Appendix.

Original fundraising book [original in English]

Whereas, the Almighty has endowed the said Hebrews of Newton with greater zeal and religious favor than worldly goods, and

Whereas, what little could be spared by individual members of the faith, has been dedicated to the founding of a Jewish Synagogue and Talmud Torah (Sabbath School), it has been

Resolved, by the members of the congregation Agudas Achim of Newton, Mass, to make known to their friends and wellwishers, their aims and aspirations.

Ever since the Hebrews first began to settle in this community, some fifteen years ago, their potency as a religious factor has been smothered by the fact that lack of means and accommodations necessitated extremely hardy measures to be adopted. Their inherent nature and nurture demanded that the Sabbath continue to be observed and that their children receive the same religious training that their fathers had received in better circumstances and perhaps more congenial surroundings. To this end, according to the Mosaic Law, religious meetings were conducted every Sabbath day and other Holy days, despite the antagonistic means and surroundings. Now here, now there, the members of the Congregation, yet without a central place of worship, contributing occasionally by the services of their houses, for religious uses.

Discouraging as such shifting methods of worship were, there was nevertheless enshrouded in this a blessing in disguise. Philosophy teaches us that the world progresses truly only after the endurance of a pain economy. That is, the burden of trials and tribulations, however weighty, are thus essentials which lead to the ultimate increase of human happiness. Thus it was with these few Hebrew endeavors. Lacking in religious atmosphere, and immediate prospects very dim, they only hoped and prayed for the time when a temple would stand in their midst that might take its place among others as a token of real reverence to the Almighty, who is One.

After all these years, under the constant leadership of their guiding spirit, a mighty effort was made and the blossom of their hope began to bear fruit. Immediate plans to for the erection of a synagogue were drawn up, even before it was known whence the funds for their purpose were to come. Disregarding this, the work was pushed, all gave what might be easily spared without detriment to the welfare of their families, and soon the realization of their highest aims was a fact. Attesting to this, there now stands in our midst, a House of Worship, simple and unostentatious though it be, a monument to those whose highest hopes and aspirations made the desire father to the fact.

Our message to our friends, well-wishers, benefactors, and all others interested is one of faith in mankind. We feel that you all as members of organized religion

and society and everyone [who] believes in the Unity of God, will do all in your power to assist a movement of this kind, that it may not fail of its ultimate success. Your beneficence will remain as a beacon-light to posterity, a veritable tower of fire in fact to guide the youth into the hallowed dominion of the Brotherhood of Man.

[The worthiness of this movement is attested to by the written acknowledgement of leading Rabbis of Boston, proof of which may be found in the back part of this volume. Rabbi Friederman and Rabbi Rabinowitz have here testified in their own hands to the sincerity of purpose of the Hebrews of Newton.] *(brackets in original)*

SUPPORT FROM THE COMMUNITY

The list of donors in the fundraising booklet, with amounts they donated, was written by one person, perhaps Jacob Swartz, the treasurer. The list is headed "Contributors [order in point of time] (brackets in original). A copy of the list is included in the Appendix.

The list notes the city of residence for some donors, and includes donations from Boston, Chelsea, Malden, Maynard, Melrose and Wellesley, Waltham and Watertown. There are one hundred fifty names on the list, some of which are multiple donations from the same person. The list specifically notes donations by twenty three married women and twelve single women.

Financial support came from the non-Jewish community as well. There are seventeen donations by men with "non-Jewish" names. Donations from non-Jews included The Honorable John W. Weeks, $100; Riley, $50; the local doctor, J. M. Gallagher, M.D., $20; J.F. Flanagan, $20; three donations of $5 each, including Alderman Licton from Waltham; and nine donations of $1.

The first name listed is Isaac Heller, a leader in the Hebrew Immigrant Aid Society (HIAS). It is surprising that a secular leader would have made the first donation but he is given that honor in the list.

There were five donations of $100 each, by Louis Baker, Benjamin Gilfix, Morris Gilfix, Jacob Schiff of New York and the Honorable John W. Weeks.

It is notable that an elected public official made a significant donation. A contribution like that was unimaginable in the Europe from which the immigrants had come. The inclusive and welcoming attitude shown by Newton's political leaders toward the small Jewish community was a revelation. It confirmed for them that they had made the right choice to leave behind family and friends and come to this new land.

Elliot Gilfix recalled, "As I remember, Mayor John W. Weeks (mayor from 1902 to 1903) was quite sympathetic." Weeks had nothing to gain from such a donation because he was no longer politically active in Newton. He had been mayor of Newton from 1902 to 1903. He went on to a distinguished political career, serving in the US House of Representatives (1905-1913), the US Senate (1913-1919) and as Secretary of War (1921-1925). His son Sinclair Weeks served as mayor of Newton from 1930-1935.

Elliot Gilfix also recalled Mayor Edwin Childs (mayor from 1914-1929 and 1936-1939). "He lived on California Street near the community and he was very friendly with quite a few of the Jews in that area. Not because he needed them politically; they were a small handful but he was a sort of democratic person. Whenever they had any sort of affairs, he always appeared. When they moved the Torah from Dalby Street to Adams Street, he led the procession with an American flag."

Mayor Charles E. Hatfield was the mayor of Newton from 1910 to 1913. He was invited to speak on the occasion of the laying of the cornerstone of the new synagogue on July 31, 1912. The local paper reported that he had "accepted the invitation to speak to the guests of the occasion, subject to his freedom from the many and various activities in which he is prominent."

JACOB SCHIFF

One of five major donors to the Adam Street Synagogue building campaign in 1912 was Jacob Schiff of New York, who donated the sum of $100.

Schiff was contacted by Charles Gilfix, an undergraduate student at Harvard, who wrote to this prominent Jewish financier to ask for a donation.

Unfortunately the letter requesting the donation did not survive in the Schiff archives or in the synagogue.

Jacob Schiff played a major role as a leader of the American Jewish community in the late 19th and early 20th century. As a wealthy German Jew, Schiff and his associates made important decisions regarding the settlement of Eastern European Jewish immigrants to the United States. At a time of increasing demand for immigration restriction, Schiff supported and worked for Jewish Americanization. Schiff believed, as did many of his fellow philanthropists at HIAS, that "Americanizing" the immigrants would reduce hostility toward them. Americanization involved teaching formal, grammatically correct, non-accented English to new immigrants, changing their style of dress to American fashions, encouraging secular education, not just religious education, and participation in civic life, by voting, for example. (The emphasis on correct English was so widespread that the children of the immigrant generation prided themselves on their beautiful accents and language skills and the fact that they sounded like well-educated Americans, and not like immigrants. To be told you looked like, acted like or sounded like a "greener," a greenhorn, an immigrant, was an insult).

Schiff believed that American Jewry could live in both the Jewish and American worlds, creating a balance that would make possible an enduring American Jewish community.[6]

Jacob Schiff

THE LAND AT 168 ADAMS STREET

On February 15, 1912, Mrs. Emma Stanton deeded the land on which the Adams Street Synagogue is built to congregant Jacob Swartz for one dollar. On February 23, 1912, Jacob Swartz gave the land to the congregation.

The deeds do not show the amount paid by Jacob Swartz to Emma Stanton. One theory is that people did not want anyone to know how much one had paid for a piece of property, so both transactions record the nominal sum of one dollar.

Based on other real estate transactions in the neighborhood around the same time, the value of the land might have been as much as $10,000. Perhaps Jacob Swartz bought the land himself and donated the land to the synagogue. Or perhaps he was acting on behalf of the congregation and did not tell Mrs. Stanton that the land would be used for a synagogue.

Using 'a straw' to purchase property was often done when it was likely that the seller would be unwilling to sell to the purchaser if they knew the true end owner or use of the property, if, for example, the seller did not want to sell to members of a particular religious, ethnic or racial group. (Our Lady Help of Christians Church, located a few blocks away from the synagogue, was purchased by a straw who turned the land over to the Church).

THE MORTGAGE

The members of the Jewish community of Newton worked hard to raise money for the synagogue but they still needed a mortgage. It was granted by the Watertown Savings Bank in the sum of $3500. The mortgage stated that the plot was "six thousand square feet, more or less," 60 feet by 100 feet. Interest on the loan was five percent per annum, to be paid on the first days of April and October.

The mortgage was granted on the 24th of June 1912 and signed by Jacob Swartz, treasurer, and Joseph Kaplan, clerk of the Congregation. The original mortgage can be found in the Appendix.

The discharge of the mortgage was never recorded by the congregation in the Registry of Deeds so we do not know how long it took the congregation to pay off the mortgage.

An article in the Jewish Advocate in December 1912 about the dedication of the synagogue stated that "a new, $15,000 synagogue" was dedicated. This suggests that the community had raised almost $12,000 and needed only a small mortgage to build the building. Elliott Gilfix thought the building was built at a total cost of around $8,000. Or perhaps someone exaggerated the cost of building the synagogue.

Respondent Elliott Gilfix estimated that when the synagogue was built, there were twenty five to thirty Jewish families in the neighborhood. "All were one hundred percent self-employed: painters, shoemakers, carpenters, junk dealers, storekeepers, drug stores, furniture stores, second hand clothing. Not any of them that I knew of worked for anybody else and almost one hundred percent owned their own homes. This made them a good investment possibility for securing financial assistance in building the synagogue."

Jewish Advocate

NEW ENGLAND'S JEWISH WEEKLY.

BOSTON, MASS. FRIDAY, AUGUST 2, 1912-5672 PRICE, $2 PER YEAR

NEWTON'S FIRST SYNAGOGUE.

The cornerstone of the new synagogue of Congregation Agudath Achim of Newton, Mass., will be laid Sunday, August 4th, at 2 o'clock P. M., at 114 Adams street, Newton.

Rabbi Friederman of Boston, the Hon. Charles Hatfield, mayor of Newton, and Abraham Alpert of East Boston, will address the audience. Mr. Isaac Heller of Boston, will preside.

NEWTON TIMES

NEWTON, MASS., WEDNESDAY, JULY 31, 1912 $1.00 Per Year.

TO LAY CORNER STONE.

Impressive Ceremonies at Site of New Synagogue to Take Place Sunday Next.

On Sunday, August 4, at 2 o'clock, the Hebrews of Newton, will celebrate a great event in the laying of the corner stone of the first Synagogue to be built in Newton. During the last fifteen years, which have seen the growth of this sect in Newton, a great struggle for religious existence has gone on continually. Small in numbers, and of limited means, the Jewish members of the community have always zealously observed their religious tenets, in spite of their limited facilities for conducting their worship. At first, the homes of the various members were utilized, for Sabbath day services, each considering it his bounding duty to as better means were afforded. Now feeling stronger and their unity of purpose being fixed, the Hebrew residents of Newton have decided to erect a Synagogue, the first in Newton, where there religious life may be cemented and its future assured.

In carrying out this purpose, a great financial hardship, is being undergone by each individual concerned, yet with high hopes and implicit trust in the community in which they reside, complete success in this undertaking is assured.

The Synagogue, which is to be erected on a plot of land situated at 114 Adams St., Newton, is to be a two-story, half cement, tile and smooth red brick finish structure. The ground floor is to be used as a Sabbath school room, vestry and meeting rooms. The upper floor and gallery is to be the Synagogue proper and place of worship. Simplicity, the universal quality of Judaism is to be the chief feature in its construction.

Leading Rabbis and Cantors of Boston and vicinity will officiate at the exercises in the afternoon. Abraham Alpert, Esq. of East Boston will act as master of Ceremonies. Rabbi Friederman will also be prominent during the services. Mayor Hatfield has accepted an invitation to speak to the guests of the occasion, subject to his freedom from the many and various activities in which he is prominent.

Other personages of local prominence are also to speak and assist during the exercises.

The arrangements for the exercises are in charge of Building committee, assisted by the Ladies' Auxiliary of the Congregation Agudath Achim.

The Building Committee of the Agudath Achim Congregation, consists of Mr. Max Silverman, Mr. Morris Gilfix, Mr. Benj. Gilfix, Mr. H. Perry, and Mr. J. Swartz, Treasurer.

DEATH REAPS

Three Prominent Newton Men
Erastus T. Colburn and
of Newton Centre--Frank

Erastus T. Colburn.

Erastus T. Colburn, a prominent resident of Newton Centre, and for thirty-eight years connected with the well known firm of Brown, Durrell of Boston, died at his residence, 1325 Centre street, Newton Centre, early this morning, after an illness of about a week.

Mr. Colburn was born in West Dedham, Mass., in 1835, the son of Mr. and Mrs. Seth Colburn. He has had his home in Newton Centre for the past 46 years and was prominently identified with the Newton Centre Baptist Church, with which he united in 1869. He was a director of the Newton Trust Co.

Mr. Colburn was a salesman with Brown, Durrell & Co. and was actively connected with the concern until about a week ago. He leaves a brother and sister, living at Holliston, Mass., and three daughters, Misses Grace T., Helen E., and Mary F. Colburn.

The funeral will be from the late residence on Friday afternoon at two o'clock, the Rev. Maurice A. Levy officiating. The interment will be at Newton cemetery.

Adolphus J. Blanchard.

TO LAY CORNER STONE

Impressive Ceremonies at Site of New Synagogue
To Take Place Sunday Next.

On Sunday, August 4, at 3 o'clock the Hebrews of Newton, will celebrate a great event in the laying of the cornerstone of the first Synagogue to be built in Newton. During the last fifteen years,which have been the growth of this sect in Newton, a great struggle for religious existence has gone on continually. Small in numbers and of limited means, the Jewish members of the community have always zealously observed their religious tenets, in spite of their limited facilities for conducting their worship. At first, the homes of the various members were utilized for Sabbath Day services, each considering it his bounden duty to as better means were afforded. Now feeling stronger and their unity of purpose being fixed, the Hebrew residents of Newton have decided to erect a Synagogue, the first in Newton, where their religious life may be cemented and its future assured. In carrying out this purpose, a great financial hardship is being under- gone by each individual concerned, yet with high hopes and implicit trust in the community in which they reside, complete success in this under-taking is assured.

The Synagogue, which is to be erected on a plot of land at 114 Adams Street, Newton, is to be a two-story, half cement, tile and smooth red brick finish structure. The ground floor is to be used as a Sabbath school room, vestry and meeting rooms. The upper floor and gallery is to be the Synagogue proper and place of worship. Simplicity, the universal quality of Judaism, is to be the chief feature of its construction. Leading Rabbis and Cantors of Boston and vicinity will officiate at the exercises in the afternoon. Abraham Alpert, Esq., of East Boston will act as master of ceremonies. Mayor Hatfield has accepted an invitation to speak to the guests of the occasion, subject to his freedom from the many and various activities in which he is prominent. Other personages of local prominence area also to speak and assist during the exercises.

The arrangements for the exercises are in charge of Building Committee. The Building Committee of the Agudath Achim Congregation consists of Mr. Max Silverman, Mr. Morris Gilfix, Mr. Benj. Gilfix, Mr. H. Perry and Mr. J. Schwartz, Treasurer.

א גרויסער יום טוב אין ניוטאן!

איבערראשענדע נייעס פיר ניוטאונער יהודים!

מיט פריידע בענאכריכטען מיר אלע יהודים פון ניוטאן און אומגעגענד אז ענדליך איז אונזער וואונש נאך פיעלע מיהע און ענערגיע ערפילט געווארען צו האבען

איינע פון דיא שיינע שוהלען אין ניוטאן, מאסס.,

און

זונטאג, דעם 15-טען דעצעמבער, 1912 אום 12 אוהר מיטאג צייט

אין 114 אדאמס סטריט, דיא וועלען מיר האבען

גרענד אפעניגג פון אגודת אחים שוהל

וואו הרב פרידערמאן און הרב ראבינאוויץ וועלען דעם פובליקום אדרעסירען

דער בעריהמטער חזן פון נארטה ראססעלל סט. שוהל, ר׳ עמאנואל שייפער מיט זיין ריעזיגען כאהר, מיט איינע פון דיא בעסטע ארקעסטער מיוזיק, וועט קאנצערט אפגעבען

דער בעוואוסטער כלל טהוער, מר. אייזיק העללער און נאך פראמינענטע רעדנערס וועלען פארטרעגע האלטע

א. אלפערט [איש קאוונע] וועט זיין מאסטער אף סערעמאניעס

עס איז ווייניג צו זאגען אז דיא קאמיטע האט געטרייעט איהר בעסט אז עס זאל זיין איינע פון דיא בעסטע ענטערטיינמענטס וואס ניוטאן האט ווען געהאט, דערום אפעלירען מיר צו יעדען אייגציגען מענש ניט צו פערנאכלעססיגען דעם געלעגענהייט און אנוועזענד זיין

דער פאראייד וועט זיך סטארטען פון 190 אדאמס סטריט — רעפרעשמענטס וועט געסערווד ווערען

ארגאנייזירט פון דער קאמיטע: זשאסעף רויטער, פרעזידענט; ס. סילווערמאן, וויס-פרעזידענט; דושיי. שווארץ, טרעזשורער, 335 וואשינגטאן סטריט

Good News for Newton

With pleasure we announce that with great difficulty we have at last been able to obtain the beautiful

Synagogue Agodas Achim, in Newton, Mass.,

SUNDAY, December 15, 1912, at 12 o'clock noon

The GRAND OPENING will take place at **114 Adams Street**

RABBIS FRIEDERMAN & RABINOVITZ will address the public, and Cantor EMANUEL SHAFER and Choir from the North Russell Street Synagogue of Boston, together with an excellent Orchestra will entertain us. The well-known Mr. ISAAC HELLER and other prominent men of Boston will address us. The Committee spared no expense to make the opening a grand success. Don't lose this opportunity, but join us and together we will have one grand time. There will be a GRAND MARCH from 19(Adams Street

Millmeister, Printer 91 Leverett Street, Boston

Refreshments will be served

Poster courtesy of American Jewish Historical Society

Poster Translation

Poster translation courtesy Rabbi S. D. Yaffe

Amazing news for Newton's Jews! A great holiday in Newton!

With great joy, we invite all the Jews from Newton and its environs. Our wish has been fulfilled after much toil and energy and we are about to have a beautiful shul in Newton, Mass.

On Sunday, the 15th of December 1912, at the hour of noon at 114 Adams Street, we will have the grand opening of the Agudas Achim shul.

HaRav Friederman and HaRav Rabinowitz will address the public.

The famed cantor of the North Russell Street Shul, Emanuel Shafer, together with his great choir, and with one of the best orchestras, will give a concert. A. Alpert, formerly of Kovno, will be the master of ceremonies.

It goes without saying that the committee tried their best that it should be one of the best entertainments ever in Newton. Therefore, we appeal to every single person not to lose this opportunity and attend. The parade will begin from 190 Adams Street. Refreshments will be served.

Arranged by the committee, Joseph Roiter, president, Max Silverman, vice president, and Jacob Swartz, treasurer.

Immigrant Jews were quickly becoming Americanized. For example, in the poster announcing the dedication of the synagogue, there were several English phrases that were transliterated into Yiddish, indicating that even native Yiddish speakers were absorbing English expressions at this date. Two examples are "grand opening" and "master of ceremonies."

THE SYMBOLISM OF THE DEDICATION ON CHANUKAH

The synagogue was dedicated December 15, 1912. Why was the dedication held in wintertime when it is likely that the building was finished and ready for occupancy earlier? The reason lies in Jewish history.

Around 160 B.C.E., the Jewish state was ruled by a Greek general named Antiochus, who persecuted the Jews, introduced idol worship and the sacrifice of pigs into the Temple in Jerusalem and tortured and killed Jews who refused to worship him as a god. This state of affairs led to a rebellion by Jews, led by a temple priest named Mattathias and his son Judah Maccabee. The rebellion was eventually successful and the Temple was purged of its idols and cleaned in preparation for its use by the Jewish community once more. The successful rebellion and the rededication of the Temple was marked by a new holiday called Chanukah.

It was an obvious symbolic decision by the Jewish community in Newton to dedicate their new synagogue on the holiday of Chanukah.

THE JEWISH ADVOCATE, FRIDAY, DECEMBER 20, 1912.

SYNAGOGUE DEDICATED AT NEWTON.

The new $15,000 Jewish synagogue Agudath Achim on Adams street, Nonantum District, Newton, was dedicated last Sunday afternoon and first services were held in the structure. Abraham Alpert of East Boston, was master of ceremonies. Isaac Heller of Boston, performed the ceremony of opening the door. The services inside were conducted by Rabbis M. J. Friedman and I. Rabinovitz, and the chanting was by Cantor Shafer of Boston and his choir.

Mayor Charles E. Hatfield of Newton was present at the dedication. Morris Gilfix, Benjamin Gilfix, Joseph Rolter, Max Silverman and Jacob Schwartz comprised the building committee.

RELIGIOSITY AND SECULARISM — DECODING THE POSTER

Who were the guests of honor at the dedication ceremony and what does their participation in the event tell us about Jewish life, both secular and religious, at that time?

In 1912, the religious and secular communities were competing for the attention and loyalty of the immigrant generation. At the dedication ceremony for the Adams Street Synagogue, the competing religious and social agendas of the community were demonstrated by the presence of two prominent Orthodox rabbis and two secular leaders from Hebrew Immigrant Aid Society (HIAS).

Every Jewish community and Jewish organization was involved in issues regarding immigrants, since the numbers of Jews arriving in the United States every year was in the hundreds of thousands. HIAS knew that virtually all immigrants would find their way to a synagogue in the process of adjusting to American life, so they made it a point to be present wherever Jews gathered and for whatever reason. The synagogue was a logical place to honor the religious beliefs of the immigrants, seek new members for HIAS and to promote their Americanization agenda at the same time.

Rabbi Rabinowitz had written a personal letter urging Jews to financially support the synagogue, but the very first donation listed in the synagogue's donation book is that of Issac Heller from HIAS. Heller was also given the honor of symbolically "opening the door" of the synagogue.

THE RELIGIOUS GUESTS OF HONOR AT THE DEDICATION

Rabbi Zalman Yaakov Friederman

One of the two rabbis listed on the poster announcing the dedication of the synagogue is Rabbi Zalman Yaakov Friederman. Immigrating to New York in 1893 from Meretz, Lithuania, Rabbi Friederman came to Boston in 1895 and settled in the North End. He accepted a position as rabbi of a consortium of Orthodox congregations known as Agudat ha-Kehilot (a collective of Orthodox religious educators and rabbis).

A notable preacher in Yiddish, he often bemoaned the condition of American Jewish religious life to his congregants, chastising them for not adhering more scrupulously to Orthodox observance. "He had a hard line opposition to any deviation from the strictest Orthodoxy. He demanded that Jews wore kippot (skullcaps) at all times, even during sleep and at the bathhouse." [8] Together with Hasidic Rabbi Pinchas David Horowitz (the Bostoner Rebbe), who emigrated to Boston from Palestine in 1914, Rabbi Friederman established a Talmud Torah where boys studied Talmud after public school hours. But the yeshiva did not receive the support of some community leaders and Orthodox rabbis who feared that a Talmud Torah yeshiva would undermine their own synagogue afternoon school programs. Without widespread support of the community, yeshiva attendance dwindled and was eventually closed.

As a traditionalist who wanted to encourage Jews in America to maintain the same religious standards they had in Europe, Rabbi Friederman was not very popular with his congregation. He complained in 1927: "The rabbis must satisfy the wants of the audience, for that is the foundation of their survival, since their prodders—the officers of the synagogue—order them, 'expand the membership of the congregation, increase the audience, attract the affluent to hear your sermons, so as to increase the income.' " [9]

Rabbi Friederman married Miriam, the daughter of Rabbi Pinchas Horowitz in 1920, in a wedding in Roxbury attended by 6,000 guests.

Rabbi Friederman maintained ongoing correspondence with many rabbis, including Rabbi Israel Meir HaCohen Kagan, commonly known as the "Chofetz Chaim." As a long time activist on behalf of religious Zionism, Rabbi Friederman also corresponded with Rabbi Abraham Isaac Kook, the first Ashkenazi chief rabbi of the British Mandatory Palestine. Rabbi Friederman died while visiting Palestine in 1934. [10]

Rabbi D. M. [Dovid Meyer] Rabinowitz

The second rabbi listed on the dedication poster is Rabbi Rabinowitz. He was born in Europe in 1863. "The year 1896 saw the arrival in Boston of Rabbi D. M. Rabinowitz, one of the first Lubavitchers to come to the United States and who became spiritual leader of the Agudat ha-Sefardim in that city." [11] He served as the rabbi at the North Russell Street Synagogue for three years, 1904-1907. He continued to serve the Jewish community in Boston but did not have another major pulpit. He maintained strong relationships with Rabbi Friederman and Rabbi Pinchas Horowitz. He also served on the Boston Va'ad Harabonim in the late 1930s. [12]

His endorsement of the fundraising efforts of the synagogue was inscribed in Yiddish in the fundraising book for solicitors to show to prospective donors.

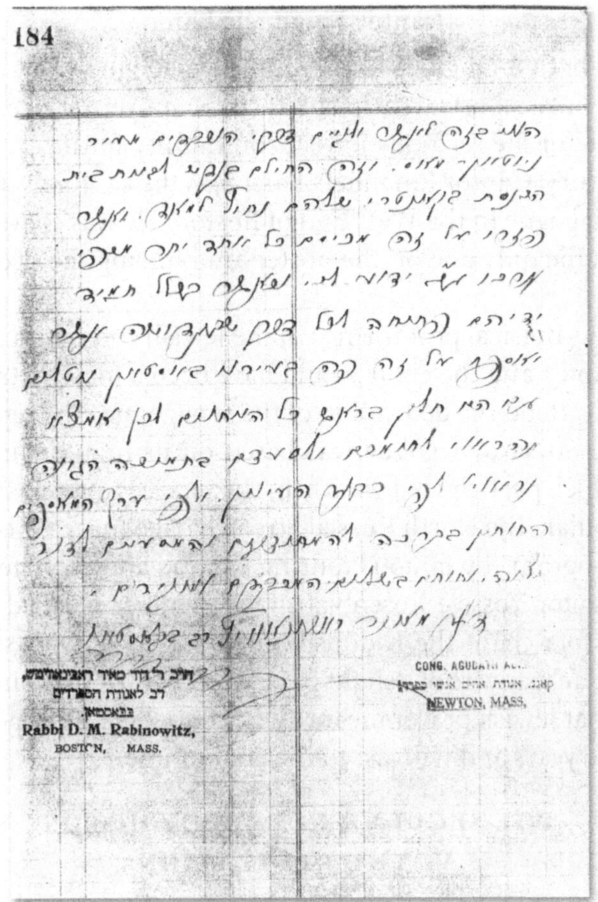

184

הרב ר' דוד מאיר ראבינאוויטש,
רב לאגודת הספרדים
בבאסטאן.
Rabbi D. M. Rabinowitz,
BOSTON, MASS.

CONG. AGUDATH
קאנג. אגודת אחים אנשי
NEWTON, MASS.

Original Yiddish fundraising letter by Rabbi Rabinowitz

Herewith I would confirm that the words of the honorable people from the city of Newton, Massachusetts. They have decided to build a synagogue in their village. It is a worthy cause and I know as a fact that they are spending, as individuals, a great sum of money for this. I also know that they are always willing to contribute and support all worthy causes. I therefore feel that they deserve all the support that can be given to them.

I sign with a blessing to all those that contribute and help support this mitzvah.

[in Yiddish] Ha Rav Dovid Meyer Rabinowitz
Rav of Agudas HaSefardim in Boston

[in English] Rabbi D. M. Rabinowitz, Boston, Mass

Cantor Emanuel Shafer

A cantor is both a religious leader in the synagogue and a musician specially trained in vocal arts to help enhance the prayer service. Cantors were the movie stars of the religious Jewish community in the early years of the twentieth century. Cantor Emanuel Shafer was the cantor at the North Russell Street Synagogue in the West End of Boston. He was so well known that his photo was the only one on the poster announcing the dedication of the synagogue.

Because of its musical prominence in the Jewish community, the presence of both the cantor and the choir would have been a major attraction for the community to attend the dedication of the synagogue. The reputation of the North Russell Street Synagogue was based on its high quality cantor and male choir, which participated weekly in the services in their synagogue and were very popular. The North Russell Street Synagogue was also well known for hosting programs by famous touring cantors and at a later time hosted the famous cantor Yossele Rosenblatt. One member recalled years later, "I once heard Sirota chant the Kiddush on Friday night with such profound sincerity that I felt shivers of delight pass up and down my spine....I grasped for all time what Jewish prayer meant and....I understood why the Jews have lasted all these years and will last to the end of time." [13]

THE SECULAR GUESTS OF HONOR AT THE DEDICATION

Abraham Alpert

Abraham Alpert served as the master of ceremonies for the opening ceremony of the synagogue in December 1912. He was always identified as the "man from Kovno."

Born in Kovno, Lithuania, Alpert immigrated to the United States alone in 1886 at the age of 13 and settled in Boston, Massachusetts.

Every day for fifty years he published articles in the Jewish press. His articles appeared in the Forward and the Jewish Advocate, among other papers. These Yiddish and English accounts of what immigrant families and groups were doing appealed to newcomers who were eager to become true Americans and remain strong in their Jewish faith. "Immigrant Jews, in the process of an inner transformation to Americanism, sought to overcome the stigma and epithet of "foreigner."

The immigrant often needed counsel from someone who knew the local politicians, could explain matters as an intermediary and could be trusted completely. Alpert served in this capacity among the plain people and never left them. His wide experience in questions of immigration, citizenship, establishment of businesses, congregational affairs or city departments made him an invaluable community resource and he was called upon to assist organizations all over the Eastern Seaboard.

Jewish Advocate

NEW ENGLAND'S JEWISH WEEKLY.

Chanucah Notes

BY ABRAHAM ALPERT

Maccabaeans or has-beens—that is the question. What is your answer?

*****

Chanucah is the only festival on which we celebrate a victory won by sword and yet, no Megillah is read, no ceremony is made, not even a real Yom Tov service is held. On Tisha B'ab, the ninth day of the fifth month, our youngsters make wooden swords and for Purim they have all kinds of weapons and devices to "rekill" Haman. Sham battles between two factions of Jewish boys are arranged, the usual result of which is that the conquered have to surrender their valuable war paraphernalia to the victors and with the

ABRAHAM ALPERT.

spoils on their shoulders, the heroes march in military order, triumphantly singing the Purim hymn, "Shoshanash Yakov," "The lily of Jacob rejoiced and was glad when Mordecai was seen in purple," etc. The vanquished ones follow behind with drooped heads and assumed bent spirit.

There is also the feature of operating Haman Klapers during the reading of the Megillah each time Haman's name is mentioned, thus expressing their wrath over the wicked plotter against the Jews. Then comes the Sudah, banquet, which is followed by such pleasant incidents as Farstelen, Salach Mones, etc. We have none of these impressive features on Chanucah, the festival of real victory, the celebration which perpetuates the memory of the Maccabaeans who haved us from becoming a people of has-beens.

I wonder why the wooden swords of Tisha B'ab and the sham battles of Purim were not displayed on Chanucah, the only Yom Tov on which we celebrate a victory won with sword and spear.

*****

Let all Israelites celebrate the "festival of lights" with pomp and ceremony. The issuing of a special number of The Jewish Advocate in honor of the Maccabaeans is a move in the right direction.

*****

It is told in the Talmud that when Aristobolus reached Jerusalem and could not conquer it, he was advised by an old man to bring in a pig in the Temple. Aristobolus complied with the old man's advice and as the pig was pulled up on the walls of Jerusalem, the Holy City was shocked.

The old man was right. The Jew will tolerate anything, but he will never stand for a pig in the Temple. Hence the objection is of Rabbi Hirsch's Hechsher for pork.

I once said that the Jew who eats lobsters is a lobster himself. What shall I say of a rabbi who issues a Hechsher for Dovor Acher?

*****

Nicholas, the second, is a prototype for Antiochus Yifanus. Our present day assimilators are no better than the Hellenists of 2100 years ago, but where are the Maccabaeans of today? This may sound quite pessimistic, but nowadays one must be either a pessi (fool) or a pessimist.

*****

Just think of it! the 90,000 Jews of Boston do not have a single representative in the city government. If we would only use our ballots as effectively as the Maccabaeans used their swords (and they were only a handful), how well we would be represented and what a splendid administration our city would have!

*****

If we have no Hannah how can we expect to have Maccabaeans? Very few of our boys receive a good Jewish education. Most of our girls receive no Jewish education at all. I once asked a number of Jewish boys who the Maccabaeans were and the answer was that they must have been Irishmen since their names began with Mac.

*****

And, to be frank, our children's fathers know very little about the Maccabaeans—Boston beans is good enough for them.

He remained religiously observant all his life but he never accepted a call to the Torah (aliyah) at any synagogue. As an American Jew, he was often asked if he preferred "Jew" or "Hebrew" as a description of his people. The local Protestant elite liked Hebrew because it sounded like the Bible but it was not to his liking. As a justice of the peace (appointed in 1897), he had the authority to administer oaths associated with many documents. A fervent Zionist, in 1909 he arranged the first public discussion on the subject in a synagogue in East Boston. The meeting was further notable because the discussion was entirely in English.

He supported himself and his family with a lunchroom/club in East Boston. Previously he was a laborer, and his first job in the United States was in the city yards of Boston, managed by Patrick Kennedy, paternal grandfather of the late President. In another incident connecting the writer and speaker to the future, the father of Leonard Bernstein told everyone that Alpert's article on Lenny's musical genius was the first public notice of Bernstein's long career.

Outside of his writing, he also rose to become a prominent national Jewish figure and leader. One newspaper wrote that there was not a synagogue on the Atlantic Coast that had not heard Alpert talk. He averaged one hundred speeches per year. He spoke in Yiddish, English and Hebrew. His speaking style was unassuming, full of humor and owed a lot to Sholem Aleichem's style of writing. He helped organize the Boston branch of the Hebrew Immigrant Aid Society (HIAS), and was active there for over 40 years, aiding over 3000 immigrants in receiving citizenship.

He was once asked why Jews registered to vote as Republicans. "The Constitution of the United States guarantees a republican form of government—which the immigrants understood to refer to the Republican party! Not until the days of Woodrow Wilson did the work democracy find wide acceptance and by then the Jews were ready to vote Democratic!" [14]

Isaac Heller

Isaac Heller was a native of Cleveland, Ohio. He was a graduate of Adelbert College (Case Western Reserve) Class of 1895 and a graduate of Harvard Law School, Class of 1898. He was vice president and member of the Board of Directors of HIAS. He advertised in the Jewish Advocate that he bought and sold real estate (including numerous parcels in Brookline and Boston) and insurance. He was a trustee of Foxborough State Hospital.

Heller performed the ceremony of opening the door of the synagogue for the first time at the ceremonies in December 1912. His donation of $50.00 to the building fund is recorded as the first donation "in order in point of time" in the fundraising record.

Among other notables associated with HIAS at that time were Louis D. Brandeis, Jacob Schiff and Rabbi Steven Wise. [15]

THE ARCHITECT AND THE BUILDER

The architect was Samuel S. Levy Jr.

Levy was born in Russia in the 1880's. Like many immigrants, he did not know his birth year and listed dates as varied as 1883, 1885, 1886, and 1890. He gave his date of birth as July 1. He arrived in the United States with his parents in 1898. His wife's name was Rebecca.

In 1915, 1916 and 1926, he is listed in Boston business directories as an architect having offices at 35 Court Street in Boston. He had already joined the residential exodus from the North End of Boston to Roxbury and Mattapan. In 1905, he is listed as a "clerk," residing on Humboldt Avenue in Roxbury. In registering for the draft in 1918, when he was 35 years old, he gave his address as 607 Morton Street in Mattapan. At that time, he was employed by the Hood Rubber Company in Watertown. In 1930, he was listed as residing at 17 Intervale Street in Roxbury and manufacturing window shades. Although information about his career is scarce, he is listed as the architect of a Georgian Revival building in Codman Square at 316-324 Talbot Avenue (1913); a Classical Revival building, called the El Paisa Butchery Building in Orient Heights (East Boston) (1914); a yellow brick Georgian Revival apartment building at 96 Bowdoin Avenue, Dorchester (1915); and the architect of a building at 1971-1979 Columbus Avenue, Roxbury (1917). None of those buildings still exist. [16]

A single reference states that he was active as an architect from about 1905-1930. Another reference to him in the architecture archives of the Boston Public Library states that "his grandson believes that Levy was active in the rebuilding of Chelsea after the great fire of 1908."

The builder of the synagogue, a young man named Isaac Fox, lived in Malden. We have been unable to find out anything about him.

The Bimah

Newton was located outside the major Jewish centers of the Greater Boston Jewish community in the early years of the twentieth century. When the Adams Street Shul was built in 1912, the center of Jewish life in Boston was located in the North End, the South End and the West End of Boston, with at least fifty synagogues, but moving rapidly toward other locations. By the early 1920's, the center of Jewish life had moved to Roxbury, Dorchester and Mattapan. Half the Jewish population of Greater Boston lived in those three communities. There were more than thirty synagogues built in those communities between 1910 and 1930.[17]

In those neighborhoods, the congregations were building new synagogues and installing elegant and elaborate new arks in them, made by a well respected ark maker, Samuel Katz.

The older members of the Newton congregation were content, indeed proud, to have built a synagogue. They were religiously observant people who didn't need and could not afford anything fancy in their shul. The members of the congregation came mostly from Ukraine and from small villages with limited resources. They were accustomed to praying in a *shtibl*, a small room furnished with a few tables and benches, a bookcase and a simple wood cabinet for an ark. They were satisfied with a chair brought from home to sit on in the synagogue and content with the Torah scrolls housed in an unadorned wooden cabinet.

But their children had been educated in the United States and exposed to a different way of life. The new synagogues that were being built in Roxbury, Dorchester and Mattapan did not have bedsheets for Torah ark curtains. If the congregation wanted their young people to stay in Newton and not move away, they would have to make certain improvements.

On February 6, 1924, the women of the congregation made a donation of $184 to the congregation, "to be used specifically [underlining in original] for the purpose of building an Oran Achodash, or Ark, in our synagogue." Elliot Gilfix stepped forward to support this effort. He wrote the donation document himself, and had it signed by "the executive committee of the Newton Junior Council" (meaning the younger members of the community) presumably to prevent the "Senior Council" from appropriating the funds for other purposes.

Elliot himself signed as Chairman. The other signers included Philip Bram, and Ida Roiter, Sarah Silverman and Hazel Schwartz, all single women. The men of the Bimah Committee, included Samuel Bram, (father of Philip Bram) and Joseph Roiter, (father of Ida Roiter), making this unusual document an intergenerational one. Furthermore, it included unmarried women among the organizers. It is significant that women, both married and single, were the movers and shakers of this effort and the first ones to sign the document. (Signator Hazel Schwartz's family owned the house at 97 Dalby Street where the Keneses Israel Anshe Sephard synagogue had been located before the Adams Street Shul was built). The other male signers were

Abraham Shrier, Louis Baker, Joseph Roiter, Morris Fried, Joseph Hoffman, H. Perry, and Louis Fried.

Elliot was a clever politician, assisting in the fundraising, writing the document, getting the major fundraisers to sign the document (to give them public credit for their work) and then getting the men to sign the document, so that they were also publicly committed to this work. The Ark, described elsewhere in this book, was completed in the same year.

We don't know the specific date when the Ark was installed in the synagogue in 1924 but judging by the straw hats worn by the men of the Bimah Committee, it would have been summertime.

The Bimah Committee, 1924

Photo courtesy of Mr. Elmer Lippin

L to R: Louis Fried, Joseph Hoffman, Abraham Shrier, Joseph Roiter, Hyman Perry, Louis Baker, Samuel Bram

To the
Agudas Achim Congregation
Newton, Mass.

We, the undersigned, as authorized representatives of the Agudas Achim Congregation have received this day a donation of

ONE HUNDRED AND EIGHTY FOUR DOLLARS

to be used specifically for the purpose of building an Oron Achodesh or Ark for the Holy Scrolls in our Synagogue.

The executive committee of the Newton Junior Council reserves the right to apply this donation for any other purpose of immediate relation to the Agudas Achim Congregation.

Signed

Attested:-
Elliot A. Silfen chairman
Phillips Baum
Ida Reiter
Sarah E. Silverman
Hazel R. Schwartz
FEBRUARY 6TH 1924

A. Shapiro
L. Baker
Samuel Brown
I. Reiter
M. Forbes
J. Hoffman
H. Perry
Louis Field

x 50

to the

Agudas Achim Congregation

Newton, Mass

We, the undersigned, as authorized representatives of the Agudas Achim Congregation have received this day a donation of

ONE HUNDRED AND EIGHTY FOUR DOLLARS

to be used specifically for the purpose

of building an Oran Achodash or Ark

for the Holy Scrolls in our Synagogue.

The executive commitee of the Newton Junior Council reserves the right

to apply this donation for any other purpose

of immediate relation to the Agudas

Achim Congregation.

Signed

Attested:	A. Shrier
Elliot A. Gilfix, Chairman	L. Baker
Phillip Bram	Samuel Bram
Ida Roiter	J. Roiter
Sarah E. Silverman	M. Fried
Hazel R. Schwartz	J. Hoffman
February 6th, 1924	H. Perry
Louis Fried	
Samuel Katz	

Samuel Katz

The builder of the ark, Samuel Katz, was born in Ukraine in 1885 and moved to Troy, New York, in 1907. He eventually moved to the Boston area where he lived until his death. He was trained as a cabinet maker, a trade he learned from his father. He made his first arks for synagogues in Albany and Saratoga Springs, New York by 1910.

In 1913, he moved to Chelsea, Massachusetts, where he opened a woodworking shop. He also worked in a furniture factory in Woburn, MA, where he perfected his furniture building and woodworking skills. He built approximately two dozen synagogue arks in the Greater Boston area, one of which is located in the Adams Street Shul. Most of his arks which survive are located in buildings which are now churches. During the Great Depression, he established a business to make refrigerator cabinets, called ice boxes.

Katz himself was an interesting man, an observant Jew, keeping a kosher home, speaking both Yiddish and English, and attending synagogue regularly. He was also a socialist, a member of the carpenter's union and a member of the Yiddish speaking *Arbiter Ring* (Workman's Circle).

To order an ark, synagogue leaders would come to his workshop to negotiate a price. The price would depend on the size, ornamentation, the number of carved animals ordered and extra pieces like the bimah, the platform for the Ark, the reader's platform and chairs for the rabbi and president of the congregation. To choose the details, Mr. Katz had a notebook in which he had drawn pictures of the various decorations that could be applied to the ark.

The average price for an ark was about $700. The average annual salary in 1924 was $1124. The cost of a new car averaged $400.

The ark at Adams Street is the chief ornament of the synagogue. The ark is made of mahogany and each piece is hand-carved and many parts are gilded by hand. The ark at the Adams Street Shul contains a unique feature that Mr. Katz incorporated into his arks and which can be seen in every photo of every ark he built. It is a pair of hands in the special position that the Cohanim use when they recite the prayers. The hands hover over a book inscribed in Hebrew with the blessing that the Cohanim recite during special times in the religious calendar. [18]

Photo courtesy Steve Rosenthal

Chambers Street Shul, West End, Boston, 1920
Sam Katz, far right.

Photo: The Jews of BostonTable of Contents

COMMUNITY

WHERE DID WE COME FROM?
THE "OLD COUNTRY," THE *SHTETL*

Many of Newton's Jewish residents came from small towns called *Shtetlekh* [Yiddish: *shtetl* (singular), *shtetlekh* (plural)]. The *shtetlekh* were small towns with large Jewish populations in Central and Eastern Europe before the Holocaust. They were located in the so-called Pale of Settlement. (The archaic English term *pale* is derived from the Latin word *palus*, a stake, extended to mean the area enclosed by a fence or boundary). The Pale extended to the western Russian border with the Kingdom of Prussia (later the German Empire) and with Austria-Hungary. It comprised about 20% of the territory of European Russia including much of present-day Lithuania, Belarus, Poland, Moldova, Ukraine, and parts of western Russia.[19]

In the early nineteenth century, the *shtetl* was a major economic engine of Eastern Europe, engaging in trade with the West and bringing new items to the large but isolated and backward area. The role of Jewish traders was restricted in the middle of the nineteenth century when the Tsarist government decided to encourage the growth of local industry by restricting imports that the *shtetl* had specialized in. By the late nineteenth century, the *shtetl,* deprived of international business opportunities, came to signify provincialism, timidity and stupidity, ghettoization, uncivilized matters, coarse accents, pedestrian thoughts, and bad taste, all qualities which were attributed to the Jews.[20] The *shtetl* was "Otherness, Old World backwardness, loudness, vulgarity, clannishness, ignorance and materialism." [21]

ADAPTING TO AMERICA: NOSTALGIA FOR THE *SHTETL*
GONE BUT NOT FORGOTTEN

The image of Jewish life in Russia is indelibly shaped for 20th and 21st century American Jews by the musical *Fiddler on the Roof.* The stage production was derived from books written by Sholem Aleichem, the popular Yiddish author. The musical presented a view of the *shtetl* as a poor, backward and desperate place but it also created a vehicle for a nostalgic memory of those villages and that way of life that had been destroyed by the Holocaust.

The author Sholem Aleichem believed that Jewish knowledge, a combination of Jewish culture and cultural memory, could be the factor that united Jews into a Jewish nation, rather than the specific acts and prescriptions of religion or the abstract principles of the Jewish faith, increasingly ignored by Jews in this changed and changing modern world. [22] Reading his holiday stories was, in its own way, holiday observance; celebrating past tradition was becoming its own means of worship." [23]

In America, there was a "previously unimaginable possibility of acceptance, and some Jews seized on it, changing their dress, behavior, reading and speaking habits, and social and professional ambitions to model more closely those of their non-Jewish neighbors."[24] "America's greatness...lay in its *beheimishness,* its hominess, its ability as a melting pot country to simultaneously transform its immigrants into ardent patriots by sharing its freedoms and allow them the opportunity to cherish the language and humor of their former lives and homes." [25]

The Jewish community of Newton kept the atmosphere and traditions of the *shtetl* alive even as their children received American educations and lived American lives. Common memories and experiences united the Jews of Newton even though their religious practices often differed. They retained a strong connection to their Jewish religious and cultural roots. This made it possible for the newcomers to successfully build new lives, to retain their strong Jewish identity, to educate their children in both secular and religious ways and to build and sustain a synagogue that was and remains a home for the entire community.

JUNK PEDDLERS AND SCRAP DEALERS

Waste was literally a dirty word in America in the latter half of the nineteenth century and the early years of the twentieth. Waste collection was by definition dirty and dangerous. It was associated in the public's mind with the desperately poor scavengers who picked up trash on the street or picked through garbage looking for salable bits and pieces. So it was open to immigrants, who were perceived as dirty and poor and therefore fit for trash collection, junk peddling and scrap collecting.

Junk peddlers, however, were businessmen and not scavengers. In the language of the turn of the century, junk peddlers traded in almost everything and scrap dealers specialized, usually in rags and paper but increasingly in metal. The peddlers and scrap dealers did not necessarily discriminate among themselves in the use of these terms. The basic skills essential to the successful scrap dealer remain the same today as in the nineteenth and early twentieth centuries. These are the ability to find, assess and sell valuable materials and the ability to cultivate relationships with suppliers and customers. Timing sales and purchases of scrap materials was and is crucial to a dealer's success or failure. [26]

The scrap trade experienced its most conspicuous growth during a period of mass migration to the United States and industrial expansion. [27] By 1900, 24.5% of New York Jews were active in some facet of the junk trade. [28] By 1920, so many Jewish immigrants had started trading in scrap that the public face of the scrap dealer was the face of a Jew. [29] Sixty eight percent of the junk workers identified in the 1920 census were from central and eastern Europe. By the mid 1930's, Fortune magazine estimated that 90 percent of the scrap metal industry was owned by Jews.[30]

In Newton, at least two of the scrap dealers turned their junk businesses into selling second hand automobile supplies and selling second hand cars (Shriberg and Yanco). A third, Philip Bram, got into the auto supply business through his father the blacksmith, who recycled used metal.

Jews also had centuries of tradition as entrepreneurs all over the world, owners of small shops and peddling in their home countries. But shops had to conform to some extent with the opening hours preferred by their customers, which might mean being open on Saturday and Jewish holidays. A junk peddler or scrap dealer had no such interference with his preferred lifestyle, if that lifestyle included observing Jewish religious laws.

Little investment capital was needed to enter the scrap trade. The low starting costs, combined with a lack of competition from established natives, made it possible for immigrants to gain footholds in the trade by becoming peddlers. One could become a peddler, which required only a sack to carry materials and rudimentary English, especially the ability to count in English. Later, one could acquire a horse and wagon and perhaps a storage shed for the collected materials.

Telephone Newton North 4321

BENJ. GILFIX & COMPANY
93 WEST STREET, NEWTON, MASS.
Dealer in All Kinds of Plumbing Lead and Solder
In Exchange for Old Junk

Date.................................193

Sold to..

Quantity	Description	Weight	Price	Amount

The Newton Journal

MAX PISCHANSKY

Wholesale and Retail-dealer to Metals, old Iron, Bottles, Paper Stock and all kinds of Second-hand Articles. Second-hand Furniture a Specialty. Orders called for and delivered. Bottles will be paid for at Market Price. Always ready to fill orders. Telephone.

316 California St., Newton, Mass

MAX PISCHANSKY

Wholesale and Retail-dealer to Metals, old Iron, Bottles, Paper Stock and all kinds of Second-hand Articles. Second-hand Furniture a Specialty. Orders called for and delivered. Bottles will be paid for at Market Price. Always ready to fill orders.

516 California Street Newton, Mass

NEWTON INVESTMENT ASSOCIATION

The founding members of Newton's Jewish community were active in the real estate market, both on behalf of two synagogues and on their own accounts as well.

The Newton Investment Association was created by a Declaration of Trust and registered with the Commonwealth of Massachusetts on February 21, 1914. The purpose of the Trust was "the collection, accumulation and investment of funds in real estate and loans to members and to others with or without security."

The signatories were Abram Shrier, Max Silverman, Hyman Meilman, Hyman Mahlowitz (?), and N. Lipcrite (?).

New trustees were elected on January 30, 1915. They were Abram Shrier, Joseph Roiter, Samuel Bram and Harry Yanco, signed by Max Cantor, secretary. In 1917, the members were Benjamin Gilfix, Harry Yanco, Julius Pass, Abraham Pass and Harry Kritzman. The last recorded election was May 8, 1926, when Philip Gilfix, Abraham Pass and Harry Yanco were elected. All of the men listed here, with one exception, were immigrants.

The records are unclear as to what they bought and sold; they might have loaned money to each other to purchase homes or business properties.

JEWISH BUSINESSES IN NEWTON

Elliot Gilfix, who was born and raised and lived most of his life involved in Nonantum, remembered the Jewish community of Newton in its earliest years.

He estimated that when the synagogue was built, there were about forty Jewish families in the neighborhood. "All were one hundred percent self-employed: painters, shoemakers, carpenters, junk dealers, storekeepers, drug stores, furniture stores, second hand clothing. Not any of them that I knew of worked for anybody else." [31]

Between 1911 and 1921, the following Jewish businesses were located on Watertown Street, then as now Nonantum's main shopping street.

307	Halperin grocery
309	Kaplan Kalman, dry goods
310	Fried's dry goods, survived until 1963
318-320	Schwartz shoemaker (his home at 97 Dalby Street was the location of an earlier congregation until the Adams Street Synagogue was built in 1912)
330	Slesinger boots

332-334	Fox Drugs, still survives on Watertown Street
339	Perlmutter's department store
341-345	Nonantum Furniture Company, later Fox Furniture Company
347	Minkowitz tailor
353-355	Swartz Hardware, still in existence, now called Swartz Ace Hardware
361	Perlmutter Real Estate
375	Finberg shoemaker
376-378	Perry Hyman dry goods
386	Bram blacksmith
456	Kligman junk

There were also numerous small businesses located on side streets, such as Louis Baker's grocery store on Chapel Street (which is still a store today). There were junk yards and many self-employed junk dealers as well. Many of them had businesses next door to their homes rather than on the main shopping street.

The ideal of being one's own boss in the first generation changed in the second generation to the ideal of having a government job which presumably would provide job security. Some of that change might have been driven by the fact that some second generation children did not want to take over the junk businesses of their fathers.

There were several second generation sons who carried on their father's junk businesses (Shriberg, Yanco) but those businesses often morphed into selling second hand cars as well. Roiter's junk paper business survived in its original form into the 1960's.

But Morris's son Hyman was a Registrar for the Draft in Newton and later a letter carrier in Newton. Charles Gilfix worked as a census taker while in college and later held government positions in Revere. Jacob Gilfix landed a job as an accountant with the railroad, but later opened and ran his own business. Elliot Gilfix was a teacher and had a real estate and insurance business as well. (Philip Bram said, "to become a teacher, that was next to God.") One Yanco son became an officer of the Newton District Court and another son became a Newton police officer.

BAKER FAMILY

The Baker family came from Vilna, Lithuania and settled in Newton around 1902. In 1905, Mr. Baker made the building at 67-69 Crafts Street into a grocery store called Baker and Bass. He and his partner Julius Bass lived in a rooming house at 11 Maguire Court. By 1907, Julius Bass had left Newton and the store now bore only Louis Baker's name. A store is still in existence today at that location.

Although his name appears as Louis in all the documents we have, in the family it was spelled Lewis. He was married twice. The name of his first wife, who died in Europe, is not known. They had two children, Muriel and Harry. He and his second wife Mary (Gotfried) married in 1898. Sylvia Baker's son Jonathan Frieze says that family history suggests that she was a niece of his first wife and much younger than her husband. They had eight children together, Minnie, Jacob/Johnny, (both born in Europe) Abie/Arthur, Henry, Ethel, Gert, Helen and Sylvia.

Muriel Baker married Samuel Cohen. They had two children, Jacob and Hannah. Hannah married Milton Brodie. They had no children of their own but adopted two children, a boy, Samuel, who died about age two and a daughter, Marjory. They had a grocery store on the corner of Green and West Streets. Jacob was called Sonny all his life but his birth certificate read "John." At the time of his birth, the clerk registering the birth was asked what the boy was called, meaning what was his name. He is called Jack, they replied. The clerk apparently decided that Jack was a nickname for John, not a nickname for Jacob.

Louis had a store and what was called an express business where he went to Boston twice a week (Thursday and Saturday nights) with a horse named Daisy. He would buy kosher food for his customers. His nephew Philip Bram would go with him to buy the food and take it to customers in Nonantum. It took two hours to get to Boston with the horse and wagon. You could not leave on Saturday before the Sabbath was over, so by the time they got to Boston, bought the groceries and were done delivering, it was 2 or 3 AM.

Louis died in an automobile accident in 1925. Mary continued to run the store for about eight years after his death, until her death in 1933.

Louis Baker served four terms as president of the synagogue, in 1913, 1919, 1920 and 1921.

My Mother's Stories

In addition to this information, we have a memoir by Minnie Baker Gerson, told to her daughter Ruth Gerson Rabinow.

I was only two years old when I came to America. I always remember my birthday because I was born in October in the last year of the century, 1899. It was around the Jewish holidays. My mother came with Jake and me and my half sister and half brother, Muriel and Harry. There was another baby who died in the old country. My mother was not much older than Muriel. They were like sisters. Muriel was a big help to her.

I was told later than when we got to Ellis Island, we had to go back to Europe because there was something wrong with our papers. So we crossed over twice. Finally, we did get to Nonantum where my father was settled. He came to Newton because he had a cousin there.

I was afraid of my father. He was very cranky. He had been living by himself and then he had to deal with all us kids. He was sweet to Muriel, though. He called her Mirrela and kissed her. She must have reminded him of his dead wife. Muriel was a good girl. She and Harry were quiet. But Jake and I always wanted to have fun.

Our first home was in Maguire Court. All the tenants were immigrants. We were the only Jews. They were Irish, Italian, French and a colored family, the Wellmans. There was a lot of name calling and laughing but we all got along. When I went out to play, I remember saying, "May I please play *mit* your *ballaleh*?" The kids laughed and had some fun with me. They said, "Say it again and we'll let you." So I said it again. Most of the kids talked a foreign language in their homes. My mother became friendly with the neighbors. They would take care of each other. Sometimes she even nursed babies that weren't her own.

When I went to school, I was told to sit there until the bell rang. When it rang for recess, I got up and went home. Somebody had to explain to me in Yiddish not to do that. Pretty soon I was speaking English. There was another girl in school whose name was the same as mine, Anna. I told them to call me by my middle name, Minnie, and it stuck. I thought Minnie was very fancy. Now some of my friends call themselves Minnette, but I'm just Minnie the Moocher.

It took a lot of effort to keep our Jewish traditions. We had to schlep all the way to the West End to buy kosher food. My father conducted religious services in our house. My mother cooked all day for the Sabbath. We would pay a gentile kid to put the lights on and off for us on Friday nights and Saturdays. After awhile, my father and some of the other men in the Jewish community bought the land on Adams Street. Later they built the Adams Street Shul. Sometimes visiting rabbis and cantors came to conduct services at the temple. We would put them up in our house. Once a colored Jew came. He was very *frum* [pious]. The shul was very Orthodox. The women sat upstairs and the men sat downstairs. In all the years since then, there has never been any vandalism at that temple. The neighborhood respected us. The shul is now a historic building as the first temple in Newton. It is still in use. My father was the first president of that shul.

We soon left Maguire Court and bought our house with the store on the corner of Crafts Street and Clinton. The store was attached to the house. My mother and father and us kids helped in the store. The store became a neighborhood meeting place. It had the only telephone in the neighborhood. Whenever there was an emergency, people came to the store.

My mother was like a saint. She was so sweet and so good. Everyone loved her. She worked very hard. She had one baby after another. She had ten children in all. One baby died in the old country and one died here. I took care of that baby. He was my responsibility. I felt that he was my baby. One nice warm day, I thought that it would be good to give him a bath. I kept him nice and warm but the next day he caught a cold. That turned into pneumonia and he died. I thought it was my fault because of the bath. I used to wake up in the middle of the night and think that he was still alive. I would look for him all over the house, in closets, in drawers, but he was gone.

I pitied my mother. She had so much to do. If I had any problems, I would never tell her. Sometimes I was sick or had nits or something embarrassing like that. I took care of myself. Although one time I remember her chasing me up a tree because I wanted to play and she wanted me to do something. She shook her finger at me and said, "*Ich vill du bald geben* [I will give you something; meaning, you're going to get it when you come down]. Imagine me being like that to that sweet woman.

My father was not always nice to her. I used to hear them fighting in their bedroom. She didn't want more children. I used to see him flirting and being so charming to the customers. It made me sick. We never felt secure. I remember all of us were so scared when the Board of Health came to examine the store. We were afraid that he would shut down the store—our livelihood.

Our father would buy these wild horses and he would train them in our yard. He would drive the wagon to Brookline and bring back kosher foods. I was a little older then and I would deliver the food to the Jewish customers on my bike. I had some funny experiences on my delivery route. One time I was told that a very famous boy violinist was staying with a relative in Newton. He had played for the Tsar. I pushed my wild hair down as best I could and tried to look pretty for Jascha Heifetz. I shouldn't have bothered because he was disgusting. He only knew dirty words in English. I ran out of there. They could keep him.

Another time when I was on my bike I thought I would stop at the house of a man in the neighborhood who had just died, to pay my respects. I opened the door and walked in. I went into the parlor and there was the coffin. I was alone with it. I looked at him and he looked at me. I ran like hell out of there!

I used to deliver kosher food to the Gilfix family. They had a million kids. Mrs. Gilfix would open the package and break a whitefish into pieces with her hands. Then she would call her kids, "Yossel, Rose, Itzik." Hands came up from under the table, another from behind the bureau, down the steps. She would shove a piece of whitefish into each hand.

I had a crush on the Irishman who would deliver milk to the store. He had beautiful blue eyes. He always joked with me. I think that he knew that I liked him. When I thought he was coming, I tried to look good and would hang around the store. One time he caught me at my worst. My hair was wild and kinky and was standing up all around my head. I was wearing an old dress and I was barefoot. I saw his wagon in front of the store and I ducked under the counter. All of a sudden I heard his voice say to my mother, "What is this, Mrs. Baker? Do you have mice?" He pulled me out of there by my dirty big toe!

Sometimes he would take my colored friend and me to school in his milk wagon. The fresh boys would yell at us all the way to school, throwing snow balls and calling out the worst worst words they could think of, nigger, mick and kike all sitting together.

By this time Muriel and Harry were married and had left the house. My father set Muriel up with a store on Adams Street. Muriel had married Sam Cohen and thought she had found a prince because he was American born. He was spoiled and liked to gamble but he was the man she loved. She worked for him all her life.

Jake and my father never got along. Once he ran away from home. He was gone for a whole week. He had traveled by hiding in the bathrooms on the trains. The day he came home, he hid until he saw me. Then he knocked on the window and asked, "Is Pa around?" My father was damned glad to see him alive. He didn't even get mad.

Baker Family, about 1912
Back row: Harry, Muriel
Front row: Minnie, Mary, Abie, Henry (on his father's lap), Louis, Jacob

Photo courtesy of Mrs. Helen Baker Norman and Historic Newton

That picture of our family was taken by the Bachrach Studio. It must have been very expensive. My mother made every bit of clothing that we were wearing there. My father wanted us to be real Americans. My father thought that I should learn to play the piano. We went into Boston and he picked out a piano. He wrote Baker on the back of it so that he could be sure that the piano delivered was the same one that he had chosen. Our name, Baker, was spelled that way but it had two little dots over the a.

I was a teenager now and everyone said I was pretty. My father took some pride in that. I bought my first grown up long dress. I remember showing it to him. He was sitting in the parlor. I carefully called from the door, "Pa, can I show you my new dress?" He motioned me in. I remember turning all the way around, self-consciously. "Good," he said. My father was much gentler with the younger kids. But I was always afraid of him.

I started to go to dances with my friends. Sometimes we went down to the Charles River to skate. In those days, you could skate all the way to Boston.

At that time, Henry Gerson, your father, visited us. We were distantly related to each other. We were all Litvaks (from Lithuania). We called him a big butter and egg man because he was doing so well and would drive up in a big car. I thought that he was pretty classy except he had an accent. My family liked him a lot and we started to date. Then we got engaged.

At that time, I was working in a factory (a sweat shop). I was working so hard that I had a nervous breakdown. I just sat there. I heard everyone but I couldn't talk at all. I heard my father talking about me to my mother in Yiddish. "Let's not waster any money on doctors. She's *meshuga*." My mother insisted that we go to the doctor. I got better but sometimes I got bad again. It was my depression. Your father knew about my depression but he wanted to marry me anyhow. I was sick on and off. You were born and then when Tiby was born, I got sick again and we had to break up our home You went to Tanta Lilly's house in Melrose and Tiby and your father went to Newton and stayed with my family.

When I recovered, we bought the two family house in Roxbury. Before that, we lived in Malden. Your father's cousin Sam lived downstairs. Once his wife called me a *meshugana* [crazy]. When your father came home and found me crying about it, he ran downstairs and gave her hell.

I used to visit my mother as much as I could. My mother started to have backaches. I took her to the doctor, who recommended an expensive corset to make her feel more comfortable. We went to a special place in Boston to get fitted for that corset. A month or so later we were sitting in the kitchen drinking tea. When she suddenly got up, ripped off the corset and said, "*In dread [to hell with] mit the doctor, In dread mit der corset*, I know what's wrong with me." She had just felt life; she was pregnant. She didn't tell the other kids about it. They didn't notice because she was getting heavy and always wore a dark loose fitting dress.

One night, my brother Abie came from a date and found all the kids sitting in the parlor crying because Pa took Mama to the hospital. When Abie called the Saint Elizabeth's Hospital, he was told that Mrs. Baker had just given birth to a baby girl. That's when your Aunt Syl was born. You were born a couple of years later. There's twenty-seven months between you two.

I was in Newton one day, showing you off to my father. I wanted you to walk for him, but you weren't quite ready. He said, "Don't worry. She'll walk, she'll talk!" Then he and Sam Gerson left for a business trip to Vermont and he never came home again. The truck went over an embankment and he was pinned under the wheel. Sam survived. He even talked to my father for a little while until he died.

My poor mother was left with a large family and the business.

BRAM FAMILY

The Bram family came from Vilna, Lithuania. The family settled in Newton because Louis Baker, who was their uncle, had settled there. Samuel Bram came to the United States in about 1907. His wife and children traveled to America on the Mauritania, landing in New York in December 1910. Philip Bram recalled that the ticket was sent from Boston to the family in Europe. Purchased from Slobodkin in the West End, it cost $50.00 per person for steerage.

The family had seven children, Philip (b. 1903), Bertha (b. 1904), Morris, Frank, Joseph, Ida, and Amy (b. 1918).

In Lithuania, Samuel Bram's father was a tavern owner.

Samuel Bram was a blacksmith. Many of the Jewish residents were peddlers with a horse and wagon, so Samuel the blacksmith had done business with them making horseshoes, as well as stovepipes and pots and pans. As the use of horses was less prevalent as years went by, Samuel sought to diversify his work as a blacksmith by going into the junk business. Blacksmiths like Bram regularly recycled old metal, horseshoes, cast iron pots, and junked automobiles, from which he made a good living.

His son Philip recalled that when they arrived in America, his mother was horrified to find her husband was going to work on the Sabbath. She told him that they would have to return to Russia if he didn't stop. She was very careful about *kashrus* as well.

Samuel died in a fire in April 1926 at the age of 47, leaving his wife Rose to raise their seven children by herself. The fire originated in his blacksmith forge and the whole horrible event was witnessed by his wife, who had a nervous breakdown and was considered unstable for the rest of her life. Despite her mental problems, Philip remembered hers as a wonderful mother, an excellent cook and very smart, although illiterate. She could speak about five languages, he recalled, which she learned by talking to customers in the stores where she worked.

Samuel Bram

Photo courtesy of Mrs. Vickie Bram

Philip recalled his life in Lithuania as a child. "We slept in the barn with the horses and cows and we had a *kammer* [an apartment] on the perimeter. And it had a sand floor. And every Friday before Shabbas and before every Yom Tov, they would sweep the old sand off and put in new sand. In the kammer, we had a ladder and we three children slept on top of the stove. It was a brick oven, a couple of feet below the ceiling." (These tall brick or porcelain stoves were prevalent in Russia and Scandinavia and sleeping on top of the stove was a privilege because it was so warm, and often reserved for the younger children).

Philip loved cars and he had a vivid memory of seeing his first car. "This magnificent automobile, with the coat and the hat and the goggles, and all the things that you know about, that you've seen in an automobile, I saw that go by, first time I ever saw anything like that, I never saw one since. But I remember vividly this magnificent piece of equipment, blowing a horn, going by our house, on the street in front of our tavern" in about 1910 while they were still in Europe. He loved cars all his life and would drive friends and relatives to go visiting, even as far as New York. In his old age, he could recall every car he had ever owned and what he paid for it.

With the death of his father, the blacksmith, Philip became head of the household at the age of twenty one. "But time was of no essence. We had everything but money. We had health, we had time, and stretching the dollar was a specialty." He recalled proudly that he "provided the money for [his sisters] to get married on." He also had an informal delivery service for groceries, similar to what his uncle Louis Baker had done with a horse and wagon. "Now the horse was so trained that it would stop. Mr. Baker would take me with him, that was a privilege, to be taken by Mr. Baker to the West End, to get stuff for my mother and all the other Jews." In later years, the women would come by trolley from the West End or South End with their groceries late on Saturday night to Watertown [where the car barn was and still is located]. I would take their bundles of food in my car and deliver it to their houses, just like we used to do with the horse and wagon. They would be so appreciative of my help that they would bless me "and those blessings are the reason I live so long." [Philip was 83 at the time of this interview].

Bram Building, Walnut Street, Newtonville, 1926   Philip Bram, left

Photo courtesy of Mrs. Vickie Bram

In March 1926, Philip opened Philip Bram Auto Supply in what became known as the Bram Block on Walnut Street near the corner of Washington Street in Newtonville. Philip first appears in the 1925 city directory as an auto mechanic. There was a lot of scrap metal in cars, such as tubs, radiators, crank cases and battery boxes, which his father had reused or recycled, thus exposing his son to the automotive business. He also ran a bicycle shop at the same site and Harry Standel remembered buying his first bicycle there.

The Bram Block has always had a clock which could be seen from Washington Street and Walnut Street and it has been a landmark in the city for many years.

Philip was actively involved in the city of Newton and Philip Bram Way, off Austin Street near the Shaw's supermarket, reflects his political influence. When the synagogue was undergoing its restoration, friends of Philip Bram donated the fire alarm system to the synagogue in his honor.

His son Richard and Richard's wife Vicki donated the Newton Room at the Newton Free Library, a reflection of Dick's interest in Newton's history and his own civic-mindedness. Richard also served as president of the Newton-Needham Chamber of Commerce.

ABRAHAM FOX FAMILY

Father, Abram/Abraham Fox and his wife Ida, had two sons, Jack and Sam. They had an uncle Alexander. The men came to the US from Russia around 1907.

They started out in the West End. When they came to Newton, they lived in Coxeter's Hotel, at 81 West Street.

Mr. and Mrs. Abram Fox and Herbert, 1914

Photo courtesy Mrs. Franklin Fox and Historic Newton

"My father opened his first furniture store, the Nonantum Furniture Company (later Fox Furniture) right across the street from the drug store [Fox Pharmacy] in Nonantum [on Watertown Street], and then he moved it to Newton Corner. They moved to the Newton area when there were only two other Jewish families, the Frieds and the Perlmutters. They both owned dry goods stores on Watertown Street."

Photo of Nonantum Furniture Company, later Fox Furniture Company

Photo courtesy of Mrs. David Dangel and Historic Newton

ALEXANDER FOX FAMILY

The pharmacy was located on the corner of Chapel and Watertown Streets. Philip Gilfix recalled that there was a Jewish doctor named Robbins and he shared the space with Alexander Fox, the pharmacist. Mr. Fox had been a pharmacist in Russia. Eventually the doctor left but the pharmacy remained.

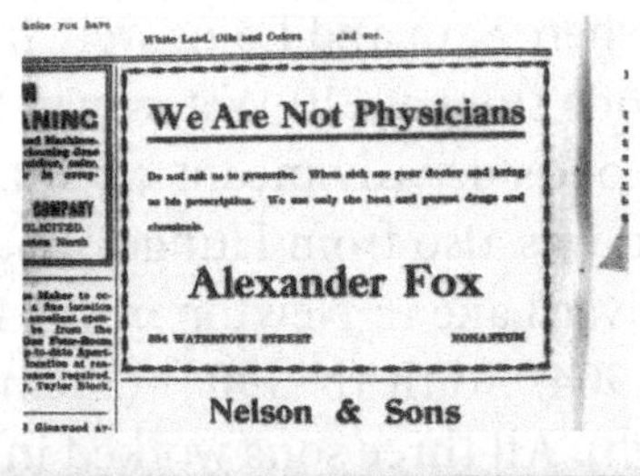

"Nonantum thanks its pharmacists for 3 generations of Health Services, March 17, 1966"
L to R: "Doc," Mrs. Frank Lombardi, Frank Lombardi, Sam Fried, M. C. Fred Fox, Mrs.Fox, Mrs. Alexander Fox, Mr. Wilfred Chagnon

MORRIS FRIED

Morris Fried arrived in the US in 1882 from Nyiregyhaza, a city northeast of Budapest, Hungary. When he arrived in America, he went to Poughkeepsie because there was a Perlmutter living there that he had known in Hungary. When he first arrived, he worked as a baker. Morris' father was a master baker in Hungary. He married Celia Perlmutter in 1893 and they moved to Newton around 1900 where Sam and Louis were born.

He opened a dry goods store at 310 Watertown Street, called Fried's Department Store. (Dry goods usually meant clothing, shoes and linens). He and his wife Celia, who was also from Hungary, had six children: Sigmond (b.1894; drowned in Silver Lake in Newton in 1904), David (b. 1896), Louis (b. 1901), Samuel (b. 1904), Ruth (b. 1906) (Shelman), Bertha (1908-1909, died of whooping cough). All three sons worked in the store.

David served with the 26th Yankee Division in France and was gassed but returned home alive. He had a 60% disability from the war and eventually died from the effects of the gas. Morris's son Louis recalled that a local boy, a Kligman, was excused from military service because he refused to eat *trayfe* (non-kosher food). The cement steps leading up to the synagogue today replaced the original set of wooden steps. The Fried family donated the steps in 1919 in honor of David's safe return from France. Louis and David married two sisters, Marion and Henrietta Lichtman.

The Perlmutter and Fried families were well off in Europe and when they came to Newton, they immediately opened stores on Watertown Street. Louis Fried recalled seven stores on the street owned by his relatives. At a time when many immigrants were struggling to establish themselves, Morris traveled to Europe every year to "take the waters" for his health at Karlsbad in Czechoslovakia.

Morris Fried was instrumental in the establishment of Keneses Israel Anshe Sephard, the first attempt to establish a synagogue in Newton, starting in 1909. Records at the Registry of Deeds show that Morris Fried was also active in the real estate market, buying and selling real estate not only in Newton but in Cambridge as well. He may have used his own money in the real estate transactions regarding Keneses Israel Anshe Sephard. His son Louis said Morris was too ill to be president of the synagogue but he was active in other ways.

The Fried family dry goods store on Watertown Street in Nonantum was well known to everyone in the neighborhood. It is now the location of Antoine's Bakery.

Family of Morris Fried, 1917
L to R: Louis, Celia, Samuel, Morris, Ruth, David

Photo courtesy Diane Lurie Berg

Morris in Karlsbad, Czechoslovakia

Photo courtesy Diane Lurie Berg

Fried's Department Store, Watertown Street, Nonantum

Photo courtesy Diane Lurie Berg

LOUIS FRIED

Joseph Louis Fried was born in 1901 in Chelsea, MA. The family moved to Newton when he was an infant. By that time the Perlmutters had established themselves in Newton. (Louis' mother was a Perlmutter). The Fried family owned Fried's Department Store on Watertown Street. Louis worked in the business which was started by his father, Morris.

As a young man, Louis played football and recalled with pride how tough they all were, with no pads. "And you played the whole 48 minutes, no replacements." Their coach was Mr. Dickinson, for whom the high school football stadium was named. He also said he played baseball and he was the catcher because he was fat and didn't like to run so much. He said he lost sixty pounds over the years.

Louis recalled that his father opened the store as soon as he arrived in Newton. He listed the stores on Watertown Street. "My uncle Abe [Perlmutter] had a store, and the store on the corner of Cook Street was vacant and that's where my father Morris set up. My mother's brother had a shoe store across the street and my uncle Will opened a dry good store, Perlmutter and Dane. My other uncle had a dry goods store also. The street was almost a family enterprise. And we did very, very well because my father was able to buy land . So my folks did very well. My father used to go to Europe every year for his health, for six weeks. The doctors told him to take the baths at Karlsbad in Czechoslovakia, that the water would melt the kidney stones. He was there in 1917 when America joined the war and he was lucky to get the last boat home. He told us that for eight or ten days there was no light on the boat and they zig zagged across the ocean to evade the U-boats. He died at age 54 from kidney disease."

Louis recalled an experience in kindergarten when they showed the children how to churn butter but he refused to eat it because he thought it was not kosher. He also went to Will Perlmutter's wedding in Roxbury and "there were colored waiters and I wouldn't eat because I was sure it wasn't kosher."

At the Stearns School, they had a print shop for the students to learn printing and he was proud to go into Boston to buy the type and everything for the school all by himself.

An active young man, Louis played football for Newton High School. After he graduated, Louis went to work in the munitions plant at the Fore River Shipyard. He was arrested and lost his job because he was falsely accused of not registering for the draft. (In fact he was not yet 18 so he didn't need to register). Then he went to work in his father's store. The store remained in business for 43 years until it was closed in 1963.

Louis and Marion Fried

Photo courtesy of Diane Lurie Berg

Louis Fried, ca 1965

Interviewed in 1986, Louis recalled that the trade was 85 % Italian, with some French and Irish customers as well. The Italians usually came without families and they would work and buy clothing and household linens to send back to their families. They would sew the items into pillowcases to mail them. They were very loyal customers.

Our Lady's Church had a Society of St. Vincent de Paul at the church. The Society would provide clothing for the poor and they bought their supplies from Fried's Department Store. "I used to go to that church every Monday night and be friends with them all, card parties, whist parties. So I was known as the best Jew in that parish and my brother Sam was known as the best Jew in the French parish (St. Jean L'Evangeliste)."

He and his brother Sam helped at least five hundred people to get American citizenship. For example, the Frieds helped the Franchi family to come to America and become citizens. Mr. Franchi [of Franchi Construction] built a big nursing home in Waban and at the dedication of the nursing home, he told everyone, "Louie, if it wasn't for you, I'd still be in Italy."

Louis's granddaughter Caryn Diuguid recalled that the Americanization process in her family was demonstrated in their dietary habits. Although they kept a kosher home, she recalled that her grandfather introduced her to seafood in restaurants. However, she said, he was the only Jew she knew who would not eat Chinese food.

There were about forty Jewish families in the neighborhood. Louis recalled that his father had been instrumental in starting a synagogue (Keneses Israel) which dissolved when the Adams Street Shul was built. Louis recalled that when the children of those immigrant Jewish families grew up, most of them moved to Roxbury and Dorchester and it was hard to maintain the congregation. The Frieds were among very few Jewish families who stayed in the neighborhood. The family lived on Cook Street which Louis recalled as being 100% Italian except for one Irishman and the Frieds. He himself never experienced any anti-Semitism.

The community did not change very much until the Depression, Louis recalled. Then there were very few new immigrants and it was hard to get merchandise but the store had done business with the city and that helped them to get supplies. During the Depression, people couldn't pay their rent and then the war came, he recalled and everyone could buy their own home.

The war years were hard for the store, again due to shortages of merchandise. Suddenly there were lots of jobs. Raytheon opened its first plant on Chapel Street in Nonantum and then a plant in Waltham. Other factories opened on Chapel Street as well. Any woman who wanted a job could get one and Raytheon even had a bus to take women workers to a factory in Burlington. This increase in jobs also gave people money to buy more merchandise.

After the war, Lou recalled, the city hired many returning Nonantum veterans as fireman and police officers. One group of local men called themselves the Lucky Seven because they all survived the war. The community had wonderful ball teams, where men in their twenties and thirties would play ball together and the police had a softball team as well.

Lou was proud to have served as president of the synagogue in the 1960s. During that time, the Post 440 [the Veteran's Post on California Street] called and asked the officers of the shul to come down. "So I called the Gilfix boys and Harry Roiter and Elmer Lippin and myself and we went down and they gave us a thousand dollars for our shul. They gave a thousand dollars to some other churches around the city and they also included us. I thought that was the nicest, nicest thing that had ever happened to us."

SAMUEL FRIED

Sam married Irene (Szathmari). Sam and Irene were cousins. They had the same grandfather in Hungary but different grandmothers.

Sam was well known in the community and his warmth and beaming smile was memorable. People enjoyed his company. Sam Fried exemplified the spirit of friendship, community and sharing. A Newton police officer, LT Charles Feeley, reminisced about the Lake and its inhabitants in a newspaper interview in 1972.[32] He noted that Sam, Louis and David were intimate friends of Father Robichaud from St. Jean L'Evangeliste Church and frequently drove him around to call on homebound parishioners. Sam even ran the bingo games at St. Jean's as master of ceremonies. LT Feeley recalled that Sam was an excellent athlete and loved sports. "He was a great salesman; he could separate a person from a dollar for a cause, sold good sportsmanship and what was more important, sold (his brother and business partner) Louis on the idea to mind the store while Sam did all these things. Sam did many grand things because Lou kept his nose to the grindstone."

In addition, LT Feeley continued, "they were saviors, godparents, mentors and teachers of hundreds of immigrants. There wasn't a week when they didn't swear out citizenship papers at the Federal Building and today there are many second generation Americans whose parents were taught the rudiments of reading by the efforts of Sam and Lou, along with the Fried's help and car, to learn how to drive, in order to make a living."

Samuel and Irene Fried

Photo courtesy of Diane Lurie Berg

Sam's granddaughter, Diane Lurie Berg, recalls that if a local boy got into trouble and was sent to prison, Sam would visit him in prison and when he got out, and would try to help him find a job. Local residents remember that Sam and Louis would see to it that children had proper clothing and shoes for First Communions and other Catholic religious events, even if the family could not pay at that time. They would provide the outfits, knowing that they would be paid when money was available.

Sam Fried's special relationship with Father Robichaud was a unique example of inter-religious friendship. When Sam died in South Carolina, Father Robichaud said a mass for him, as a parish benefactor, and one who was like many in the Lake, a good man and a good neighbor.

Sam's interest in sports gave him an interest in the Boys Club. He believed that sports taught boys sportsmanship, kept them healthy and kept them out of trouble. He used to say, "sports minded means clean minded." Along with the YMCA, located on Washington Street, the Boys Club was a major source of Americanization for the children of immigrant families. The Boys Club was founded in 1899 on Dalby Street and offered the opportunity for athletically inclined young men in the various immigrant communities in Nonantum to play sports. The Boy's Club sponsored many athletic teams. Many of the Jewish second generation students recalled playing baseball, football and boxing. The Club changed its name to Boys and Girls Club and moved to Watertown Street in the 1990s.

ISAAC GILFIX

Rose Gilfix Schribman recalled the stories of her ancestors that her parents told her in an interview with her daughter, Jean Birnbaum.

Isaac, the father of Morris and Benjamin Gilfix and Goldie Silverman never came to America. He died at the age of forty two. He may have been tubercular or asthmatic, as he always had a constant, severe cough. (Many of his descendents are asthmatic as well). His wife Shaindel was an orphan who was raised by relatives after the death of her parents. Her daughter-in-law Sarah (Benjamin's wife) remembered her as a sad person who always felt belittled because she had no parents and had to live on the bounty of her relatives.

Isaac and Shaindel had seven children, ranging in age from sixteen year old Morris to baby Joseph. Of the seven, Morris, Tzippeh, Benjamin, Libby, Golda emigrated to America. Their sister Elka Shifra remained in Europe. Joseph died in Russia after a fall from a wagon at the age of thirty five. Eerily, his sister Golda had dreamed that he would die in such an accident. Shaindel never came to America, although almost all her children were here. She lived to a very old age.

The house that Isaac and Shaindel lived in was in a village called Colchin, in Volina Gubernya. The house had a dirt floor and a small garden where they grew vegetables. It is not known what they did to support themselves but they may have had a business selling paints or dyes. That is the business that Shaindel operated after Isaac's death. Everyone had to work, even the small children, in order to earn enough money to live. Girls in poor Jewish families often went to work as servants in the homes of other Jews. They would never work for non-Jews because they would not be able to get kosher food. Colchin was primarily a farming community and the boys could work on farms or in local factories.

The local mills processed local agricultural products. There was also a rope mill. Some rope mills used horses to turn the wheels which turned and twisted the straw into rope but other mills used boy power, including Benjamin. No boy was too young to work as long as he could contribute. Benjamin became a wheel turner at the age of eight. Sometimes he would fall asleep from sheer exhaustion from pushing the wheel round and round but he would be roused by a blow from the mill owner.

There was no public education for Jewish students so the boys were taught in *cheder* (a Jewish one room schoolhouse) by a local Jewish man who knew how to read and write. It was essential that the boys knew Hebrew so that they could read the prayer book. Sometimes girls were taught to read also.

Many of the Jews could speak Russian but not necessarily read it. Knowing the local language was essential to conducting business with the local people.

Market days in Kolchean (alternate spelling) took place every week. Farmers and business people would come from outlying areas to buy and sell, even in the wintertime. The women were often the ones who ran the market stalls. They would have little pots of coals underneath their long skirts to try and keep warm standing outside all day.

BENJAMIN GILFIX

Benjamin (known in Yiddish as Beryl Dovid and in Hebrew as Dov Ber) was born in Ukraine in January 1869.

Military service was compulsory in Russia at that time and Benjamin was drafted into the Army at the age of 21 for a four-year tour of duty. He served in the fortress of Kiev. However, if there was not a war, each year the recruits drew lots to see who would be released after only one year of service. Benjamin was lucky to get one of the early releases. When he was released from the army, he tried to earn a living as a "runner," connecting buyers and sellers and earning a small commission on each transaction that he put together. He decided to come to America when he realized that he could not earn a living in Russia.

He wrote to friends who were already in America to ask for advice. They wrote back saying, "if you have unpeeled potatoes (a supply of food), stay where you are but otherwise, if you no longer have unpeeled potatoes (no food surplus), come, but don't think you'll have it easy here." He didn't come right away but he could see only a dismal life ahead of him if he stayed.

He married Sarah Y'hudis Moran (or Maran) (b. April 1874) in Colchin in 1894 and he came to America in 1895. The marriage was arranged by a matchmaker. Benjamin's mother was very upset that her tall, handsome son was being offered a match with this "*pitzsileh* [very tiny]" woman but Benjamin liked her so they got married. Later in life, his daughter Rose described her parents: "He was tall and very straight backed and had red hair and a red beard and a temper to match. She was very small, but pretty. She looked like a little doll and was very mild mannered."

Sarah's father Mordechai was reputed to be a very good looking and very haughty man. He was also a very scholarly man and a scribe who devoted his life to the study of Torah and to teaching others. They owned a five room house (very large for that time and place), in which all the rooms were rented out, including the kitchen which served as a sleeping space at night. In that way, he managed to support his family without resorting to work which might have taken him away from Torah study.

Benjamin's oldest child, Rose, was born in 1895 in Chon, Russia. His wife Sarah and their daughter came to America on the Pretoria in 1899. At 59 Clinton Street, Benjamin put in running water and a toilet right away. There was no electricity at first, only kerosene lamps. The chimneys of the kerosene lamps had to be cleaned every night as they got all sooty. It was a dirty and difficult chore as the chimneys often broke and then you had to run to Swartz Hardware to buy a new one before dark.

Benjamin and his wife had ten children, seven of whom lived to adulthood. They were Rose (b. 1895), Isaac (b. 1900, died in 1919 of congenital heart disease), Joseph (b. 1901), Jacob (b. 1902), Philip (b. 1903), Molly/Malke Faige/Mary Fannie (b. 1905, died 1905. age 10 months, of convulsions), Adele Sophie/Udel Shifra/Ida Sophia (b. 1906, died 1910, age 4, from burns), Allen (b. 1908), Irving (b. 1910) and Isabel (b. 1912).

Benjamin and his wife both died in 1935.

Benjamin was a junk dealer specializing in metal of various types. One of his daughters in law commented that "he had the neatest junk yard you ever saw, with everything neatly arranged in bins and boxes." A successful junk dealer would not immediately sell what he collected but would wait for the best prices.

When they came to Newton, they lived at 59 Clinton Street, a four room house. In 1908, there were at least ten people (two adults and eight children) living in a four room house, with two rooms on the first floor and two rooms on the second. A toilet was added in the basement and eventually a bathroom was added off the kitchen. Benjamin kept his horse and wagon in the barn at 93 West Street after they moved but earlier must have boarded the horse since 59 Clinton Street had no land for a stable or junk yard.

Benjamin was instrumental in the founding of the Adams Street Shul and is the first name listed of the incorporators. His home at 93 West Street was listed as the location of the founding group. He was a follower of Rabbi M.Z. Twersky, the Talner Rebbe. The rebbe came to stay in the Gilfix house, sometimes accompanied by his *gabbai* (assistant) and young son, later Rabbi Doctor Isadore Yitchak Twersky. The rebbe would teach and provide religious guidance and counseling for members of the community who sought his advice.

Philip Bram recounted his opinion about the Gilfix family. "Mrs. Gilfix was a lovely woman. Benjamin was a tyrant. But he had one son, Isaac, that had congenital heart trouble. A wonderful young man, hung around the house, couldn't go anywhere. And his father, I think that put him in a terrible frame of mind to have that boy so ill. Isaac would cough his head off. But he had a wonderful family, Joseph and Philip, Jay and Sruli, Al."

The house at 61 Clinton Street was owned by Morris Gilfix, Benjamin's brother. The boundary between 59 and 61 Clinton Street was marked by a grapevine, remnants of which survived into the 21st century. Everyone who remembers the homes on Clinton Street remembered the grapevine and the aroma of the ripening grapes. Benjamin's grandson Marshall Schribman recalled that they used the grapes to make wine by squeezing the grapes by hand. Marshall recalled that the recipe called for ten pounds of grapes and five pounds of sugar and that the wine was very, very sweet. Marshall's sister Jean recalled that the inside of the grapes were very sour but the skins were sweet to eat. The wine making took place at the home of Jack and Rose Schribman, Benjamin's son -in-law and daughter, who lived at 83 West Street.

Benjamin had a house built at 93 West Street in about 1909. The house was made of stucco, which was considered very avant garde at that time. He planted pear trees and plum trees and black cherry trees in the back, as well as a grape arbor and kept chickens as well. Jean Birnbaum, a Gilfix granddaughter, recalled that off the kitchen on West Street was a screened or glass enclosed back porch. "Here our grandmother had wooden kegs in which she made sour pickles and tomatoes as well as sauerkraut. When these items were ready to eat, she would give my brother Marvin and me (aged about six and seven at the time) a hunk of black bread and a fork and turn us loose, and we would eat to our heart's content of these goodies. The sauerkraut was unbelievably delicious and was my favorite. Through the years I have tasted a lot of store bought sauerkraut but none has even approached the taste of hers."

Family of Benjamin Gilfix, about 1906
L to R: Joseph, Sarah Y'hudis, Rose, Jacob, Philip, Benjamin, Isaac

Photo courtesy of Beryl Gilfix

Benjamin was very patriarchal and authoritarian, not an understanding person. His eldest child, his daughter Rose, was taken out of school at the end of eighth grade to stay home and help her mother take care of the other six children. To her brother Jacob, she was as prominent in his memories as his mother, taking care of everyone. Despite her intelligence (Jacob thought she was the smartest of all the children), she was denied education. It was customary for many children at that time to leave school at the end of eighth grade; the boys would be sent out to work. At the turn of the 20th Century, it was common for high schools to have entrance examinations which restricted entrance to fewer than 5 percent of the population in preparation for college. Most were expected to be ready for a job or a family after junior high school. So Benjamin's action was not unusual, except that it was unusual in the Jewish community. There were instances in the community of girls who chose not to continue their education but it was very rare for such a decision to be imposed on the girl by her family. And how did Rose feel about this?

There is a photo of her eighth grade graduation class. All the girls in the class are dressed in white, except Rose. She sits on the ground in front of group, dressed entirely in black.

The speed with which the Jewish community of Newton changed from around 1900 to the early 1930s was very marked. By the 1930's, when Marshall Schribman (a Gilfix grandson) was a child, there were only three Jewish children in the four-room Eliot School. The 5th and 6th grades were housed in the Stearns School. Marshall's family moved to Newton Centre in 1938 because by that time the Adams Street Shul was open only on holidays. Marshall believes his brother Marvin was the last person to be bar mitzvah in the synagogue (1938).

The house at 93 West Street was much larger than the four room house on Clinton Street. It made it possible for the family to host visiting charitable collectors when they came to town, as well as visiting rabbis.

Mordechai and Chana Bela Moran, parents of Mrs. Benjamin Gilfix

Photo courtesy of Beryl Gilfix

RAGS TO RICHES, OR THE ROAD TO THE MIDDLE CLASS

Benjamin Gilfix came to Newton in 1896 and settled into a four room house at 59 Clinton Street in Nonantum, a house owned by his brother Morris who lived next door. The house had two rooms on the first floor, a kitchen and a "parlor," which could serve many different purposes. There were two bedrooms upstairs. The house sat at the back of the lot, with just enough room to walk around the sides and back of the property. There was a small front yard with its famous grape arbor. He brought his wife and infant daughter to this house in 1899 and worked as a junk peddler. By 1909, there were two parents and eight children living in that house. Reading this list of facts might suggest a poor man who could not speak English and who struggled to support his family in the new world.

But add to this image the fact that in 1908 and 1909 Benjamin bought two parcels of land on West Street, totaling over 7,000 square feet. It is frustrating that the two deeds are for "one dollar and other valuable considerations," so we don't know how much he paid for the land but it was one of the largest lots in the neighborhood. We don't know how much he paid to build the house. But it was a congenial neighborhood for him and his family since the 1910 census shows that the Pass, Yanco, Mielman, Shriberg, Greenwald and Cantor families were living there as well.

59 Clinton Street

93 West Street

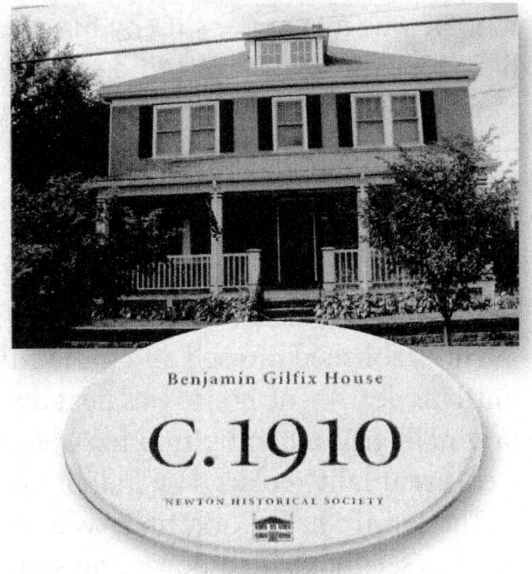

Photos courtesy Beryl Gilfix

The records show that he obtained two mortgages from two different banks in order to build the house which is now numbered 93 West Street. In November 1908, he obtained one mortgage for $1300 from the West Newton Savings Bank. In the same month, he obtained a mortgage from the Newton Cooperative Bank for $800. In June 1910 he also borrowed money from his cousin Samuel Rosenbaum in the form of a mortgage of $800. All these mortgages were paid in full by 1917.

Records show that he borrowed money freely and that he was considered to be a good credit risk, because the Newton Cooperative Bank loaned him $1500 in 1925, which he repaid in two years.

MORRIS GILFIX

Morris/Maurice (Moshe or Moishe) Gilfix was one of the charter members of the synagogue.

His daughter Dr. Brenda Gilfix Foner, has done extensive research on the family's geographic locations and history. Morris was born in Ukraine in May 1856 in Khmelnytskyi Oblast in the Volyn Highland (Volynia Gubernia) on the Bug River. The town, called Colchin, was located roughly 60 miles north of Proskurov. He died in Newton in 1936. His father Isaac died in Russia in 1864 when Moishe (as he was known in Yiddish) was eight years old.

Morris arrived in the United States in August 1888, landing in East Boston. He was met at the ship by his sister Libbe (or Leah) who had preceded him. He lived in the West End of Boston until about 1897 or 1898, when he moved to Newton. He became a citizen in 1899. His wife Frayda (b. September 1863), whom he married in 1880, died in 1921.

Morris and his wife had nine children, Hyman/Hymie/Hart, Charlie, Eva (Standel), Leah (Poutasse), Lily, Elliot, Helen (Berman), Leo (mentally disabled, he lived in a group home in Hopkinton) and Rachel (died young). Lily, Leah, Leo and Rachel died without children.

He established himself and his family at 61 Clinton Street, where he lived until his death. The house was next door to his brother Benjamin. The house originally had a hand pump for water in the kitchen and gas lights, which were eventually replaced by indoor plumbing and electricity.

The family name originally was Alter or Alten or Alder or Alden. No one has seen it written down and so the pronunciation is in question. They all mean "old." (Moishe Alter and Elliot Alden). Frayda's maiden name was Alden, so they may have been related.

Moishe's mother Shaindel lived until at least 1915 (Leah used to write to her in Russia). Shaindel never came to America, even though all but one of her children were here and she was a widow.

Morris was missing the thumb on his right hand. The family story is that it was amputated when he was an infant so that he could not serve in the Russian Army. Or he might have maimed himself as an adult to avoid service in the Russian army. Although not especially religious, he always wore a black, pillbox style yarmulke, and was involved in the founding of the synagogue.

Eva was one of Morris Gilfix's daughters. She told her grandson Harry Standel this story about her father. Morris came to the United States and settled in the West End, where there was a small Jewish community. He was contacted by a local horse trader because he had been a horse trader in the old country. Morris went to meet the fellow in his stable in the South End. The stable owner brought out a horse and asked him to describe the horse and Morris did. I guess horse traders in those days were akin to used car salesmen, but after Morris described several horses, he was offered a job and he went home and told his wife, "great news, I've got a job!" And she said "what are you going to do?" and he said "I am going to be checking horses." She said "where is this job?" and he said" it's in Colorado." She said "where is Colorado?" and he said "I have no idea." She said "is there a shul?" and he said "I don't know." She is said "is there a rabbi?" and he said "I don't know." She says " is there a *shocket*? (a religious slaughterer of beef and chicken)" and he said "I don't know." She said "is there a *mohel*? (to perform a circumcision)" and he said "I don't know but I will find out." So the next day he went back to the South End and talked to his prospective employer and the prospective employer said "I know there are Indians there but I don't know if there are rabbis or shuls. I've just been buying horses in Colorado and they are delivered by train here to Boston and sometimes I get this bad group of horses and I want someone out there to check them out before they are delivered." So Morris went home and told his wife and she said " that's the end of the good job in Colorado. We are not going to Colorado."

So Morris became, for want of a better word, a custom peddler. He was given a pack and he walked from East Boston to Watertown and Cambridge and Newton and that was his route. He would knock on doors and offer pins and needles and whatever else housewives needed in those days. At some point Morris said to his family, I don't want to live in the dirt of the city any longer. I want to live in the country where the farms are and where there is clean air. At the time Newton was that place, so they moved here.

He moved to 61 Clinton Street in Newton and that peddling is what he did all of his life. His descendent Harry Standel visited 61 Clinton Street and remembered a big grape arbor and sitting under that grape arbor and picking grapes with his aunt Lillian, who died quite young.

Moshe and Frayda Gilfix

photo courtesy of Brenda Gilfix Foner and Stephen Gilfix

Morris was listed in the Newton City directory as a junk peddler but he also had a delivery service utilizing his horse and wagon. His horse was named Fitzpatrick. Fitzpatrick lived in a shed at the back of 61 Clinton Street. Morris often took the horse and wagon to the North End from Newton to get kosher meat. His granddaughter Brenda Gilfix Foner remembered going with him and the horse and wagon to deliver milk in and around Newton when she was very young.

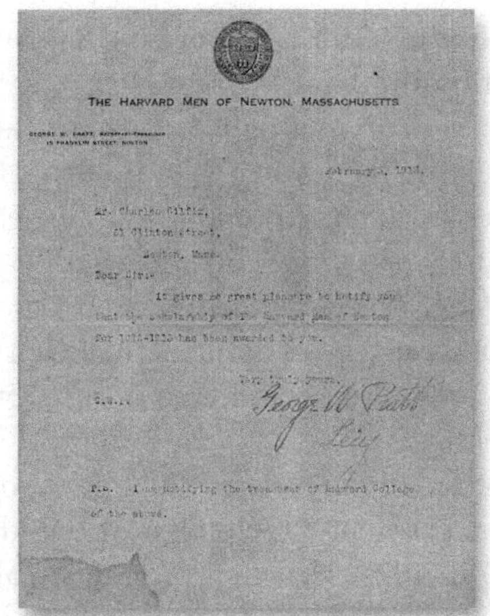

THE HARVARD MEN OF NEWTON, MASSACHUSETTS

[illegible], [illegible]

Mr. Charles Gilfix,
[illegible] Clinton Street,
Newton, Mass.

Dear Sir:-

It gives me great pleasure to notify you that the scholarship of The Harvard Men of Newton for [illegible] has been awarded to you.

Very truly yours,
[illegible]
Secy.

P.S. I am notifying the treasurer of Harvard College of the above.

Charlie Gilfix, Harvard College, Class of 1913

photo courtesy of Brenda Gilfix Foner and Stephen Gilfix

His sons Charlie and Elliot were both graduates of Harvard College. His son Hymie was the first Jewish postman in Newton. Philip Bram recalled "the Gilfixes on Clinton Street, their oldest boy Hymie was a letter carrier. And that was the greatest in that era and awe to think that anybody could get a job in the Post Office. There was nothing like that around." The idea that a Jew could get a government job impressed even the second generation.

Morris's son Charlie was born in Ukraine in 1888 and came to America around 1896. He graduated from Harvard College in 1913. He died in 1949. He lived most of his life in Revere. His son Charlie Junior graduated from Harvard in 1941. Junie, as he was known, died in 1993 of Alzheimer's. The third generation of that family to graduate from Harvard, R. Charles Gilfix, graduated from Harvard in 1993. The family saved the graduation cap and gown that the first Gilfix wore and each subsequent generation has worn the same gown to their Harvard graduation.

Morris' son Elliot graduated from Harvard in 1922. He earned a master's degree in education from Harvard in 1932. Elliot's son Matthew also graduated from Harvard College in 1958 and Harvard Business School in 1961. His daughter Brenda graduated from Radcliffe College before going on to medical school.

JACOB GILFIX

Jacob Louis Gilfix was born in Newton in 1902, the fourth child and third son of this immigrant family. His father was a junk peddler who specialized in metals. Born in a four room house at 59 Clinton Street, there were five people living there when he was born. He was so blonde that his nickname was Weisse (Whitey, pronounced Vice-eh). There were eight people living in the house when the family moved to 93 West Street in 1909. Clinton Street was a very crowded residence, but it had wooden floors and an indoor toilet. His mother had been born and raised in a house in Ukraine with dirt floors and an outhouse, so although it was crowded, it was a big step up from her life in Europe.

Educated in the Newton Public Schools, he received a degree in accounting from the Bentley School of Accounting and Finance (now Bentley University) in 1923. He often proudly recalled that he had studied with Mr. Bentley himself, who had many new and modern ideas about accounting.

In 1929, he married Judith Gorin. His marriage was not accepted by his family because of an old Jewish superstition, which said that a man should not marry a woman with the same name as his mother. His mother, Sarah Y'hudis, had the same name in Hebrew as his wife. So Judith was never accepted in the family until the death of her in-laws in 1935, when the children of his family (now all adults) welcomed her and their son.

Jay had a wonderful personality and had an endless fund of terrific stories and jokes. He was the center of attention at every social event. Handsome and gregarious, he also was very well read and had a photographic memory, so he could call up an appropriate quotation for almost every occasion. He especially enjoyed poetry and philosophy. On long drives in the country in the summertime, he would stop at a scenic spot and recite poems that he had memorized. All the Gilfix boys, as they were known in the neighborhood, could cook something, in order to help their sister, Rose. Jay was famous for making potato latkes for the annual family picnics every year. Philip learned to make challah.

In contrast to his brother Philip, he did not recall anti-Semitism and physical attacks. This may have been because he was big and strong and less likely to be assaulted than his slender brother. And he loved to recount how strong his father was. He claimed that Benjamin could bend horseshoe nails with his bare hands and bend horseshoes as well. He also told a story that someone said to his father, "can you hold this up?" and handed him a rifle. In those days, the rifles had wooden stocks and were very heavy. Benjamin was able to hold the rifle by the barrel and hold the rifle straight out in front of him. So no one ever gave him a hard time.

Jacob and Judith Gilfix

Photo courtesy of Beryl Gilfix

Jay also enjoyed the varied ethnic groups that lived in the community and learned to speak Italian, French and some Greek from the neighbors and other children in the schools. Jay also recalled positive relationships with the neighbors, including a widowed Italian woman who lived nearby. She was concerned about her son and his future and asked Jay to employ him in the newly formed G & S Paper Company, with the hope that steady employment and the good example of the Jewish family would keep the young man on the "straight and narrow." Jay did employ Danny Leone, who ended up as manager of the warehouse and truck fleet of the business for nearly forty years.

In order to earn money, all the children in the family had to work. While in high school, Jacob worked for an early car company which was located in Newton, the Stanley Motor Carriage Company, colloquially called the Stanley Steamer Company. The Stanley family had a mansion on Sargent Street.

He learned to cut fish and also worked in the Brighton abattoir (slaughterhouse), hauling slabs of beef around, a job that required great physical strength. He went to college during the day (it was located in downtown Boston) and then worked at the abattoir from 3 to 11 PM. While looking for a job, he ran an ad in the newspaper "young man will sell anything, go anywhere" and he worked for a short time at the Botsford Paper Company in Boston as a salesman. He also worked part time for a Mr. Mintz at 101 Tremont Street in Boston as an accountant.

Like many children of immigrants, he wanted a job with stability and long term prospects and he thought he had found his dream job with the Boston & Maine Railroad. That was considered a plum job, as the railroad was one of the major corporations in the United States and a job there was expected to last a lifetime. But he encountered the casual anti-Semitism which was very common in those days when he informed his employer that he would not be in to work on the upcoming Jewish High Holidays. He was told that if he did not come to work, he would be fired. He did not go to work; he was fired. He decided at that point to go into business for himself. He incorporated the G & S Paper Company on July 8, 1924.

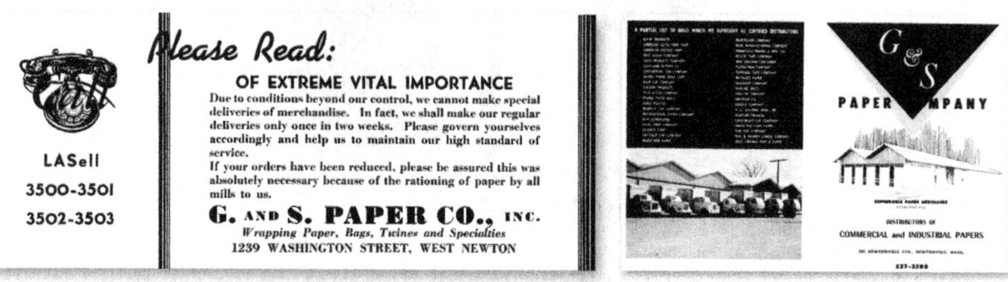

The family story is that his father said to him, "why don't you go into the paper business? People always need paper; you use it today and you need it again tomorrow." Jay started by loading a pushcart with paper cups (a new innovation), twine, wrapping paper and other paper goods) and going from store to store in Newton and Watertown. One of his first accounts was a grocery store on Mt. Auburn Street owned by Mr. Mugar (which became Star Market), an account he kept until his retirement. Another account that he kept all his life was Raytheon, whose first plant was located on Chapel Street in Nonantum, within walking distance of his home on West Street.

A company selling paper products, even if only from a pushcart, was both a big leap from junk peddling and yet somewhat familiar. It was more physically demanding in some ways; there was no horse to move the cart from place to place. Some of these products were new to the market and did not yet have wide customer acceptance but he was young and strong and had a wonderful personality, which made it easy for people to like him and to want to do business with him. Although it was challenging, he was able to keep the business going through the Depression and World War II, when consumer products were hard to obtain. The business prospered and eventually employed all the members of his family and lasted until the middle 1990s, long after his death in 1976.

PHILIP GILFIX

Philip recalled building the synagogue, with twelve to fifteen members of the congregation who were "handy" doing much physical work, aiding a young Jewish builder from Chelsea named Isaac Fox. Many immigrants at that time had building and maintenance skills. It was cheaper if your family could do the work instead of hiring a specialist and sons especially were encouraged to know carpentry, general plumbing and electrical work. One cousin, Lou Silverman, recalled helping to lay the floors in the women's balcony.

"The building of the synagogue was a labor of love, something dear to all our hearts. All the fundraising was done by the membership. If such a profession as professional fundraiser existed, they didn't know about it."

His nickname was Duke. No one knows why he had that nickname. Philip, like many Newton youths, attended sports classes at the YMCA and the Boys Club. He boxed and wrestled and ran track and played baseball. Phil wanted to be a dentist but could not afford the tuition at Harvard. But he learned through the YMCA in town about a one-year course at the Y which would lead to entrance to Northeastern University. He took a business course and received a BA from Northeastern in 1925. But he kept a lifelong interest in science and medicine.

He had an interest in photography and worked for Bachrach's, then the leading photography studio in Boston. His brother Joe also loved photography and founded a photography studio of his own in Philadelphia. Phil intended to stay at Bachrach's as a steady job. His brother Jay had just founded the paper company that would eventually employ all the family members. Jay had an emergency appendectomy and Phil left Bachrach's to take care of the business "temporarily" and never went back.

Philip recalled the house at 93 West Street which his father built in 1908 or 1909. In an interview, he said, "That was not just a house; it was a home. We had three kinds of pear trees, several kinds of apple trees, plum and cherry trees. And a grape vineyard that was very big. Papa built it up so that it was like a closed room with one side open and great big blue Concord grapes and that was where we had our *sukkah*. We could pull a rope to open the roof and we could see the stars and we could close it if it rained.

We had a garden on the other side and we grew all our own vegetables, corn, peas, beans, gooseberries, etc. We made our own sauerkraut, made our own wine, made our own farmer's cheese. Had our own chickens, we had a horse and wagon. The horse was kept on the right hand side. We used the manure to fertilize the garden. On the left hand side was copper, all the copper and brass. Later all kinds of junk; old horsehair cushions, usually horsehair which we would pull apart with our hands. There was bronze, copper and iron. We sold the metal to Rosenbaum Smelting Company in Watertown, a cousin. The Rosenbaums used to take mostly copper and make ingots and sell abroad to Japan and other places.

We worked. When we could barely walk, we learned to work. We worked in the yard, breaking up automobiles, tying up paper, putting bottles in barrels and sorting them out. You would separate the horsehair from the car seats. White horsehair was more expensive and therefore more valuable. Champagne bottles were the most expensive at that time and had to be separated and sold to be sterilized and used over again. We did whatever had to be done. If you wanted a sled, you got boards and baby carriage wheels and made it.

As kids, if you had a dime or a nickel, you could get an ice cream cone. And Hymie Shrier would not spend a nickel and after we finished our cones, he would say, "See, your nickel is gone but I still have mine."

There was a stove in the kitchen with wood and coal. We would sift out the coal from the ashes and take it into the back yard and sift it again for the tiny pieces of coal and then put them back in the stove. You didn't waste anything.

On Fridays, Rose and Mama would be up before dawn, *"smollahing"* the chickens over an open flame to burn off the feathers and hair after which the feathers were "flicked" off. They would buy a whole fish and open it and clean it and "*chack* it (chop it) to make *gefilte* fish. In Brighton for five cents you could buy a heel or foot from a calf, and blacken the bone in the stove. Then they would crack the bone and make calf's foot jelly.

He recalled his father peddling with a horse and wagon buying rags and bottles and finally metals. "It was a privilege and a treat to go on the wagon with him. If you had a store, you had to be open on the Sabbath. Being a junk dealer was lower class but they broke the Sabbath and we didn't."

He had nine brothers and sisters. Two of the sisters and one of his brothers died young. He recalled his childhood and school years and said it was not comfortable to play with the children of the Italian, Irish and French neighbors. The most animosity he experienced was from the Irish, who were vocal and offensive, verbally and physically. But he also recalled that their family's *Shabbas goy* was a man named O'Brien who went on to become a Catholic priest and who used to come back to the neighborhood to visit them. [A Shabbas goy was a gentile who came to Jewish homes to light fires in the wintertime or to feed the horses or other chores that were forbidden to Jews on the Sabbath. The Shabbas goy was usually a teenage boy from the neighborhood who was paid a nickel or a dime for these chores]. Not everyone in the Jewish community recalled physical or verbal abuse from their neighbors. It is possible that girls did not experience this as much as boys. And there were families who felt very close to their neighbors of different ethnic backgrounds.

Philip remembered two Black families who lived on Adams Street who liked to associate with their Jewish neighbors. One of those families, the Rollins family, had a big garden and every year the young men from the synagogue would go to their house near the corner of Adams Street and collect the corn stalks for the synagogue to be used as "*schach*," the branches covering the ceiling of the *sukkah*. This custom lasted into the 1980s.

"You could call them colored," he said, "but you would never dream of using any offensive words about them. Some colored people haven't prospered as much as others, even though they had the ability to succeed. The immigrant Jewish families in the neighborhood were willing to sacrifice a whole generation in order for their children to succeed, to achieve a higher standard than their parents."

unidentified   Louis Fried   Rabbi Samuel Chiel   unidentified
at the Adams Street Shul

As the son of a very observant Hasidic father, expectations of religious observance were very high. "My house was a very synagogue in itself. Religion was a part of growing up; it was just there. My mama would get up before dawn to prepare for the Sabbath and make *challah*. She would chop the gefilte fish and cut the *lokschen* (noodles) by hand. The household was transformed into a different atmosphere, a completely different environment. We would eat the fish, then sing *zemiros* (Sabbath songs) and then chicken soup and the rest of the meal. It was a feast every Shabbas. After Shabbas was over on Saturday night, we would go to Newton Corner and the West End to shop." It was a big deal when a kosher baker opened in Waltham in 1912.

The family was proud of their reputation for honesty and religious observance. My father used to say, "I've got a good name in this town. Don't you spoil it."

In the interview with Historic Newton, Philip recalled the relationship between Temple Emanuel and Rabbi Chiel and the Adams Street Shul. Phil: My brother Irving belongs to Temple Emanuel and he got about 25 or 30 people to come in and become members of the shul. They pay $25 bucks per year. Before that, we couldn't get a *minyan* and Irving told me to approach Rabbi Chiel and have a breakfast and invite him down with his whole entourage, which consisted of Reverend Louis Lourie and Cantor Gabriel Hochberg and Rabbi Samuel Chiel. So Irving brought the tables and chairs from Temple Emanuel because we didn't have any and Rabbi Chiel brought about 85 people over and Rabbi Chiel told them "They are in desperate need of members here for a *minyan*. I would like you fellows to help him out." He offered his own people from Temple Emanuel and that is how we are functioning now (1986). Now generally we have about 40-45 people come for services on the holidays thanks to Rabbi Chiel."

ROSE GILFIX

Rose was born in Russia and came to the United States with her mother in 1899 at the age of three. They were passengers on the Pretoria. She married her second cousin Jacob Schribman in 1924. They had four children, Marvin (b. 1925), Jean (b. 1926), Marshall b. 1928), and Sylvia (b. 1930). She reminisced about her life with her daughter Jean Birnbaum.

"I attended the Adams School (located at the corner of Watertown Street and Bridge Street. I then went to Horace Mann which was then situated on the corner of Watertown Street and Walker Street. I graduated from that school at the end of ninth grade in 1909 and that was the extent of my schooling. I wasn't enthused with school and was quite glad to stay at home after graduation and help my mother, who really needed my help.

We lived in a four room house (59 Clinton Street) with a kitchen and dining room downstairs and two bedrooms upstairs. The toilet was in the cellar. We had only cold water and used a coal stove. The coal was kept in the cellar and had to be carried up to the kitchen in a hod. We used kerosene lamps for light. There was also a pump in the yard where we got water and a well from which we brought up the clearest and coldest water I have ever seen or drunk.

If you can visualize this, you will have an idea what we had to contend with. To wash clothes, we had a large wooden tub which we set on two chairs, the seats facing each other, heated water on the stove, poured it into the tub, and rubbed the clothes on a washboard. While we were washing the clothes, we put a copper bottomed oval boiler on the stove with water in it and put the rubbed clothes into the boiler where it boiled for at least half an hour, then back into the tub with clear water for rinsing, then into a large basin for bluing [to whiten the clothes], and then hung outside on a line to dry. Compare this procedure to the present day with washing machines and dryers! [There were nine people living in the house when they moved in 1909, seven children and two adults].

Free time? Don't make me laugh! Who had free time? From school we had homework. We had to learn the definitions of the various parts of speech in grammar, which it wouldn't do today's children any harm to learn! Even today, I like correct grammar, but who speaks English correctly any more?"

Jean: "My mother told me that from the time she was nine years old, she had to do the weekly shopping for the food for the family. Her mother would put her on the trolley to Roxbury to go shopping on Blue Hill Avenue where all the kosher stores were. Her aunt, Libby Berman, our grandfather's sister, would meet her at the stop and then take her to the stores to shop. When finished, she would take her back to the trolley to head home and her parents would meet her when she got back. She told me that her mother couldn't do the shopping because she had to stay home and take care of all the small children. Now I wonder about who did the shopping before my mother was able to do it."

ELLIOT GILFIX

Elliot was a very important member of the second generation of Newton's Jewish community.

Two of Elliot's sisters, Lily and Leah, remained in the family home at 61 Clinton Street and Elliot maintained his two unmarried sisters and their home. Although he moved to another part of Newton after his marriage, he continued to be involved in the community and the synagogue. Elliot graduated from Harvard College and became a teacher. He was employed as a public school teacher in Boston. His wife Ruth was a graduate of Radcliffe College. He also ran a real estate business and an insurance business on the side. From his contacts in the neighborhood, he spoke fluent Italian, and had many Italian insurance customers. He had a nickname, Pete. Later in life he formed a real estate business under the name Peter Elliot.

As the second member of his family to graduate from Harvard and a modern person, compared to the immigrant generation, Elliot understood and appreciated the need to do things differently from the earlier generation, with their junk businesses and horses and wagons. Elliot was deeply involved in two major events after the building of the synagogue, the first in 1924 and the second in the 1930s.

Elliot saw that many of his contemporaries had moved to Roxbury, with their more elaborately furnished synagogues, while he remained in Newton. He understood the need to modernize or update the synagogue. In 1924, he became involved in a plan to raise money to build an ark. (See the Bimah Committee section of this book).

The second time that Elliot decided to get involved was in 1933.

Elliot described this event in a tape recording made by Historic Newton in 1986.

"There was a little bit of hostility between the builders of this building and the second generation, since they felt that we were not quite up to their standards in many respects, in conducting religious services, and were not very happy with our presumed interest in the building.

Elliot and Ruth Gilfix

Photo courtesy Brenda Gilfix Foner and Stephen Gilfix

We were interested presumably and quite honestly from a social point of view. The young men and women in the community felt that a place for meeting would be a desirable further use for this particular building but since the basement had never been completed, we took it upon ourselves to do so. Besides, the women who were running the philanthropic end of the work [The Newton Hebrew Ladies Aid Society] also needed an adequate meeting place. In order to further this end, the young folks ran dances and shows and all the receipts were turned over to refurbish or to furbish the synagogue. The ark was built, pews were brought in (I believe the original pews which were nothing but a combination of a desk and a chair, came from LaSalle Seminary or some such seminary). These were used for quite a few years until Temple Kehillath Israel in Brookline was refinishing their chapel and were able to donate these new pews to the temple. [There is some confusion in the memories of various respondents about when the pews currently in use came into the synagogue. One respondent says that the desk/chair combination was still there in 1938]. That, plus the new ark, lent a little status to the interior of the building. Now the young folks, in order to achieve their aim, had to win over the older people in the synagogue who were not too happy with the turn of events. They felt that the synagogue was a synagogue and nothing else. We thought that it was a place for social activity and betterment of the community. Quite a number of young men, who are now professionals and in business, joined the synagogue and more or less took over the building for a year, during which time the basement was redone, ceiling, walls, floors, new heating system, new daily meeting hall and so on. What we did was the younger men got together to try to finish the building. But we couldn't get permission from our parents.

So what happened was they inveigled me into becoming president for one year. We got enough new members to swing the vote, paid for remodeling the basement, put in a new heating system. After this was done, it was then returned to the original owners and designers of the building itself. The young folks met there as the YMHA, the women met there as the Newton Ladies Aid, which is now part and parcel of Temple Emanuel, in an attempt to engage the third generation in the activities of the community.

I would say that the real reason this building has continued to be successful as a synagogue is the friendly relationship between the older Jews of this era with the Italians and French of the neighborhood. There was never, to my knowledge, any hostility of any kind. In fact, we always felt that the neighbors took care of the building when the Jews were not in attendance."

Eliot recalled that then Mayor Charles Hatfield attended the dedication ceremony of the synagogue in December 1912. [Mayor Hatfield served as mayor from 1910-1913]. Future mayor Edwin Childs [who would serve as mayor of Newton from 1914-1929] took part in the parade of moving the Torahs from Dalby Street to the new building. He marched with them with the American flag. "He lived on California Street and he was a very democratic person, and whenever they had any sort of affairs, he always appeared."

HARRY STANDEL

When my great-grandfather Morris Gilfix retired around 1912 there was no social security and so he called his children together and he said to them, I have decided to retire and each of you will kick in x dollars per week and that was his retirement. So he came to the synagogue every day; it was more than anything a men's club. This organization was, I am sure, what a shul was like in 19th century Russia or maybe even earlier than that. I remember there were no pews, just those desks and one time someone in back of us spit on the floor and my grandfather said, "what are you doing? you can't spit in the shul" and the man said, "I spit at home and I can spit in the shul." If you can imagine such a thing, like a person spitting in Temple Emanuel, he'd be arrested.

(A different respondent told the author that the event described above took place in the early 1930s. The man who did the spitting was almost forced to leave the synagogue permanently but it was decided to allow him to remain. It was a very big scandal. And in the opinion of the respondent, the spitter was an uncouth man).

We do not know if the action that Harry Standel recorded about a member of the congregation spitting in the synagogue was a reflection of the following custom or merely uncouth behavior. A web site, Jewniverse.com, explains: "Jews would (surreptitiously) spit on the ground when passing by a church. They also spat on the floor of synagogue while reciting the line in the daily concluding prayer *Aleinu* about those 'who pray to the emptiness and void and bow down to the god who does not save.' Although censors had long crossed this line out and forbidden Jews to reprint it in prayer books, it nonetheless remained in the oral culture. Another theory is that the reason for spitting is a desire to not benefit from the saliva formed in the mouth when recounting idol worship."

I never realized this as a kid but this shul was a place where people came to meet and talk with each other as much as to worship. It wasn't a sanitized version of what we expect now; it was pretty earthy stuff. But they knew what was going on in the service. They knew how to find their way around the *machzur* (prayer book) and what page they were on. My father was bar mitzvahed here. I remember as a kid my first introduction to Jewish religious ceremonies was here. I don't know how old I was but it was about 70 years ago and for years I thought this was the way it was [that all synagogues were like this] and it was kind of a shock [to see another congregation]. This congregation was very poor and they were only open on the high holidays. I think my dad attended a *cheder* (Hebrew school) here but I went to Temple Bnai Moshe in Brighton and there were pews there and there was decorum there and people would open their books and they would listen to the rabbi, Rabbi Joseph Shubow, and there was a cantor. B'nai Moshe was a standard procedure Jewish synagogue but this place was not.

The best way to describe the congregation here was semi chaotic. Let me explain how. We'd arrive usually on the high holidays because the synagogue wasn't open much else and since there was no rabbi, there was a hired gun who would come in and do the services. There was always an argument about who to hire and how much money to spend and they would usually get the cheapest guy. They hired the same guy over and over and when people arrived they would say, oh no, not him again. So we'd come in and sit down. They would begin the service and for awhile there would be a certain amount of decorum and then after a while someone would turn to my grandfather Max and say, "Max let me tell you what happened to me last week" and then someone else would join in the conversation and one person after another would join in and at some point everyone would be talking. It would spread like a disease and everyone would be talking with everyone and of course the women were upstairs talking to each other as well. At some point old Mr. [Joseph] Roiter would lift the cover of his desk and slam it down like a thunderclap and everyone would immediately spin around and ask what page are we on and they would get back to business and this would continue for another five or six minutes and then it would start again. The topics of discussion, this was a once a year event, so with all the pent up dirt that had built up over the year about who was doing what to whom and who bought a new car and what children had been born and so forth. This was more a place to show off your kids and catch up on the news and talk and socialize as much as the religious aspect.

There was always an anticipation of the blowing of the *shofar* and it was typical that the individual who was hired to lead the service was incapable of blowing the shofar properly. When they begin *tkiyah*, blat, splat, and eventually it worked but people were rolling their eyes and chuckling and laughing but this was an annual event: waiting for the blowing of the *shofar*. If it ever worked correctly, it would be a shock.

I have two snuff boxes that belonged to my grandfather. They have his initials MG. These were kept in the desks along with the tallis and prayer book and when they felt tired or weak, say on Yom Kippur, they would take a pinch of snuff. They are made of ram's horn with a wooden base. They are homemade; people made their own.

My best memories of Yom Kippur as a young kid: of course we were hungry during Yom Kippur. My mother and grandmother were up in the balcony because of course women could not sit downstairs. They would bring a picnic basket with them with chicken legs and apples and oranges and when I would get hungry I would go upstairs. It was a sewing circle up there. There were a few women who would religiously look at the book and *daven* but most of them were coffee klatching. If God forbid a child came up there they would pass this kid around and *kvell* over the little children and me with a chicken leg. Did the women have the same desks as the men? No, the women had old wooden folding chairs.

I remember there was a boy my age named Glen Shriberg and Glen and I used to play outside. We were about 12 years old and we would get hungry and we would walk down the street all dressed up in suits and ties and go to Lombardi Drug on Watertown Street and we would ask for a coke and Mr. Lombardi would say "no food today, back to shul" so everyone was wised up, even the Italians.

My grandfather Max was a junk man and grandfather had a horse and wagon and he had one of the first junk licenses in Watertown. He had a route that he would take his horse and he had a big barn in back of the house, He was never a particularly ambitious guy and he would trot along on his routine and the horse knew where to stop and Max was a kibitzer and he would take more time than normal kibitzing and the horse would turn around and go home and my grandmother was sitting in the house and this horse would be coming down the driveway pulling the wagon and he'd go into the barn by himself.

My grandmother Eva Gilfix had to leave school when she was 14 because they needed money and piled her hair up on her head to make her look older and she went to work in one of the mills to help support the family. My dad David went to Northeastern law school and he dropped out of law school during the Depression, saying, "I see lawyers on the bread line, so what am I doing here?" I was the first one to go to college.

My family bought the house on Morse Street in Watertown in 1912, using the money earned as a junk peddler and they stayed there until they moved to Florida in 1969. My grandparents lived on the first floor and we lived on the second floor. My grandmother was always a bit embarrassed that she lived in Watertown and not Newton. She had stationary printed up with her address and a Newton zip code.

Dr. Shrier was our doctor and he would just walk over to the house and say I just wanted to see how Harry was. He never asked for money and you could just walk into his office on Pearl Street. I had a rash and I went to the office and he would show me a big book with pictures and say "do you think your rash looks like this?"

I think Nonantum was a pretty even mix of Jews and Italians. But all was not fun and games in those days. Anti -Semitism was rife and lots more so in Watertown, where I lived and went to Watertown public schools. As a kid I remember one day playing outside of the shul and a couple of Italian kids walked by and said "what are you Jews doing in there, kissing the devil's ass?" I was about eight years old at the time and I still remember that day and what a shocker it was to hear someone say that. I fought my way through school. I remember coming home one day and saying to my grandmother "what's a kike?" I was hearing a kid saying you killed Jesus and asking my mother "who's Jesus, what's a Jesus?"

The Shriberg's junk yard was called West Street Auto Parts, and Willy did very well but Jane was always a bit embarrassed by Willy because he had dirt under his fingernails. I was more connected to my mother's family. My wife was not Jewish, she was Italian. Harry Roiter married a non Jew, married his secretary; that was a scandal. I met my wife in the 60s; my mother's brother William Polishuk went to Harvard. He married a Delano and he was disowned by his family for marrying her. He founded Brandywine College in Pennsylvania and was wealthy and successful but the family was never reconciled.

My grandmother was beside herself because I married a non Jew. But my wife became very close to my mother and they got along very well. My cousin Leah married a non Jew also. One day my wife said to me that she was going to convert on her own and she went to Mishkan Tefilah and we had a second marriage, a Jewish marriage. We had been married for ten years at that point. My daughters thought this was standard procedure.

Eva and Max Standel

As people succeeded financially, they migrated away from this shul and my kids went to Temple Emanuel for Hebrew school and we went there also.

It was busier here when I was much younger. I first came here before WW II. My parents moved to Florida in 1969 and my dad died in 1989 but they continued to come here so we were still coming here in the late 1980s. My name is Harry Morris Standel and Morris died a year or so before I was born.

Both my parents spoke Yiddish fluently, and neither of them had accents in English even though my mother was born in Russia. My grandfather came from Shepatovka and my grandmother came from Colchin which were close to each other. My grandfather spoke of an automobile as a "machine" (the Russian word apparently). My mother wanted to teach me Yiddish and my father said " no, he's an American I don't want him to speak Yiddish. I don't want him to be a *greener* (an immigrant). I want him to be an American, not a Jew (in the sense of an old country kind of Jew)." My family always spoke Yiddish, especially when they didn't want me to understand what they were saying.

I was in Russia with my business partner and his mother, a Russian pediatric neurologist, asked if I spoke Russian and I said no and she asked "*ken retten Iddish*?" [can you speak Yiddish] and I said "*a bissel*" [a little] and for the first and only time in my life I had a conversation in Yiddish, dredging my vocabulary up from my childhood.

Archbishop Cushing was at my bar mitzvah at Temple B'nai Moshe. He and Rabbi Shubow were friends. It turns out that my father's brother Ruby was a motorman with the MTA and he drove a bus. We lived in Watertown and occasionally I would come home and see a bus parked outside my house. It was a narrow street and it was a sight to see this big orange and yellow bus parked outside the house. It was my uncle Ruby visiting my father. It turned out that one summer Ruby taught a seminary boy who went to work for the MTA how to drive a bus and the seminary boy's name was Richard Cushing. They became very close friends; they worked together every day for the entire summer. I remember one day when Ruby met Archbishop Cushing when he had all his finery on and Ruby said to him, " I don't know what to call you" and Cushing said "what do you mean, you don't know what to call me? You call me Dick."

I think that time heals over scars and I am not sure I want to go back to what it was like then. It was an experience that shaped my life to a large extent. When you mention religion and Judaism the immediate connection I have is this shul and what went on here. One of the things that did go on here was the Chasidic ritual of the *Cohanim* putting the *tallesim* over their heads and it was spectre-like. It seemed to me the individuals here were not Orthodox or Chasidic Jews but they continued this ritual they remembered from the old country.

GOODMAN FAMILY

The Goodman family came to Newton from Kiev in Ukraine around 1903. Abraham was a shoemaker. His wife's name was Dora. Abe (1869-1932) and Dora (1870-1930) had six children, Joseph Hyman (b. 1892-1957); Rose Mildred, (b 1895); Nelson Oscar/Nate (b. 1898); William Lewis; Thomas Merrill; Ida. The family moved back and forth between Boston and Newton before finally settling in Newton. They first lived in what is now a park between Lowell Avenue, Watertown Street and Walnut Street. "There used to be a big tenement house on that street."

When asked what Abe did for a living in Europe, his son Nate told the following story. "When you ask someone what they did for a living when you couldn't figure out how they managed to get by, that was the standard story: He went out at night with a *shtrikle* (a piece of rope) and came back in the morning with a horse."

He told his children that his real name was Kivie but when he came to America, his friends said that was not a good American name and so they called him Abe. He somehow learned English and became a citizen. Early in his life in Newton, he did shoe repair for the McCammon's Shoe Store in Newton Corner. He would pick up shoes to be repaired and take them to the house in Auburndale where they were living and fix the shoes. Later he had a shop on Walnut Street, in what is now the Bram Block Street. His son Nelson Oscar (known as Nate) recalled with pride that his father invented a new kind of shoe for a man who had a crippled leg. The new shoe made it possible for the man to walk normally.

Nate Goodman

Nate was an electrician who lived on Lowell Avenue in the neighborhood and was active in the shul for many years. Nate had one of the first Master Electrician's licenses in Massachusetts, obtained in 1920 (number 9). He was a wonderful story teller and with his serious demeanor, there was a delayed reaction before the listener realized the joke and broke up laughing.

When Nate first went to work, he worked in local factories that made adding machines. When World War I broke out, he got a job in a factory that made Browning machine guns. The inspector on the Newton draft board told him, "Boy, they will draft the president before they will take you." After the war, there were troubled times in business and industry and he was out on strike for a long time. Dissatisfied with the way his work life was going, he left to start a radio business in Brockton but did not succeed. So he came back to Newton.

His father was not a regular shul goer except on the holidays. As a young man, Nate recalled, the boys would misbehave in shul. It was the custom on the High Holy Days for the men to take off their shoes when they went up on the *bimah*. So he and his pals tied the shoelaces together so one man's shoes were tied to another man's shoes. Then they filled the shoes with water. And they never figured out who did it! (Nate says it was his brother Joe and Dave Fried).

"The Jews in Newton, the natives, can be very proud of what they've done. They always worked hard, always took care of themselves, never became a burden or beholden to anyone, and they did it all by themselves. Later on I was one of the very first to join Temple Emanuel. And Mrs. Schribman says to me, "Oh ho, Adams Street isn't good enough for you?" Well, I said, this is handy for me and the next year, I see Mr. and Mrs. Schribman are members of Temple Emanuel."

The family lived in Auburndale and Nate did not have any Jewish classmates until he got to high school. The house on Lowell Avenue was almost a farm and they had chickens, ducks and geese. They also grew vegetables and one time they bought a goat but did not know how to control it. They tried holding each leg to milk it, but after the goat kicked over the milking can, it was returned to its owner. While he was in high school, he was incubating chickens and "twice a day you have to roll the eggs over like a chicken when she gets up off her nest, she shakes and rolls the eggs over; it keeps the yolk from settling on one side of the eggs. So twice a day I had permission from the high school to come home during lunch period to turn the eggs. Then we tried duck eggs to get ducklings. The incubator was run on kerosene lamps and it got so hot the duck eggs got cooked! Then I got a job with a store that sold eggs and milk and one day, they asked me to take the milk delivery route. When I said I didn't know the route, they said, 'You just start. The horse will stop at every house. And he did. And when he got through, he took me right back to the barn again."

He recalled the 1930s when he and others like Elliot Gilfix worked to fix up the shul. They ran dinners to raise money and invited speakers. They created a YMHA (Young Men's Hebrew Association) which met in the newly built social hall in the basement in 1933. And it was also a place for the Newton Hebrew Ladies Aid to meet. Nate was the treasurer of the shul when Elliot was president.

He recalled that Edward Swartz, brother of Hazel Swartz Santis, was a graduate of MIT. Edward founded a company called Keystone Camera which was very successful. Nate stated that Edward paid off the shul mortgage and the community celebrated with a big party.

GREENWALD FAMILY

There were three sisters, Rose, Saide and Bertha Greenwald who were part of the Nonantum Jewish community and they never married. They were also unique in that they lost their mother when she was very young (age 44) so they didn't have the typical family life.

Their father Morris (1873-1933) went to Poughkeepsie NY when he first arrived in 1891 perhaps because he knew a Perlmutter from Hungary who had settled there. Morris' father had died young and he was raised by an older brother, whose name is unknown. Their mother Katherine Grossman (1873-1917) was from Hungary also. The parents met and married in New York in 1902 when they were about 29 years old. When the Perlmutter family moved to Newton, Morris moved with them and lived in their home when they first settled in Newton.

When they first arrived in Newton, Morris opened a hardware store on Watertown Street but he closed the store and became a junk dealer. Where did he keep his horse? Here on West Street. Everything took place on West Street. Louis Fried recalled that Morris used to come to the Fried house to take a bath every Friday afternoon.

Bertha was the only sister who graduated from high school. Saide was taken out of school to run the house when her mother died and Saide was in the eighth grade. Rose dropped out of school after the eighth grade. "She simply was totally uninterested in school and wouldn't go on."

Recalling her education, Saide noted that the Italian children were, in her opinion, juvenile delinquents. She was very respectful of the teachers. "I had my own trinity, God, teachers, parents." Bertha recalled "I went to the Elliot School and there was this great big room off to the side where we hung our coats. There was something in that room that was always covered up and one day one of the kids said 'that's the teacher's toilet.' I was just stunned. It just never occurred to me that teachers went to the bathroom. Teachers and millionaires just didn't have intestines, I thought."

Recalling the synagogue, Bertha said that if you were a Jew, you were accepted in the community but at the same time, there was a lot of infighting. She remembered times when they would stop *davening* in the shul to have a fight.

But what the sisters remembered most was the preparation for the Sabbath. "It was a religious community, it really was. In the winter they got through early and God forbid, those men never, never worked on a Friday afternoon because they cleaned up their act for the weekend. Our mother got up at 5:00 AM to get the old coal stove going. When we got up to go to school, things were already started. I know that when I got home from school, the whole thing was complete. The floor was shining bright white, the stove was like a mirror and she bought a white apron a bit like linen, like the table with the white napkins and the challah and of course the whole bit with the wine. And it was beautiful, those Fridays, and the aroma from the fish, the soup, the chicken, the *tzimmes*. She made marvelous coffee cake. She did all her baking on Friday, making *challah* and her own noodles. Every Jewish woman did."

All the kids in the neighborhood, when I saw them, the first thing they said was, do you make the *pogatchlick* (?) that your mother made? It's a Hungarian butter cookie. Nobody knows how to make them now. The ingredients were butter, flour, eggs, cream. They were criss-crossed, then egg washed and then had a fancy design on it.

Where did your family shop? "Every Thursday and Saturday, like the postman, sleet and rain wouldn't stop them. They would go down to the West End Thursday night to shop for Shabbas. And then Saturday night for the week. Remember we didn't have refrigeration. You couldn't buy that much because it wasn't going to keep all that long. So they bought what they needed and the little delicacies, like lox, cream cheese, butter, a little piece of herring. Cottage cheese with scallions and cucumber especially in the spring." Bertha recalled going with Rose Gilfix to the West End by streetcar to shop one Thursday night and Rose had a live chicken with her that she was taking to the *shochet* (kosher slaughterer). And the chicken got loose in the streetcar and they were chasing the chicken all over the streetcar. The last streetcar was at midnight from Newton Corner and if you missed it, you were out of luck and had to walk home *shlepping* all those bundles.

The women remembered a great deal of anti-Semitism and being embarrassed about being Jewish in a very Catholic neighborhood. Bertha especially recalled having only Christian friends. Saide was very careful to avoid fights, even if they were of the "you sheeny," "you guinea" variety. She remembered stones being thrown at her.

Even using the word "rabbi" was something you didn't say out loud. The only Jewish girl she knew (and she would not give her name) insulted and abused her and Bertha didn't know how to defend herself. We had just lost our mother and Saide had taken over and become the mother and it wasn't a pleasant time. This girl would come into the house and make nasty comments.

Saide was a freshman in high school when their mother died of cancer at the age of 44. She was immediately taken out of school to become her family's housekeeper and a second mother to her two younger sisters. Says Bertha, "and Saide got very little help from us, I can tell you that." Bertha was the only sister who graduated from high school. Their sister Rose graduated from the ninth grade and refused to go on to high school.

Bertha worked as a secretary in Newton for awhile and gave up that job to take care of her father when he became ill. Sadie and Rose supported the family by working part time at the Earnshaw Mills in Newton. After Mr. Greenwald died in 1932, Bertha went to work for G & S Paper Company, owned by Jacob Gilfix. In 1950 she took at job as a social worker with the welfare department working in Newton City Hall. She worked there until her retirement. She had a hard time at work because she did not have a college degree and because she was a Jew. "The welfare department at that time had a solid group of Irish Catholics who really stuck together. They drove out an Italian girl because they were so mean to her. I determined that they were not going to drive me away!" Bertha recalled the constant nasty comments about her Jewishness and the comments when she took the day off to go to shul on a Jewish holiday. Finally, one day she said to Lil Shea, "Lil, I have two propositions for you. You can convert and celebrate with us. Or you can get the legal department to open the office on Christmas Day and I'll come in and work. That shut her up."

She planned to study Italian, "having lived all her life in an Italian neighborhood, it would be nice to speak the language of her environment. She recalled someone coming into G & S Paper Company and saying, "Hungarian? Well, then you are not a Jew."

After their mother died, the girls and their father did very little together as a family. They were all very sad. Saide recalled that her father "absconded, he really did." He worked. And you know *Shabbas* had to be observed so that was the one time we were all together. He was just earning a living. He worked long hours. But the effect was that the girls had very hard and very sad lives and very little money. None of the three sisters ever married.

HOFFMAN FAMILY

Joseph Hoffman was born in Yaroslavl, Russia in 1863. He arrived in Boston in 1895 and moved to Newton in 1899 because his doctor told him he needed to move to the country for his health. He was a voter in Newton in 1899 (he paid a so-called poll tax to the state of $1.00 and a county tax of $1.00). At the time he and his wife Freida (Fanny) (born 1862) were living at 39 Crafts Street. In Russia, Freida's father owned a tavern.

The Hoffman family had five children, Anna (Goldstein), Samuel, Harry, Maurice (Mendell) and Minnie. They bought a house at 470 Watertown Street, which was the gathering place for the whole family. Maurice became a lawyer and one other son became an accountant. A great grandson, Charlie Fogel, lives in Israel. The family was very long lived, with three female grandchildren living well into their nineties.

Joseph was a junk peddler with a horse and cart and his family recalled a house full of "bric a brac" that he picked up on the street. His granddaughter Barbara Adams recalled, "He was a junk dealer. But I think he dealt in antiques and used furniture because he had a kind of business card that said so."

Betty Hoffman (daughter of Anna): "Well, grandpa lived for the synagogue. He was there all the time, constantly. The synagogue was his life. What did people have? You worked and went to synagogue." He is one of the members of the congregation involved in the building of the Ark for the synagogue in 1924. Betty recalled the family Passover seder which went on until midnight. And after the seder our grandfather would sit us on his lap and tell us stories about the Bible.

She mentioned the old families, the Brams, the Frieds and the Perlmutters, Meilmans and Shriers. The Bakers had a grocery store, and Mrs. Baker always had a barrel of pickles that she preserved and "I would sit on the stoop and eat those pickles and to this day nothing has ever tasted as good as Mrs. Baker's pickles."

Family of Joseph and Anna Hoffman, 1939
L to R: Anna Hoffman Goldstein, Joseph Hoffman, Harry Goldstein, Freda Bordman Hoffman, Mendell Hoffman
Kneeling in Front: Ruth, Betty and Barbara Goldstein Adams

Photo courtesy of Jane Fogel and Barbara Adams

His granddaughter Barbara Adams (daughter of Anna) recalled that he quiet and good looking. He was very gentle. He had a barn behind the house where he kept a horse and wagon. There were differing memories about their grandfather from Betty Hoffman: You must have paid attention (at the seder). Barbara: We had no choice. We were scared to death of him!

They were so happy to be Americans. That came first before Judaism. The family was very progressive and Americanized. The family owned a piano, that symbol of middle class respectability, and it was kept in "the music room." Joseph also played the accordian. Their daughter Anna (Goldstein) lived a very American life. She worked at Filenes and during the summer, she and a female friend rented rooms in Revere.

KLIGMAN FAMILY

Jacob Kligman was one of the signers of the charter of the Adams Street Synagogue. He was remembered by his decendants as being very religious. His great-grandson Daniel Green recalled seeing a photo of Jacob which had been taken in Ukraine, of a young man with a black hat, beard, visible *peyes* (ear locks), and a long black Chassidic-style *kapote* (coat)with a *gartel* (belt) tied around the waist. He made his living as a junk dealer in metals.

The Kligmans were from Ukraine. The census records that Jacob was born around 1870 and came to the United States in 1891. Jacob grew up in an extremely religious (mostly Chassidic) shtetl called "Dinivitz" (Dunaevtsi in Russian).

His relative, Janet Bloom, daughter in law of Esther Bloom, shared her research on the family. Jacob and his wife Chana (Meilman) came to America on the California, which sailed from Hamburg, Germany. His wife returned to Ukraine in 1897 and returned to the US on the Saint Louis in July of that year with two children, Avrum (age 3) and Joe (age 2). The boys were always referred to as their children but the ages of the two boys when they came to the US suggests that they were adopted, perhaps from a family member still in Ukraine.

Anna Kligman, wife of Jacob Kligman

Photo courtesy of Janet Bloom

The family lived on Derby Street and West Street and eventually bought a home at 456 Watertown Street. They had ten children, and several of the grandchildren held jobs in science and engineering fields. Abraham/Avrum (b. 1893), Joseph (b. 1895), Ida (Savage, b. 1899) (Ida's son Melvin worked for NASA in the Apollo program), David (b. 1901), Moshe/Morris (b. 1904) (his son David was a mathematician at Lincoln Labs), Reuben (known as Ruby) (b. 1906), Fannie (called Fay) (b. 1908), Charles (b. 1912) (mechanical engineer), Peretz (Bob) (B. 1913) and Esther (Bloom, b. 1915).

The tradition for the men in the family was to study at yeshivas to become rabbis and cantors. At least two of Jacob's sons, Moshe and Peretz, formally studied in yeshivas. Moshe (Morris) reportedly had *smicha* (Rabbinic ordination) from Yeshiva University.

Jacob died in an automobile accident on January 25, 1938.

In the Yad Vashem online database, there is a page of testimony regarding the murder of Meir Kligman from Dunaevitsi. His profession is listed as "cantor." He might have been a relative.

Daniel Green recalled that his grandfather David told him how fortunate his father Jacob felt that the Adams Street Shul had been so well-protected by the neighborhood. His family could walk to and from shul unmolested. In Ukraine, the Gentile neighbors would severely harass and molest Jacob Kligman and his family by throwing stones at them and beating up my great-great grandfather, breaking bones and cutting off his beard. Jacob specifically fled after Dinivitz was hit by pogrom(s).

Around 1990, Daniel was at the Adams Street Shul and an elderly member, Mr. Pacey Mielman, conveyed to him a very interesting fact about Jacob Kligman. The Mielmans are related to the Kligmans. Pacey told me that he grew up going to the Shul with my family and remembered that Jacob Kligman was the *baal koreh*, who read the Torah in the shul every *Shabbes* and *yontif* from the shul's founding until his death.

ELMER LIPPIN

Elmer Lippin was born in 1908 and died in Newton in 1987. He is buried in the cemetery in Everett. His wife's name was Ethel. They had no children. He had two sisters, Lucy (Lasoff) and Rosalie and a brother, Joe, who moved to California and lost touch with the family in Newton.

Elmer owned local property and like many immigrants, was a jack of all trades, capable of fixing almost anything. And since he was self-employed, he had time to devote to the synagogue and its maintenance. Elmer's father was very involved in the day-to-day life of the shul. If you asked Elmer why he also was so devoted to the shul, he would reply that his father on his deathbed had made him promise "to always take care of the shul," a promise

Elmer kept until the day he died. Elmer devoted years of his life to running the synagogue, fixing it, cleaning it, opening and closing it for services, sending out notices of services, arranging kiddush after services, hiring a cantor for the High Holidays, raising money to pay the bills, etc.

His nephew, Mark Needleman, helped Elmer in the maintenance of the building. "To say that the shul was very important to him, doesn't begin to describe it", Mark reported. The atmosphere of the synagogue was awe inspiring, quiet and mysterious. Mark was thunderstruck by the ark the first time he came in at the age of six or seven. This was the first place he actually saw a Torah scroll close up. Mark's family were not regular synagogue attendees and the reverence and awe with which Elmer held the Torah made an indelible impression on the children. "My brother and I were enveloped by the community. When we were young, we were the youngest people in the building by many years and it was very welcoming and very comforting. We looked forward to coming to Newton." When the boys reached bar mitzvah age, Elmer would drive to Framingham and pick them up and bring them to Newton to help make a minyan if someone he knew would be saying kaddish.

Mark had vivid memories of Elmer up on a ladder, with a little paint brush and a can of brown paint, touching up the stenciling on the walls, while Mark and his brother held the ladder.

Without Elmer's attention to the synagogue, the congregation would have ceased to exist in the 1950s or 1960s when the original immigrant families had all passed away and their children no longer lived in the neighborhood. If Elmer had not taken it upon himself to send out notices for services for every holiday, had not hired a cantor, had not raised the money to pay for heat and lights and water, and to do everything necessary to keep the congregation coming back every year for every holiday, the building would have been abandoned. Even at the end of his life, if someone volunteered to help him with any of the responsibilities for the synagogue, he would politely refuse or ignore the offer altogether. He had made a deathbed promise to his father and he kept that promise faithfully until his own death.

Philip Gilfix talking about Elmer Lippin—Interview by Historic Newton, February 1986:

"This man has spent his entire life taking care of the synagogue. He washes it, he cleans it, he papers it, paints it, he washes the floors, he fixes the roof, he does everything you can imagine to keep that synagogue going. He has done it for 35 years. If this man decides he wants to go to Florida and retire, the synagogue, well, you might just as well board it up and forget it.

Now what's going to happen to it? Who's going to take title to it? I guess if a few people who are left are willing to go in there and claim they are the board of directors and they'll give the title to the Italians or the French or Irish to make a club out of it. That's why it's really important to have it a national historic landmark. We feel that if there's some way we can perpetuate at least that particular synagogue, even if it has to be destroyed, and just make a park out of it, and have a monument or something and give all the *oren hakodesh* [Holy Ark] and the *Torahs* and holy books so we can at least perpetuate it in some way. It shouldn't just be destroyed and thrown away."

Elmer: I know what he's talking about because I have somebody that wants to buy the land. they've been after and after me, and they get very angry with me. They want to buy it and put up an office building.

Philip: He could get a good price, $200 or $250 thousand. That's what I had in mind.

Elmer: There is nobody to take care of the shul or do a darned thing. The reason we are functioning now only on high holidays and other holidays is because of the people that come down from Temple Emanuel and from Beth El. I am the treasurer but if you haven't got any money in the treasury how can you function? We need a fence so I see that the carpenter wants $1500 and I don't have it so I do it myself. My father was a contractor and I worked with my father most of my life as a contractor. So the idea is that I have the tools to repair things. I don't go to anybody and ask for money. Three years ago I tried to quit and said I can't take this any more. Let somebody else take over. And Phil (Gilfix) said to me, you can't quit. We have nobody to take your place. If you need money, we'll get it for you.

Elmer Lippin

Photo courtesy Historic Newton

Elmer talked about how he came to be involved. This was about 1951. Louis Fried was the secretary of the shul and when he got hurt about 1951 he asked Elmer to take over. When Elmer asked about the checkbook and the money, Louis replied, " I don't know. Mr. Roiter took care of everything." Joseph Roiter was president and treasurer at that time and Louis Fried was the secretary. Harry gave Elmer the original donation book which is now in the archives of the American Jewish Historical Society. "I went over to the shul and see what my duties are and what I have to do. And I find an empty shul with no heat in the building and the furnace is broken down, all rusted away and they are meeting in a little room on the first floor with a little heater and that's where they have their services. Now when I came there I said, I've got to put this shul on its feet. They need heat. So I went round to several Jewish homes on a Sunday rapping on the door, "*a beyten oyf nedove*." A plea for money. I begged for money and I collected $600. The local company wanted $1500 to put in the heating system so one of the big shots in the shul gave me the money in advance and they put in a new heating system and I was able to repay the donor. When I first came there, Mr. Joseph Roiter was there, he opened the door and he had the key. I didn't have a key. We would sit there and no one would come and I said "what's the sense of opening the shul?" and he replied, "on Shabbas if you have services or not, a *shul muss sein offen* (a shul must be open). "

So I instituted a system of a Board of Directors. I knew how to do these things because I had been the secretary of the union at Raytheon in Waltham. And for a Jewish boy that was a big honor. In our shul Dr. Shrier was the chairman of the board and we had six or seven other members and we would meet once a month.

MEILMAN FAMILY

Max Meilman was born in 1871 and died in 1939. He arrived in the US from Zitomir Russia in 1890. His wife Sarah (Neiberg) was from Zitomir also. They married in 1893. They had six children, Martha, Dora, Lewis/Label, Bessie, Emma/Mina and David (born 1906). Max was a junk peddler and was remembered by his family as very religious. He first appears in the Newton City Directory in 1899. He became a citizen in 1906.

Hyman first appeared in the City Directory in 1903. Jacob and Joseph (Zadek) first appeared in the Newton City Directory in 1907.

Hyman and Joseph were charter members of the Adams Street Shul. All four brothers were junk peddlers.

The family name is variously spelled Meilman or Mielman.

PASS FAMILY

Abraham Pass arrived in Newton around 1911. Abraham lived on Cook Street and had an Italian grocery store there until about 1930. Starting in 1934, he and Ida Pass operated the Nonantum Spa on Watertown Street, an Italian style restaurant. During the war, because of rationing, someone remembered that he bought a carload of sugar for a company he called the Newton Sugar Company.

The City Directory lists Julius Pass, arriving in 1907 and living at 81 West Street. Julius is Abraham's brother. Sam Pass recalled the story about how his uncle got to Newton. "My uncle Julius came to Newton in 1907 from Russia. He didn't know where he was going and some guy saw him with his bag and he put him on a bus and gave him a nickel and said to the conductor, "Make sure you let him out on the corner of Watertown and West Street and cross the street with him and tell him where to go and someone will see him" and that's how he got to his brother. His brother Abe (Abraham) had a grocery store on West Street, way down, near the Gilfixes."

Abraham and Ida Pass

Photo courtesy of Betty Pass Roffman

By the time Ida came in 1910 or 1911 Abe had rented a house on Cook Street and had a horse and wagon and was peddling fruit and vegetables.

They opened a store around 1911 until 1930 on Cook Street. In 1911, the City Directory lists Mrs. Ida Pass, running a grocery at 91 West Street and living at 81 West Street. Abraham Pass is still listed as having a store on Cook Street.

Abraham Pass, the Nonantum Spa, Watertown Street, Nonantum

Photo courtesy of Betty Pass Roffman

Louis Fried recalled "Abraham had a little grocery store on Cook Street and he was friendly with a lot of the Italians. Abe would trust them from winter until they went to work in the summertime. They were all outside laborers, so they did nothing from, say December until April and he would run charge accounts with them all."

SAM AND RUTH PASS

Ruth (Yanco) Pass: Both our families were members of the shul but Sam's father Abraham Pass at one time was El Presidente [of the shul].

When we first applied for the National Register [of Historic Places], we were told the building was not old enough. I was the one who tried to get that going.

Ruth on learning Hebrew. "There was not a regular Hebrew school. They would hire someone and he used to slug the kids and they swore at him. You learned nothing. It was sad. Another time, they thought the teacher didn't speak English and said many bad things about him. And when they were done, he told them that he spoke English and then he reached out and hit them both. There was no supervision, no planned education. The teachers were knowledgeable but they didn't know how to apply it."

The president of the shul was Mr. Baker. There was no election. The president stayed until he passed away.

Ruth Pass: My father was a very kind man named Harry Yanco. He was a peppery man, an amputee who had lost his leg in a streetcar accident. My father was sent from Ellis Island to a town owned by Mr. Chapin and called Chapinville near Worcester. There was a company town and a company store. The rent was taken from the money they earned and the food too. My grandmother could not speak English so the first time she went to the store, she would point to what she wanted. Then she saved potato peels, egg shells, onion skins, so that the children could now go to the store and pick stuff for her. Not one Jewish person to say a word to. I thought that was cruel, to send them out to a God-forsaken country.

Ruth and Sam Pass

Finally they came to Newton and he worked in one of the mills. My father would come home every day about how he had an argument with the boss. My mother saved her nickels and dimes and bought him a horse and wagon because she couldn't stand listening to him complain any more about how much he hated the mills. He could not take this from anybody and he couldn't take orders. He became a junk dealer. There were many of them. Eventually the junk business became a used car lot as well as junk from cars.

Ruth said, You knew you were a Jew. Well, they let you know. At the Stearns School, I was always being told that I killed their God. How I hated that but I didn't know how to defend myself. I was too young. Sam remembered playing on the sidewalk and some fellow went by, I don't know who he was and he looked at me and said, "little Christ killer." And then he walked away.

Ruth: There was a big mansion where the JFK Housing for the Elderly is now. My father dismantled cars and sold the parts for junk. My brother Herb took over that business. My older Albert brother was a policeman and retired as a captain on the Newton Police Force. Herbert worked up at the Courthouse.

Sam: They had an "Italian" grocery store which he opened around 1911 or 1912. Yes, they were open on Saturday but my father was not a real religious fellow. When it came to a Jewish holiday, my father would tell his customers, "The holiday starts on Thursday. Wednesday you have to buy all your supplies because I won't be open until Saturday night." And that the way it would be. But you know, most of the Jewish people belonged to this particular little Orthodox shul because they had nothing else. But they couldn't be religious; it was that kind of neighborhood.

Sam: I can remember when my father knocked off Friday afternoon always. He was religious. He really was. Sincerely. I can remember sitting with my mother in the kitchen in the dark, until my father came home from church (sic). They wouldn't even put on the light. When my father got sick, he would ask me to put on his *tallis* and *tefillin*. And finally I said, "Pa, I am not going to do this any more. If you want to *daven,* you can *daven* sitting down. God will listen to you just as well." And from that day on, he did not *daven*. The children of immigrants were taught that if you couldn't do it "correctly," {that is, very religiously}, don't bother to do it at all.

PERLMUTTER FAMILY

The Perlmutter family came to America from Hungary on the Edam, arriving on September 11, 1896 with five of their eight children. They arrived in Newton around 1903. They were related to the Fried family. The Frieds came to Newton because the Perlmutters were already established here.

Lorincz (d. 1901) and Esti/Esther Weinberg Perlmutter (d.1913) had eight children, Edward (b. 1872), Celia (Fried) (b. 1876), Harry (b. 1878), William/Farkas (b. 1880), Bertha/Betti (b. 1885), Morris/Maurice/Moritz, (b. 1888), Herman/Haiman (b. 1890), Abraham/Abish (b. 1894). Three of their children, Harry, Edward and Celia were already in America when the rest of the family arrived.

William and Julia Perlmutter, 1907

Photo courtesy of Judy Perlmutter Sugarman

Around 1903, Harry became a shoemaker and had a shop on Watertown Street. In 1905, Edward and William had dry goods stores on Watertown Street but at two different addresses. In 1909, William and Maurice and later Edward joined together to form Perlmutter Bros, a dry goods store on Watertown Street. Their sister Bertha worked in the store also. She married Morris Pactovis (born in Hungary in 1883).

A family tragedy: two relatives, Abraham Perlmutter and Sigmond Fried (uncle and nephew—mother and daughter had sons the same year) drowned in Silver Lake in a skating accident in 1904. Both boys were about ten years old. David Fried was also there but he was saved and did not drown. In the confusion and distress of the families at the time, both boys were named Abraham on the death certificates but the Fried boy's name was always given as Sigmond. Sigmond was the oldest child of Morris and Etta Fried. The event was covered in all three of Newton's newspapers as well as the Boston Globe.

NEWTON BOYS BREAK THROUGH ICE TO DEATH

Charles Dunn Makes Heroic Efforts to Save Abraham Perlmutter and Hickmot Fried, Who Had Been Skating on Silver Lake.

TEN DEAD WEEK'S RECORD OF SKATING ON THIN ICE.

Nov 11—Keene N. H., Wilfred Huard, 11 years
Nov 18—Amesbury, Arthur Page, 10 years
Nov 18—Haverhill Romeo McLish 11 years
Nov 18—Lowell, James R. Larnin, 8 years
Nov 19—Lynn Edward Carey George B. Nov 20—Worcester Ragnar Nelson, 10 years Stiles Burt H Houkes all 14 years
Nov 20—Nonantum, Abraham Perlmutter, Hickmot Fried, both 11 years

With a score of persons looking on, two boys, Abraham Perlmutter, aged 11, son of Mrs Esther Perlmutter of 387 Watertown street, and Hickmot Fried, aged 11, son of Morris Fried of 7 Cook street, Nonantum, broke through the thin ice while skating on Silver Lake, within sight of their homes, yesterday afternoon at 4 30 o'clock, and were drowned notwithstanding the heroic attempt to rescue them by Charles Dunn of 97 Adams street, Newton, who is now at his home under the care of a physician

Since the recent freeze the boys living in the neighborhood of Silver Lake have spent most of their time on the ice, although they had repeatedly been warned by the police that the ice was not thick enough to bear their weight Yesterday afternoon Mrs Perlmutter refused to let her son go as she had just read of the drowning of three Lynn boys while skating

She Let Them Go.

She kept her son in the room with her until her nephew Hickmot Fried came to the house and wanted the Perlmutter boy to accompany him to the lake The boy's mother consented, and the two little fellows ran off in high spirits.

They joined a crowd of companions on the ice and were soon skating some distance from the shore when, without an instant s warning the thin coating of ice gave away and both boys were struggling for their lives in the cold water, which at that place was about eight feet deep Young Fried caught hold of the edge of the ice, and grappling the coat of his companion tried to pull him up alongside The ice then broke again and both boys went down.

Dunn Plunged In.

One of the spectators of the accident was Charles Dunn, who as soon as the boys broke through, started to their rescue He plunged into the lake, and breaking the ice with his arms swam out about 150 feet to where the boys disappeared He then tried to find the bodies but they had been carried by the current under the ice

Dunn feeling his strength going tried to make his way back to the shore and was pulled out within a few feet of the landing by a friend, in whose arms he became unconscious.

In the meantime the Newton police had been notified, and Sergts Purcell and Burke with half a dozen patrol men, secured a boat and grappling hooks with which they pulled out the bodies about an hour after they had gone down

Newton Boys Break Through Ice To Death

Boston Globe, November 25, 1904

With a score of persons looking on, two boys, Abraham Perlmutter, age 11, son of Mrs. Esther Pelmutter of 387 Watertown Street, and Hickmot Fried, son of Morris Fried of 7 Cook Street, Nonantum, broke through the thin ice while skating on Silver Lake, within sight of their homes, yesterday afternoon at 4:30 o'clock and were drowned notwithstanding the heroic attempt to rescue them by Charles Dunn of 97 Adams Street, Newton, who is now at his home under the care of a physician.

Since the recent freeze the boys living in the neighborhood of Silver Lake have spent most of their time on the ice, although they had repeatedly been warned by the police that the ice was not thick enough to bear their weight. Yesterday afternoon Mrs. Perlmutter refused to let her son go as she had just read of the drowning of three Lynn boys while skating.

She Let Them Go.

She kept her son in the room with her until her nephew Hickmot Fried came to the house and wanted the Perlmutter boy to accompany him to the Lake. The boy's mother consented and the two little fellows ran off in high spirits.

They joined a crowd of companions on the ice and were soon skating some distance from the shore when, without an instant of warning the thin coating of ice gave away and both boys were struggling for their lives in the cold water, which at that place was about eight feet deep. Young Fried caught hold of the edge of the ice, and grappling the coat of his companion tried to pull him up alongside. The ice then broke again and both boys went down.

Dunn Plunged In.

One of the spectators of the accident was Charles Dunn, who as soon as the boys broke through, started to their rescue. He plunged into the lake, and breaking the ice with his arms swam about 150 feet to where the boys disappeared. He then tried to find the bodies but they had been carried by the current under the ice.

Dunn feeling his strength going tried to make his way back to the shore and was pulled out within a few feet of the landing by a friend, in whose arms he became unconscious.

In the meantime the Newton Police had been notified and Sergts Purcell and Burke with half a dozen patrol men, secured a board and grappling hooks with which they pulled out the bodies about an hour after they had gone down.

One of the granddaughters, Esther (daughter of William and Julia) never married. She joined the WACS in 1943 and was stationed at Fort Oglethorpe, Georgia, working in "classification." Before enlisting, Esther was head of the West Newton Branch Library. Her cousin Judy remember Esther having a gorgeous figure and looked stunning in a uniform.

Free! **Free!**

100 Special Hand Painted Pictures mounted on plate glass to be given away FREE to the first 100 customers making a purchase of One Dollar, and bringing this coupon printed herewith.

GOOD FOR ONE ONLY
FREE FREE
Perlmutter Bros.
One Handsome Hand Painted Picture, The Young Mother

The following is a partial list of our offerings for the next 3 days:

[illegible]

Special Reduction on Shoes

Perlmutter Brothers

Department Store

337-339 Watertown St., Newton

FREE DELIVERY Tel. 890 N. N. SATISFACTION GUARANTEED

Shoehorn from the store of Harry Perlmutter
Owned by Judy Perlmutter Sugarman

PERRY FAMILY

One of the Hungarian Jewish storekeepers on Watertown Street, Hyman Perry opened his shop in 1909, sharing space at 376 Watertown Street with Edward Perlmutter. Edward later left to join his brothers at Perlmutter Brothers.

Perry's Department Store

Photo courtesy Mrs. David Dangel

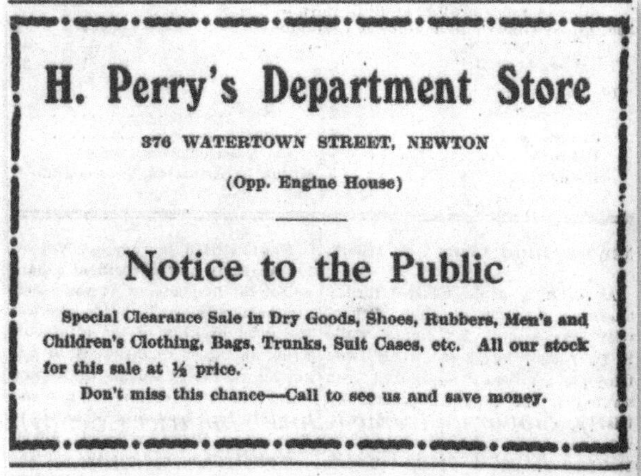

ROITER FAMILY

The Roiter family came to the U.S. with the Meilman family, perhaps from Kiev or Odessa, no one is sure, around 1910. The Roiter name is visible in the synagogue in several places, as the family remained connected to the synagogue all their lives. Joseph and Zipporah Roiter had seven children, Bertha (1895-1993), Ida (Cohen) (1900-1992), Celia (1901-1992), Harry (1902-1994), Fanny (1907-1994), Maurice (Mendy) (1913-1999), and Irving (Chick) (1916-2002). Joseph died in 1954 and his wife outlived him by many years. Joseph had a brother named Moishe/Morris, born in 1876, who arrived in the US on the Cleveland, sailing from Hamburg, in 1913. In 1918, both brothers registered for the draft. Morris described himself as a "junk collector" and Joesph described himself as a "junk dealer." When he arrived, Morris gave his brother Joseph's address as Maguire Court in Newton. The registration card for the draft for Morris Roiter bears the signature of the Registrar, H. Hart Gilfix.

Front Row: Fanny, Zipporah, Irving (Chick), Maurice (Mendy) Joseph, Harry
Back Row: Celia, Bertha, Bertha's husband, Ida

Joseph made at least two trips to the United States, the second trip presumably to bring his family with him. Of their seven children, only the two youngest were born here. His youngest son Irving often recalled with great emotion how kind his father was, inviting strangers to his home for Shabbas and holidays and how revered he was in the community and how humble Joseph was.

Joseph served as president of the congregation at least three times, in 1917, 1927 and 1929. His brother Morris served as secretary for the congregation in 1919, 1920, 1921, 1923, and 1925.

The immigrant parents were very observant all their lives but their children were very Americanized. Chick, the youngest, played hockey and Harry had his own horse, kept in a barn behind the house on Adams Street. And Chick was the only one to obtain a college degree. He had hoped to become a doctor but could not afford it so he became a pharmacist. He was also the only child to move away from Newton, to Newport, RI. Cynthia Cohen Spritzer, a cousin of Eric's, was born in 1935 and she recalled how she was "the only child with a flag, an apple and a candle on *Simchat Torah.*" Cynthia was educated at Stern College, married a rabbi and made aliyah to Israel in 1953, influenced, she said, by her grandfather Joseph.

Joseph, like many of the other immigrant members of the community, was a junk peddler. His grandson Eric Roiter recalls that "Grandpa Joe did something environmentalist before his time. He recycled paper." Joseph's son Harry took over the business which survived into the 1960's before he sold it to two Harvard Business School graduates.

Eric, now a resident of Newton, recalled his grandfather with these words, "What daring, what imagination it took to create a synagogue out of nothing. But compared to enduring persecution back in the Ukraine, living every day not knowing if there would be a pogrom, to get on a ship and come to America and start with nothing, the idea of starting a shul probably was not that daunting an enterprise."

Hiddur Mitzvah–Beauty Enhances Good Deeds

by Cynthia Cohen Spitzer, December 2014

Jewish tradition recognizes and encourages the inclusion of beauty-enhancing good deeds by appealing to the senses. Beautiful sounds and pleasant fragrances, tastes, textures, colors and artistry contribute to human enjoyment of religious acts, and beauty itself takes on a religious dimension. The idea of enhancing a deed through aesthetics is called Hiddur Mitzvah. The idea is derived from Rabbi Ishmael's comment on the verse "This is my G-d and l will glorify Him" (Exodus 15:2).

What this really means is, I shall worship Him in the way I do good deeds. There seems to be reciprocity of beauty through the power of deeds. The Jew becomes beautiful as he/she performs a mitzvah. But conversely Israel beautifies God by performing the commandments in the most beautiful manner. Bezalel and Ohab, we are told, in The Five Books of Moses, were artists filled with knowledge, wisdom, and understanding, called upon to do the work of building The Sanctuary. Thus, artists are called to be on the cutting edge of Jewish life. Thus we have this beautiful shul.

However, in the US when Jews leave an area, the synagogue building is usually sold as a church; with rare exceptions it does not stay as a Jewish house of worship. I was fortunate in growing up in a gem of a congregation that has now come full circle. The synagogue was built by my grandfather and others. My grandfather was president for several years until he died in 1953. My grandmother who died at the age of 100 was the oldest remaining member. Mr. Elmer Lippin had the key and opened up the shul for many years waiting for a minyan to show up on Sabbath mornings. None came. My uncles Harry and Mendy took care of the building, making sure it didn't collapse, put up a fence, carried out regular maintenance. Eventually the National Register of Historic Places recognized this gem. Many years later Jews were looking for affordable housing in Newton and a miracle happened.

Once again there is a congregation in full bloom. Many people participated in this good deed, from my grandparents until this day. This Shul was willed to me "in perpetuity". No, I do not own the shul, but what an inheritance I have. I believe I am one of the oldest living members of the original families (age 79).

While I was growing up, every Friday afternoon my Grandmother, Mother, Aunts and I would polish the brass and shine the wood so that it gleamed in our synagogue. Little did I realize that this was a good deed. I spent my early years sitting on my grandfather's lap on the bimah. Later I was relegated to the upstairs women's section where my grandmother reigned supreme in her black feathered hat and fox stole (complete with the eyes) . Third seat, first row. Most of the women did not know how to daven. Some had siddurim in Yiddish, some mouthed the Hebrew. I recall one Simhat Torah where I was the only child running around with my flag, apple, and candle. [There were other small children at various times at the synagogue. Jean Schribman Birnbaum recalled there was a paper flag with an apple impaled on the top of the stick. A space had been scooped out of the apple as a holder for a lighted candle and the children all followed the Torah and marched around the shul. Surprisingly, she said, there was never a fire.]

There were 55 peddlers registered in Nonantum. Everyone listed peddler as their occupation. How they progressed seems strange to me. They knew no English. My grandmother never learned a word of English. Aside from making a living, the founders had problems adjusting themselves and their children to America. The children had to go to public school. Many were sent to work after they learned to read and write. The other worry was the Americanization of the children. No hats, riding on Shabbat, electricity. Slowly the women uncovered their heads. Children were not marrying; where would they meet someone? They started a youth group. My aunt Celia was chairman. They went to Norumbega Park, and Nantasket. The large part of the female daughters of the founders either married very late, had a shidduch, or remained alone. The last three daughters were at my first wedding Sadie and Bertha Greenwald, and Minnie Hoffman.

There are many ways to apply the principle of this mitzvah. I had been blessed with being fortunate enough to be in the right places at the right times when there was a need for Hiddur Mitzvah in building and polishing sanctuaries. How fortunate we are with this inheritance. I am thrilled that there is a Roiter amongst your ranks again. My cousin Eric, who has the joy of *Hiddur Mitzvah.*

Kiddush cup, silver, 6 inches high Inscribed: Presented Oct 19, 1947
Presented to Joseph Roiter, Pres. Cong. Agudas Achim Ansei Sfard

Courtesy of Eric Roiter
Photo: Zara Tzanev, zaraphoto@gmail.com, Boston, MA

Medal presented to Joseph Roiter, 1935
Inscribed: Presented by Cong. Agudas Achim Anshe Sfard 1935

Courtesy of Eric Roiter
Photo courtesy Zara Tzanev, zaraphoto@gmail.com, Boston MA

SHRIBERG FAMILY

Philip and Etta Shriberg's family came to US in 1895, settled in West Newton on Pine Street and later moved to West Street. He became a citizen in 1902. Jane Shriberg recalls, "My father in law Philip created quite a metal business, let's put it that way, and later he took on the automobile business. It used to be known as the West Street Used Auto Parts Company. My husband inherited the business and finally sold it after many years. The family lived next door to the business. Will could not go to college because he had to go to work to help his father in the business."

Jane was a trained singer, born and raised in Randolph, Maine. She attended the University of Maine for "a couple of years." But she had a female relative who had been at the university and "she fell in love with someone and she got married. My mother didn't want me falling in love with anyone. She just wanted me to go to school. So my mother made me come home so I would not run off and get married."

She studied voice in Maine for five years, including time with Berji Ottie (sp?) who was a famous teacher in New York and he came to Maine once a week to give lessons. Jane came to the Boston area while she was a teenager. She was invited by a relative of hers, Mrs. Louis Levine, who lived in Newton Corner, to give a concert at the synagogue. Jane later received a letter from Mrs. Levine inviting her to come back to Newton because Willie's father Philip came to her and said Willie had fallen in love with her! She moved to Newton in 1927 and they were married for fifty nine years.

Jane: The Shribergs were pillars of the synagogue down here and I went to services there. They had a beautiful ark there and I think it's gorgeous and I had never seen anything so beautiful, you know, coming from the sticks we didn't have a synagogue, though I was the daughter of a scholar and my father taught us at home. Anyway they had this little white curtain on the ark. I don't know how old it was but it was in shreds and I said, well anything as beautiful as that, isn't that a shame that they have anything that ragged, and I said, well I'll put $5 or $10 of my own and then I'll walk around the area and so I rapped on every door and I raised $50. And then after I had the $50 I didn't know what to do with it. So I went to Mrs. Fried (Louis' mother) and I asked her to take this money and buy whatever they call this thing, the curtain? I didn't know a lot of this when I first came here because I had been raised among gentiles. But I had raised enough money to buy a velvet one, you know things were cheap in those days for the $50 I got a beautiful purple one with lions and the torahs done in gold. I was never thanked for what I did. I'm still looking for a thank you. Then later they needed a cloth to cover the *bimah* and I asked my very wealthy friend and she donated it. She was very glad to do it. She even wanted to renovate the whole synagogue. (Jane didn't want to give the name but it was Sadie Helman).

Philip and Etta Shriberg

Photo courtesy of Anne and Robert Chavenson

JACOB SCHRIBMAN

Jacob Schribman was one of the last Jewish immigrants to come to Newton. Jacob was born in Krisilov Volin Russia in 1889 and arrived on the Aquitania in May 1921 in New York where his brothers had settled earlier. He came to Newton to visit his relatives. He married Rose Gilfix, his second cousin, in 1924. The first part of his story is a history of what happened to Jews who stayed in Russia.

Jacob's original name (on his passport) was Jankiel Grummer. When he became a citizen, his citizenship papers stated that he was changing his name to Jacob Schribman. Where did the names come from?

His daughter Rose explained that their common ancestor Yaakov Leib Alder had a daughter Elka Shifra, who married Mendel Shreibman. Mendel's family's name had originally been Gruver or Groyer (meaning the gray one), so it is possible that the first Gruver turned gray at an early age. So he was called Gruver the Schreibman (scribe). No one knows when they dropped the Gruver part of the name or why Jacob spelled it differently on his citizenship application. Most of Jacob's family continued to be called Schreibman but Jack was always Schribman.

Jacob Shribman

Photo Courtesy of Marshall Shribman

Jacob (known all his life as Jack) was drafted into the Russian army probably in 1914. He served for three years in order to get a pair of boots. His unit invaded Austria and near Vienna he ended up in a POW camp, where he worked as a kitchen hand. The soldiers were repatriated; the Russian government had commandeered a train to take the soldiers back to Russia. The soldiers were not well treated; the officers stole their rations. He told his children that he was treated very well in the POW camp and in fact, he confided to one of the German officers that he wanted to escape and the officer helped him to do so.

While in the Army, Jacob had a dream one night. In this dream, his grandfather came to him and told him that the Germans were going to attack the next day. But, his grandfather said, if you hide in a certain place [which his grandfather described], he would be safe. The next day the Germans did attack but he was safe, although he was captured at a later time.

In Russia, Jack lived near Shaindel, the widow of Isaac Gilfix. (She was the mother of Moishe and Dov Ber). Jack was her great nephew. Jack returned to Russia after his military service. His family was well off and owned a nice home and a lumber yard. The house was taken by the government to be its headquarters during the civil war. The town had a beet sugar mill which was taken over by the communists and the local economy collapsed. Jack said that the tsar didn't care about the people and the tsarina was very unpopular.

Two of Jack's brothers were already in the US, settled in New York, so he decided to emigrate as well. Jack repaired sewing machines in Russia and in New York. Workers owned their own machines and would carry them from job to job. He liked outdoor work and there was not enough sewing machine repair work in Boston.

When asked questions in later years about his life in Russia, he would reply, "if everything there was so nice, I would have stayed in Russia. It was not nice. I am here and I don't want to talk about what it was like there." But as a younger man he often talked with his children about what life was like in Russia. He used to read them the stories of Sholem Aleichem in Yiddish and his daughter Jean remembered that the stories were very different in Yiddish from what she later read in English. They were much funnier in Yiddish and there were many ideas and actions that did not get translated or were not understood by the English audience.

He told his son Marshall that Sherpaktova was the nearest big city to Chon and Colchin. He also said that if you wanted a train, you had to go to Starokonstantinov.

Marshall recalled his father Jacob Schribman going to the Rebbe (Rabbi Twersky) to ask him what he should do, because he had to work on the Sabbath and this bothered him greatly. The Rebbe said to him, you must earn a living, so when you are able to stop working on the Sabbath, you should do so, but now you have no choice.

SILVERMAN FAMILY—LEWIS (LOU) AND ROSE

Lou's brother Isaac (Ike) thought that the boys went with their father Morris Silverman to help lay the floor in the synagogue.

Lou: my father Morris was a carpenter in the old country, but when he came here, he couldn't get work because he did not speak the language. He was very close to Benjamin Gilfix who helped him to get settled here in America. Benjamin was fond of his sister Goldie, who was married to Morris Silverman. My father had to do something that he wouldn't have to work on the Sabbath. Now what can you do in this strange land? Either you forget all about your religion and work any time and any day you could and this was the easiest way out. He became a junk dealer because he wanted to observe the Sabbath and that's why they pushed so hard and sacrificed so hard. By a strange coincidence, the Hungarians were not so Orthodox. They were merchants, the Perrys, the Perlmutters, the Frieds and they did work on the Sabbath. Not that there was anything bad about them as far as that was concerned but that was their way of life and I don't think the synagogue was that important to them except possibly on holiday times.

Lou recalled growing up in Nonantum and the anti-Semitism he encountered. "You see, when you have only one or two token Jews, they are tolerated and in fact they are honored. The minute we get to be little more numerous, and you present some kind of economic threat to them, then these people come out from under their stones."

Lou recalled coming home from school and picking up a baked potato on a cold winter's day. You'd put one in each pocket to keep your hands warm as you walked down the street and then going to the shul where one of the instructors was Harry Roiter's uncle.

Both Rose and Lou are lawyers. She went to law school nights and Lou went to BU and then to BU Law School and they were both members of the Massachusetts Bar. She worked at City Hall in the Engineering Department.

Rose: I was president of Newton Hebrew Ladies Aid for many years. Nathan Goodman's mother was the first president for about ten years and Marion Fried was president for about ten years and I followed and I was president for at least four years.

The cover on the bimah at the synagogue was given by Sadie Grossman Helman in memory of her husband or her parents. Sadie Helman donated the Memorial Book to celebrate her 25th wedding anniversary. Bookbinder was the name of the man who did the calligraphy for the memorial book.

Lou recalled that he was a Cohen and Mr. Roiter was a Levi. It was the custom in the Orthodox shul for the Cohanim to stand before the congregation and bless them. "But there's a washing of the hands and a removing of the shoes. The Levi washes the hands of the Cohanhim and I remember as a very young boy, just after my bar mitzvah, that Mr. Roiter thought it was an honor to wash my hands."

SILVERMAN FAMILY—MAX AND GOLDIE

Their son Ike was interviwed by Jean Shribman Birnbaum.

Max Silverman and Goldie (Gilfix) Silverman had five children. Goldie was Benjamin and Morris Gilfix's sister. Max's parents were Reuven and Socia Bayla. Reuven was a baker in Russia.

Isaac (Ike, b. 1899), Mary (Mae Nankin) and Sarah (Sally Tack) Silverman: Ike and Mae and Sally were born in Russia; Bessie (Betty Matulsky) and Labie (Lou) were born in America, at home, not in a hospital. Ike recalled that Sally had something wrong with her eyes and was detained with the family in Galicia for about ten weeks before they were allowed to leave for America, because the steamship company knew they would not be admitted until it was cleared up. They traveled through Germany to Holland. The name of the ship was the Arabic and they traveled from Rotterdam to England and eventually landed in Castle Island in Boston. The trip in steerage took about seven days. Ike was about five years old when he came, and Mae was about four and Sally about two years old.

Max had been in the Russian Army for about four years and when he got out of the Army, he got married, in 1898. He ran away from Russia about 1904 around the time of the Russo-Japanese War to avoid being called up again and we came about a year or two later. Max went to New York first where he had a brother Harry but by the time we came, he had moved to Newton.

They came from Kolcheen—old name Crosintee. There was a river at the bottom, like a lake; we had to go down a hill to wash our clothes and to bathe and they used to deliver water to people's houses by wagon. They would put the clothes in to soak, and then boil them and then rinse them and then take them down to the river and washed clothes by beating them on the rocks with a stick. There were no pogroms or ghettos but the Jews lived together for self-protection.

The house we lived in was an ordinary house, with one floor and a dirt floor. My father Max was a carpenter with a shop in a separate part of the house. He married at the age of 25 in 1898. Our mother Goldie could read and write Hebrew [probably Yiddish.] My grandmother Shaindel had a business in Russia dying clothes for people to earn money.

Ike recalled that when people in the community wanted to send a letter to the old country, they wrote the letter and then Murray Nussinow used to address the letter in Russian, because the Russian postal authorities would not accept letters with English addresses. Many people could read and write Yiddish and Hebrew and speak Russian but very few knew how to write Russian.

Our father was the vice president of the shul. The laying of the cornerstone was August 4, 1912.

Ike married Molly Kaufman and they had two children, Sandra Ethel (b. 1934) and Leonard Edward (b. 1938). Ike and Murray Mussinow operated Silver Lake Radio on Lincoln Street in Newton Highlands and later Murray left the business and Lou joined him.

SHRIER FAMILY

The Shrier family first appears in the Newton directory in 1901. Avram was originally from Kiev. They first lived at 127 Bridge Street and moved to Chapel Street around 1917. He was a junk peddler and his wife Rebecca ran a small grocery store at 229 Chapel Street. They had four children, Eva, Max, Goldie and Hyman.

Avram and Rebecca Shrier, 1938

Photo courtesy of Dr. Peter Shrier

Max established a printing business in Newton Corner called the Newton Corner Press, which survived into the 1990s when ill health forced him to close the business. The Press did the printing for the synagogue until it closed.

Hyman Shrier, MD

Photo courtesy of Dr. Peter Shrier

The classic Jewish immigrant success story, Hyman attended a combined BA/MD degree program at Tufts University and Tufts Medical School and graduated from medical school in 1928. He became a surgeon and practiced on Pearl Street in Nonantum. In addition to his practice in Newton, he had an office on Beacon Street near Kenmore Square and for some years was on the faculty of Tufts Medical School. He also served as chief of surgery at the Brookline Hospital.

Hyman married Pauline Kravitz in 1936. She had graduated from Boston University School of Music in 1934 and had also received a Bachelor's degree from the Hebrew Teachers' College (now called Hebrew College) in the same year. She was a classical pianist.

Hyman was devoted to the synagogue and in 1951 he paid to install a new hot air heating system in the synagogue so that his son David could have his bar mitzvah in the synagogue. That was where he himself had been bar mitzvah and he wanted his son to have the same experience. His son Peter (also a doctor) recalled that when he was a young man they were still using the old school desks for seating. His family donated a magnificent silver Torah crown to the synagogue, which is still in use.

JACOB SWARTZ FAMILY

Jacob Swartz was born in 1867 in Germany and came to the United States early in the great wave of Jewish immigration to the Unites States. He became a citizen in 1887 in Boston. In 1898 he married Julia Ida Appleton. She was born in Russia in 1878 and stated that her maiden name was Appleton. (This suggests that her family had also arrived early in the great immigration and changed their name, since it is unlikely that a person named Appleton, a very "Yankee" name, would have married a Jewish immigrant). They had five children, Lillian (b. 1900), Gertrude (b. 1901), Henry (b. 1903), Eli (b. 1904) and Gerald (b. 1906).

Swartz Hardware was started in 1890, but the store did not begin as a hardware store. Early records in 1901 and 1905 describe Swartz as engaged in selling "fancy goods," probably meaning clothing. In 1911 and 1917 the store was still described as a variety store. But in 1921, he had added hardware to the variety store. "In those early days, the business was like a general store that stocked seed, fertilizer, toys, sleds, and all manner of hardware and fasteners, plumbing supplies, and industrial tools and parts for local mills and manufacturers. Nails were purchased by the 100 lb. wooden keg, and there were fireworks on sale for the Fourth of July."

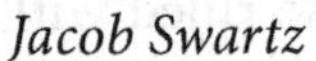

Jacob Swartz

Julia Appleton Swartz

Photo courtesy Michael Swartz

Jacob Swartz, the founder of the store that today bears his name was a critically important member of the group that united to build the synagogue. It was he who donated the land on which the synagogue is built to the congregation. He died in 1922, aged 55 and his wife Julia took over the business. Known as Mother Swartz, she successfully ran the business until she passed it on to her sons Gerald (Jerry) and Eli in the 1940's. Stories of that early time describe her sitting on a nail keg outside on the front stoop in the summer, holding court with her customers, helping with their personal as well as their hardware problems. In the winter, the pot bellied wood stove in the middle of the store served as a gathering place in the community. A local police officer, Lt. Feeley, recalled in a newspaper interview, "Swartz Hardware, where Model T. headlight (lamp) lenses were available as late as 1955. Mother Swartz knew where every bit of hardware was located and Jerry and Eli, as knowledgeable as they are, could never have the computer precision mind that Mrs. Swartz had in keeping track of thousands of items." [32]

Lt. Feeley recalled, Mr. Gerald Swartz, at the time the Lake was about to lose its branch library, entered the battle, kept our library open, moved the fire department to Crafts Street, and in a sense mothered our fine library at Bridge and Watertown Streets. [The location of the library, on the corner of Bridge Street and Watertown Street, was originally the Adams School and then a fire station]

Jacob's grandson Mike, Jerry's son, took over in 1995. In 2013, he retired and sold the business after 123 years in the family.

LILLIAN SWARTZ

LT Feeley recalled, in an interview in 1972: "The hardware store was the mercantile branch of the Swartz family.

"But there was another Swartz, one that had a love affair with every child grown in the Lake for better than thirty years. Miss Lillian Swartz, who was the playground director at Hawthorne, was leader, teacher, mother, aunt and referee to thousands of good young citizens who were better off for the association. The love and interest she had for each of them, many of whom looked upon Hawthorne as a day care center, without knowing it. While her family dealt in hardware, Lil dispensed Heart. Her family took care of those seeking hardware. Lil sought out those needing her software of direction, love and understanding." [33]

Mike Swartz, her nephew, and the last Swartz owner of the hardware store, recalled his aunt with great affection. She ruled with an iron fist but we kids learned what a good person she was and what she did for everyone. She was as good to her nieces and nephews as she was to the neighborhood.

Lillian Swartz

Courtesy Historic Newton and Swartz Hardware

Mike recalled Lillian taking him to the airport to watch planes take off and land and for his birthday, she took him to the Statler Hotel for lunch. As director of the Hawthorne Playground recreation department, she made herself available to kids who needed her guidance, took kids under her wing. People respected her and she gave her life to the community. She lived most of her life in the family home on Faxon Street.

SAMUEL SWARTZ FAMILY

Sam and Bela Raisa Swartz came from Lithuania or Latvia. He was a shoemaker. Sam and his brother had a shoe store on Watertown Street. He came to the United States before his wife and children, who arrived in Newton in 1900. They had seven children. The three oldest, Dora (b. 1896), Eddie (b. 1898), and Hazel (b. 1900) were born in Europe. Herman (b.1902), Myna (b. 1904), Louis (called Lukey) (b. 1906) and Merrit (b. 1908) were born in Newton.

Herman graduated from MIT with a degree in construction engineering and went on to found a successful magazine devoted to the construction business. Lukey's wife Etta was a Perlmutter. Lukie's family and Myna and her husband (also Herman, but called Bob so as not to confuse him with his brother-in-law), lived in New York and were involved in the automobile business, perhaps as car dealers or selling auto parts. Eddie was also a graduate of MIT and for a while he taught at Newton High School. Merrit and Eddie got interested in cameras; Merrit worked for Revere Camera and Eddie worked for Keystone Camera. Some members of the family spelled the name Swartz and some spelled it Schwartz.

Hazel was a lifelong resident of Newton. In her later years, she was active in Temple Emanuel, serving as president of the Sisterhood. She and her husband Julius donated the Eternal Light that originally hung in the main sanctuary at Temple Emanuel and is now used in its Chapel.

She recalled attending classes at the Stearns Settlement House (there was also an elementary Stearns School in the neighborhood). The school taught knitting and how to become a successful housewife. The teachers were volunteers from Wellesley College.

The family bought the house at 97 Dalby Street in 1917 that had originally housed Congregation Kenesas Israel Anshe Sfard. It remained in the family until the early 1990s and Dora lived there until her death.

Hazel's mother would not allow anyone to paint over the Biblical verses painted on the walls of what they called the living room, but which had been built onto the house to serve as a synagogue. Those verses remained as long as Bela Raisa was alive; she died in the middle 1940's. Visiting rabbis sometimes stayed in their home. It was a source of pride as well as a big honor (*koved*) for the family that their level of *kashrus* and religious observance was recognized by the local religious community.

She recalled looking forward to Friday, when there was a real holiday spirit every Friday night. Her mother, like other observant women in the community, would start cooking at 4 or 5 AM in order for the challah and other special foods to be ready in time for the Sabbath at sundown. But Hazel recalled Pesach as "not a fun holiday," when her mother "tore the house apart" and repainted the kitchen for the holiday.

She recalled that you could hire a "day woman" to help clean and do laundry for $2 per day, but all the children still had to do chores every day.

Hazel remembered the synagogue as the center of the family's social and religious life. Periodically they would hire a teacher to teach the children to read and write Hebrew. People were proud of the synagogue building.

People were devout, respectful and friendly to each other. Hazel recalled going door to door for the Newton Hebrew Ladies Aid to collect money for the poor and for Israel (it was still Palestine at that time) as well. And they had good relations with their French neighbors, urged on by the priest at the French speaking Catholic church (St. Jean L'Evangeliste) in the neighborhood. Hazel's family lived at 97 Dalby Street, next door to St. Jean's.

Father Robichaud admired the home life of the Jewish families in the neighborhood and encouraged his parishioners to accept their Jewish neighbors. She did not recall any anti-Semitism in her youth. In fact, the relations between her family and the neighbors was such that the women traded recipes. She recalled learning a different style of baking, such as frosted cakes instead of sponge cakes. That kind of cooking was also promoted by the Stearns Settlement House. The settlement house movement believed that accepting "American" food was an important milestone in the Americanization process. But kosher food could only be obtained in the West End or the North End and local Jewish resident Louis Baker would take orders and go into town to bring back bread and rolls for the neighborhood. Hazel also made her own clothes, a skill she learned from her mother.

Hazel attended Boston University for two years and learned bookkeeping but she dropped out as she wasn't very committed to her education. Many of her friends attended Framingham State Teachers College because they could get there by bus.

Nate Goodman recalled that Edward Swartz founded a company called Keystone Camera which was very successful. Nate stated that Edward paid off the shul mortgage and the community celebrated with a big party.

Hazel Swartz Santis

Photo Courtesy Phyllis Santis Stewart Smith

YANCO FAMILY

Harry Yanco was married to Sarah. They were the parents of Herbert, Albert, Annette (Feldman) and Ruth (Pass). Harry started a used car business called the Newton Used Car and Parts Company. He was also a scrap metal dealer. If he couldn't sell a used car, he would dismantle it and sell it for scrap. One of the boys enlisted in the Army Air Corps the day after Pearl Harbor and came out of the service as a captain.

Philip Bram recalled the Yanco family. "Harry was wonderful, handsome looking man, and his wife was a beautiful woman. Harry Yanco got a job and the story is that the first day he got on the streetcar, he slipped on some ice or something and the streetcar cut his leg off. And all his life Harry Yanco had to live with a wooden leg that created pain all his life. And he was difficult to do business with because he was in pain all the time. But he ran a wonderful business, a junk business first. He was very generous to customers and neighbors, in the same way as the Frieds, offering credit and good deals to local people. The business, which had three acres of land off Pearl Street, was taken by the city by eminent domain in December 1941 to build senior citizen housing (now JFK Circle)."

The family was very well off, Herbert told an interviewer. " We had a mansion to live in. I got a new Ford in 1931 for my sixteenth birthday. The house was so big that there was a room with TWO pool tables! We didn't know about the Depression." After the business was dissolved when the city bought the land, Herbert became a court officer in the Newton District Court.

Herbert's brother Albert Yanco was a Newton police officer and ended his career as a captain in the Newton Police Department.

CULTURE

HEBREW IMMIGRANT AID SOCIETY OF AMERICA (HIAS)

Over two and one half million Jews came to the United States between 1880 and 1924, mostly from Eastern Europe, Ukraine and Russia. In Boston, the Jewish population increased from 20,000 in 1895 to 40,000 in 1900. [34] Assisting immigrants absorbed every Jewish organization, religious and secular, in the early years of the 20th century, until immigration was brought to a screeching halt by federal legislation in 1924.

It is important to understand the social and political pressures that motivated the founding of HIAS. The first Statement of Purpose below is specifically designed to address non-Jewish concerns about Jewish immigration to the United States. Each segment of that Statement responds to a particular concern of the so-called Nativists (whites who opposed immigration). Many white Anglo-Saxon Protestants (WASPS) believed that the presence of so many Jewish and Italian immigrants (all of whom were considered non-white), and who were especially visible in the big cities on the East Coast, threatened "white American" culture. The second Statement of Purpose is addressed to the Jewish community.

"HIAS Statement of Purpose: To facilitate the lawful entry of Jewish immigrants at the various ports in the United States, to provide them with temporary assistance, to prevent them from becoming public charges, to discourage their settling in congested cities, to encourage them to follow agricultural pursuits, to prevent ineligibles from emigrating to the United States, to foster American ideals, and to instill in them a knowledge of American history and institutions and to make known the advantages of desirable immigration."

HIAS Statement of Purpose: "The Hebrew Immigrant Aid Society (HIAS) was formed in 1889, to facilitate legal entry, reception and immediate care for Jewish immigrants. The bureau provided translation services, guided immigrants through medical screening and other procedures, argued before the Boards of Special Enquiry to prevent deportations, lent needy Jews the $25 landing fee and obtained bonds for others guaranteeing their employable status. The Society also made great effort to search for the relatives of detained immigrants in order to secure the necessary affidavits of support guaranteeing that the immigrants would not become public charges. By 1914, HIAS had branches in Baltimore, Philadelphia, Boston and an office in Washington." [35]

The Galveston Movement, also known as the Galveston Plan, was one of several immigration assistance programs operated by Jewish organizations between 1907 and 1914. The purpose of the Galveston Movement was to try to spread Jewish immigration all over the country, instead of having it concentrated on the East Coast. This program paid the passage of these immigrants to Texas. During its operation, ten thousand Jewish immigrants passed through Galveston, Texas, with many of the new immigrants moving north along the Mississippi River toward the bigger cities of Saint Louis and Chicago. New York financier and philanthropist Jacob Schiff was the driving force behind the effort, which he supported with nearly $500,000 of his personal fortune. [36]

Increasingly anti-immigrant ideology resulted in the passage of increasingly restrictive immigration legislation, beginning in 1906 and culminating in the 1924 Immigration Act. Only twenty five years after the first HIAS Statement of Purpose quoted above, federal legislation was enacted that significantly limited the numbers of Italians and Eastern European Jews who would be admitted each year.

IMMIGRATION BY THE NUMBERS

Some facts about immigration to the United States before 1924:

Between 1820 and 1880, over 85 % of immigrants to America came from the British Isles, Germany and Scandinavia. [37]

Between 1860 and 1920 about 30 million immigrants came to the United States. [38]

Between 1880 and 1920 about six million immigrants came to the US each decade. [39]

"While the vast majority of immigrants prior to 1882 had come from Northern and Western Europe and were predominantly Protestant, by 1907, three out of every four immigrants were Catholics and Jews from Southern and Eastern Europe." [40]

From 1900 to 1909, more than eight million immigrants arrived, most of them settling on the eastern seacoast. [41]

About 2 ½ million Jews immigrated to the United States before 1924.

For comparison purposes, between 1890 and 1924, 4 million Italians came to the United States. Between 1900 and 1910, 10 percent of the Italian population moved to the United States. [42] In the first decade of the 20th century, an average of 200,000 Italians had entered the United States each year. With the 1924 Act, the annual quota for Italians was set at less than 4,000. [43]

In the years prior to implementation of the 1924 act, immigrants from Latin America represented approximately 30 percent of total immigration. [44]

IMMIGRATION AND EUGENICS

Around the turn of the twentieth century, new immigrants from Europe tended to concentrate in the major immigration ports of New York and Boston. Their visibility, due to their large numbers and differences in speech, clothing, behavior and personal appearance, fed a scientifically fashionable racist hysteria called the eugenics movement. The eugenics movement proclaimed the genetic superiority of the so-called Nordic races, and stated that only the so-called Nordic race was fit to rule. Starting in the middle 1890's, the Immigration Restriction League, founded by several Harvard graduates, began to publish pseudo-scientific papers proclaiming the superiority of the WASPS and lobbying members of Congress to adopt their ideas.[45] The major publication of the eugenics movement was *The Passing of the Great Race* by Madison Grant, published in 1916. The German translation of Grant's book was so dear to Adolph Hitler that he called it his "Bible." [46] Jews and Italians were not considered "white" in the United States until after World War II (see *How Jews Became White* by Karen Brodkin). And do not forget the racism against blacks and Asians who were not allowed to immigrate at all. An article describes how a South Asian immigrant and World War I veteran was sought citizenship because he was "Aryan" and therefore, in the "racial science" of the day, Caucasian and therefore "white." But the Supreme Court in 1923 ruled that "the great body of our people instinctively recognize and reject the thought of assimilation."[47]

GETTING TO AMERICA

The immigrants arrived by ship. Movies like "Titanic," for example, emphasized the wealthy first class passengers. The ships advertised their elegant surroundings and fine dining, and treated first class passengers as well as they would have been treated at the finest hotels in Europe and America. But the reality is that the ships of the White Star Line, like all passenger liners at that time, were built to bring immigrants to America. On the Titanic, for example, there were 319 first class passengers, 272 second class passengers and 709 passengers in steerage.

Conditions for those traveling in steerage were anything but elegant. Steamship tickets for immigrants were sold without reservations so the ship would crowd in as many passengers as had tickets. Tickets were often sold by traveling salesmen in towns and villages all over Europe. In America, relatives could buy tickets from local salesmen and send them to Europe. The overcrowding, the stench, the foul food and the discomfort of ocean travel, made steerage a sickening experience for many passengers. The cost was about $50 per person but the ships estimated they spent only sixty cents per person per day for food, so most immigrants brought their own food (including Jews, who would not eat non-kosher food). The profit to the shipping line was about $70,000 per trip.

Two examples: The Cedric, a White Star Line ship, brought Judith Gilfix to New York. It was built in 1903. It traveled from Liverpool, England to New York. A round trip took about one month. It carried 365 first class passengers, 160 second class passengers and 2352 third class or steerage passengers. The Pretoria, which brought Rose Gilfix Schribman to America, was a Hamburg-American Line ship, built in 1897. It sailed between Hamburg and New York. It carried 160 first class passengers, 190 second class passengers and 2400 third class or steerage passengers.

SS Cedric, White Star Line, built 1903

THE CITIZENSHIP PROCESS

Becoming a citizen was a priority for members of the Jewish community and a goal of the Americanization process encouraged by HIAS. It was common for new citizens to proudly display their citizenship papers on the walls of their homes where everyone could see them. This was in contrast to the fear of the government that many Jewish immigrants had felt in Russia, where political, educational and social discrimination against Jews were official policies of the Russian government.

What was (and is) the process to become an American citizen? The original United States Naturalization Law of March 26, 1790 (1 Stat. 103) limited naturalization to immigrants who were free white persons of good character. It thus excluded American Indians, indentured servants, slaves, free blacks, and Asians. [260 U.S. 178, 193]. In 1868, through the 14th Amendment, those of African nativity and descent were granted citizenship.

From the first naturalization law passed by Congress in 1790 until the 1920's, an immigrant could become naturalized in any court of record. The names and types of courts varied from state to state, and during different periods of history, but included the county supreme, circuit, district, equity, chancery, probate, or common pleas court. There were over 5,000 jurisdictions where a person could become naturalized. Today all citizenship processes take place at the federal level.

General Rule: The Two-Step Process

As a general rule, naturalization was a two-step process that took a minimum of 5 years. After residing in the United States for 2 years, an immigrant could file a "declaration of intent" (so-called "first papers") to become a citizen. After 3 additional years, the immigrant could "petition for naturalization." After the petition was granted, a certificate of naturalization was issued. In the early years, these two steps did not have to take place in the same court.

Exceptions to the General Rule

Having stated this "two-step, 5-year" general rule, it is necessary to note several exceptions. The first major exception was that "derivative" citizenship was granted to wives and minor children (under the age of 21) of naturalized men. From 1790 to 1940, children under the age of 21 automatically became naturalized citizens upon the naturalization of their father, if they were included by name in the application for citizenship. From 1790 to 1922, wives of naturalized men automatically became citizens after filing the appropriate paperwork.

The second major exception to the general rule was that, from 1824 to 1906, minor children who had not been listed on their father's application for citizenship but who had lived in the United States 5 years before their 23rd birthday could file both their declarations of intent (first papers) and petitions for citizenship at the same time.

The third major exception to the general rule was the special consideration given to veterans. An 1862 law allowed honorably discharged Army veterans of any war to petition for naturalization—without previously having filed a declaration of intent—after only 1 year of residence in the United States. An 1894 law extended the same no-previous-declaration privilege to honorably discharged 5-year veterans of the Navy or Marine Corps. Over

192,000 aliens were naturalized between May 9, 1918, and June 30, 1919, under an act of May 9, 1918, that allowed immigrants serving in the U.S. armed forces during "the present war" to file a petition for naturalization without making a declaration of intent or proving 5 years' residence. Laws enacted in 1919, 1926, 1940, and 1952 continued various preferential treatment provisions for veterans. [48]

IMMIGRATION ACTS

Immigration Act of 1906

Originally, immigration procedures in the United States were handled locally and regulated by the Commerce Department as part of the customs procedures. Anyone who had the fare for the ship could arrive at an immigration port and be admitted.

Between 1820 and 1906, passenger lists were compiled on board the ship and provided to the Commerce Department upon landing. Information included the following on each passenger: name, age, gender, occupation, country of origin.

In 1906, the first federal Naturalization Rule was enacted, which consolidated all immigration and naturalization procedures in a newly created federal Department of Immigration and Naturalization. The most immediate impact of the Act of 1906 was to create the requirement for a Certificate of Arrival for each immigrant when they applied for citizenship.

The 1906 Immigration Act required the following information on each passenger: name, marital status, previous residence, final destination, language spoken, ability to read and write, relatives in the United States, how much money the passenger had, and if they had a train ticket to their final destination. But aside from health checks (both physical and mental), arrivals were still allowed to enter without restriction.

The implementation of the new rules began with the moment of arrival, when the new immigrant was interviewed by a federal agent. The examiner sought to determine if the immigrants were capable of supporting themselves or if someone would be responsible for them. HIAS would "guarantee" the Jewish immigrants who did not have sufficient money with them (sufficient funds was defined as $25). Women who came to meet their husbands had to meet the same standards. If a passenger was deemed ineligible to enter the country for any reason, his return passage to Europe was the responsibility of the steamship company. The owners of the steamships therefore examined passengers before they boarded to try to ensure they would not be refused entry into the United States upon arrival.

Immigration Act of 1917

The Immigration Act of 1917 represented the first broad attempt to restrict immigration into the United States. In the decades prior to 1917, what was effectively unrestricted immigration allowed nearly ten million people to immigrate to the United States. Many of these immigrants came from eastern and southern Europe and Russia. The major impetus for the Immigration Act of 1917 was the large influx of eastern and southern Europeans.

The new regulations required that the head of the household or individuals over the age of sixteen traveling alone would have to be literate and demonstrate basic reading comprehension in any language. Jews were almost universally literate as they had to be able to read the prayer book. During the last year in which the Act of 1917 was law—July 1920, to June 1921—only some fourteen hundred immigrants were denied entry as a result of illiteracy, compared with more than one million who attempted to enter. Unaccompanied children were denied entry, so children traveling alone tried to be listed as the child of a traveling family, or to lie about their age to be admitted as adults (age sixteen or older).

The onset of World War I and the subsequent entry of the United States into the war in April 1917 resulted in a nationalistic fervor within the Nativist American population that in turn resulted in drastic modifications to existing immigration laws. The effect was to significantly alter the demographics of those who would be permitted to enter the country.

Beginning in 1918, the United States also required all arriving aliens to present a passport issued by their government or by some other agency. The "Nansen Passport" was the name for a series of documents issued by the High Commissioner for Refugees for the League of Nations, used during the period between World Wars I and II as identification and travel papers for refugees. They were initially issued to Russians fleeing the civil war after the overthrow of the tsarist regime, but were eventually distributed to many refugee communities.

Immigration Act of 1921

More than 800,000 immigrants were admitted to the United States during 1920-1921. According to the anti-immigrant forces, those numbers illustrated the failure of restrictions on immigration imposed by the immigration law of 1917. Of particular concern was the fear that immigrants from Russia or eastern Europe, many of them Jewish, were Bolsheviks or other kinds of radicals. The Red Scare (1919-1920) represented a growing concern that the revolutions taking place in Europe could spread to American shores. The

Immigration Act of 1921, merely a stopgap until more encompassing legislation could be passed, reflected that fear. The 1921 Act limited the annual number of immigrants from each country to 3% of that nation's nationals present in the United States according to the 1910 U.S. Census. Total immigration was set at 357,000 persons.

Immigration Act of 1924

When the Congressional debate over immigration began in 1924, the idea of a quota system was so well-established that almost no one questioned whether to maintain it, but rather discussed how to adjust it.

Senator Henry Cabot Lodge, (R, MA), Congressman Albert Johnson (R, WA) and Senator David Reed (R, PA) were the main architects of the Act. There were only nine dissenting votes in the Senate and a handful of opponents in the House, the most vigorous of whom was freshman Brooklyn Representative Emanuel Celler. Over the succeeding four decades, Celler made the repeal of the Act his personal crusade, which finally succeeded in 1965.

The Immigration Act of 1924, or Johnson–Reed Act, including the National Origins Act and Asian Exclusion Act (enacted May 26, 1924), was a United States federal law that limited the annual number of immigrants who could be admitted from any country to 2% of the number of people from that country who were already living in the United States in 1890. That was a decrease from the 3% cap of that nation's nationals present in the United States according to the 1910 U.S. Census set by the Immigration Restriction Act of 1921. The effect of that change, using the Census of 1890, was deliberate.

The 1924 law traced the origins of the whole of the American population, not just immigrants, including natural-born citizens. The new quota calculations thus included large numbers of people of British or Northern European descent whose families were long resident in the United States. Significant immigration by Southern European and Eastern Europeans did not really include large numbers until the middle of the 1890's. As a result of the quota system, the percentage of visas available to individuals from the British Isles and Western Europe increased and the percentages of immigrants from eastern and southern Europe decreased. Asians were specifically excluded from immigration.

The Act was aimed at restricting Southern and Eastern Europeans, mainly Italians from southern Europe and Jews fleeing persecution in Poland and Russia, who immigrated in large numbers starting in the 1890s. The Act also prohibited the immigration of Middle Easterners, East Asians and Indians. According to the U.S. Department of State Office of the Historian, "In all its parts, the most basic purpose of the 1924 Immigration Act was to preserve the ideal of American homogeneity."

The National Origins Formula had been in place in the United States since the Emergency Quota Act of 1921. The Emergency Quota Act, also known as the Emergency Immigration Act of 1921, the Immigration Restriction Act of 1921, the Per Centum Law, and the Johnson Quota Act (May 19, 1921) had restricted immigration into the United States. The 1924 Act "proved in the long run the most important turning-point in American immigration policy" because it added two new features to American immigration law: numerical limits on immigration from Europe and the use of a quota system for establishing those limits. These limits came to be known as the National Origins Formula.

Proponents of the Act sought to establish a distinct "American" identity by favoring native-born Americans or Northern Europeans like Scandinavians or residents of the British Isles over Southern and Eastern Europeans in order to "maintain the racial preponderance of the basic strain on our people and thereby to stabilize the ethnic composition of the population." Senator Reed (R, PA) told the Senate that earlier legislation "disregards entirely those of us who are interested in keeping American stock up to the highest standard – that is, the people who were born here." Southern and Eastern Europeans, he believed, were illiterate, unfamiliar with democratic ideals and institutions, and sick and starving, therefore less capable of contributing to the American economy, and unable to adapt to American culture. (The Emma Lazarus poem, inscribed on the Statue of Liberty in 1903, included the line "the wretched refuse of your teeming shore." To many Nativists, that expressed their opinion of immigrants perfectly).

In addition to fears about radicalism, some congressional leaders were concerned about the large influx of workers willing to work for substandard wages. For that reason, among the supporters of the bill were the leaders of the growing labor unions of American workers. During World War I, large numbers of Latin American workers, particularly from Mexico, had entered the United States to supplement the labor force related to war industries or farming, especially in the sparsely populated Southwest. The importance of these workers was reflected in their exemption from the quota system as established by the Act. In the years prior to implementation of the 1924 Act, immigrants from Latin America represented approximately 30 percent of total immigration. [49]

The consequences of this Act would reverberate before and during World War II. Once the United States entered World War II, the State Department, headed by special assistant secretary of state Breckenridge Long, practiced stricter immigration policies, allegedly out of fear that refugees could be blackmailed into working as agents for Germany. Between 1933 and 1945 the United States took in only 132,000 Jewish refugees, only ten percent of the quota allowed by law. Ninety percent of the quota places available to immigrants from countries under German and Italian control were never filled. If they had been, an additional 190,000 people could have escaped the atrocities being committed by the Nazis.[50] Reflecting a nasty strain of anti-Semitism, Congress in 1939 refused to raise immigration quotas to admit 20,000 Jewish children fleeing Nazi oppression. As the wife of the U.S. Commissioner of Immigration remarked at a cocktail party, "20,000 children would all too soon grow up to be 20,000 ugly adults." [51] This Act remained in effect until 1965.

The Immigration and Nationality Act of 1965 (enacted June 30, 1968), also known as the Hart–Celler Act, abolished the national origins quota system that was American immigration policy since the 1920s, replacing it with a preference system that focused on immigrants' skills and family relationships with citizens or U.S. residents. It was proposed by Representative Emanuel Celler of New York, co-sponsored by Senator Philip Hart of Michigan, and promoted by Senator Ted Kennedy of Massachusetts. [52]

"CITIZENSHIP PAPERS"
Naturalization Certificates

Here are the "citizenship papers" (the commonly used term) for the official naturalization certificates for Jacob Schwartz, Philip Shriberg and Benjamin Gilfix.

Jacob Swartz's citizenship paper is the most straightforward and headed "United States of America." There is no reference to renouncing allegiance to any foreign ruler. Philip Shriberg's states that he is a "free white person." Also, there were so many English, Irish and Scottish immigrants coming to the United States at that time that his preprinted form asked applicants to renounce allegiance to the king of England. Benjamin Gilfix's citizenship paper is headed "Commonwealth of Massachusetts." Some variations of those forms also required applicants to renounce "any titles of nobility." . In the case of Judith Gilfix, she had to swear that she was not a polygamist. These documents illustrate the variety of forms and locations that existed until 1906, which centralized all citizenship documentation at the federal level.

Several of the families interviewed for this book testified that they were responsible for many people "getting citizenship." What did they do? They would accompany the applicant to the courthouse or federal office building to complete the Petition for Citizenship, where they would act as character witnesses for the applicants. The witness would testify that the applicant had been resident in the United States for five years, was of good moral character and not planning to overthrow the government. One could be a witness for any number of people. In some cases, the federal examiner would ask non-family members to be witnesses. In other cases, a family member was acceptable. After assisting the applicant in filing the petition, everyone would return home to await the official notification that the application had been approved and they would be summoned to be sworn in as citizens.

The record of Judith Gilfix illustrates the entire process required of individuals who wanted to become citizens after the Immigration Act of 1906: ship passenger manifest, Certificate of Arrival, Declaration of Intent (to become a citizen, so-called first papers), and Petition for Citizenship (there is a mandatory three year waiting period after filing the Declaration of Intent) and Certification of Naturalization.

Note also that Judith Gilfix's place of birth was listed as Vilna Lithuania Russia on the Declaration of Intent in 1928 and she was asked to "renounce all allegiance to the State of Russia and the Republic of Lithuania." In 1935 she was asked to "renounce all allegiance to the Republic of Poland."

United States of America.

CIRCUIT COURT, U. S. MASS. DIST. SS.

To all People to whom these Presents shall come . . Greeting.

KNOW YE, That at a **Circuit Court of the United States,** begun and holden at Boston, within and for the Massachusetts District, on the ~~fifteenth~~ six- day of May, in the year of our Lord one thousand eight hundred and eighty-seven

To wit: on the 27th day of September A. D. 1887

Jacob Swartz

of Boston in said district, Carpenter

born at Russia

having produced the evidence and taken the oath required by law, was admitted to become a citizen of the said United States according to the Acts of Congress in such case made and provided.

In testimony Whereof, I have hereunto set my hand and affixed the seal of said Court at Boston aforesaid, the day and year last above written, and in the one hundred and twelfth year of the Independence of the United States of America.

Benj H Bradell

Deputy *Clerk of the Circuit Court of the United States for the District of Massachusetts.*

Citizenship paper for Jacob Swartz

106

[Form 2. After prior declaration.]

UNITED STATES OF AMERICA.

To the Circuit Court of the United States, *holden at Boston, within and for the District of Massachusetts:*

Respectfully represents Philip Shriberg residing at No. 77 West Street, Newton Mass in said District, occupation Junk dealer, an Alien and a free white person; that he was born in Russia on or about the 12 day of November in the year of our Lord eighteen hundred and Seventy and is now about Thirty six years of age; that he arrived at Boston in the State of Mass in the United States of America, on or about the 15 day of October in the year of our Lord eighteen hundred and Ninety five; that he made a primary declaration of his intention to become a citizen of said United States, before the Honorable United States Police Court, of Newton Mass on the 17 day of November A. D. 1902 in which he declared on oath that it was his bona fide intention to reside in and become a citizen of the United States of America, and to renounce all allegiance and fidelity to every foreign Prince, Potentate, State or Sovereignty whatsoever—more especially to ~~Edward VII., King of the United Kingdom of Great Britain and Ireland,~~ Nicolas II Czar of Russia whose subject he had theretofore been.

And the applicant further represents that he has resided within the United States for the five years preceding this application, and within the State of Massachusetts one year preceding the same; that he has never borne any hereditary title, or been of any of the orders of nobility; that he is ready to renounce and abjure all allegiance and fidelity to every foreign Prince, Potentate, State or Sovereignty whatsoever — and particularly to

Citizenship paper for Philip Shriberg

No.

Commonwealth of Massachusetts.

MIDDLESEX, ss.

TO THE JUSTICE OF THE POLICE COURT of Newton, holden at said Newton for the transaction of criminal business, within the County of Middlesex.

Respectfully represents Benjamin Gilfix petitioner of Newton, in the County of Middlesex, Junk Dealer ~~laborer~~, an alien, and now residing within the judicial district of said Court, to wit: in the house situated and numbered 55 in Clinton street in said Newton, that he was born at Russia ~~in the County of~~ in ~~Ireland~~, on or about the ~~tenth~~ sixth day of November in the year of our Lord one thousand eight hundred and Sixty being now about thirty-one years of age; that he arrived at (New York), ~~Boston~~,

in the United States of America, on or about the 15th day of June in the year of our Lord one thousand eight hundred and ninety-five ~~then being a minor under the age of eighteen years~~, and that it then was and still is his bona fide intention to become a citizen of the United States of America, and to renounce forever all allegiance and fidelity to every Foreign Prince, Potentate, State, and Sovereignty whatever, especially and particularly to Nicholas II Emperor of Russia ~~Victoria, Queen of Great Britain and Ireland, and Empress of India~~,

whose subject he has heretofore been; all which appears by the record of ~~this~~ the Court of the U. S. Mass. District Court on the 29th day of October in the year of our Lord one thousand eight hundred and ninety-eight *a certified copy of which said record is now on file in this said Police Court.*

And the said Benjamin Gilfix petitioner further represents that ever since his arrival at said (New York) ~~Boston~~ he has continued to reside within the jurisdiction of the said United States, to wit, at Newton aforesaid, and that he has never borne any hereditary title, nor been of any of the orders of nobility; that he is ready to renounce and abjure all allegiance and fidelity to every Foreign Prince, Potentate, State, and Sovereignty whatever, and particularly to Nicholas II Emperor of Russia ~~Victoria, Queen and Empress as aforesaid~~,

whose subject he has heretofore been; that he is attached to the principles of the Constitution of the United States of America, and well disposed toward the good order and happiness of the same; Wherefore your petitioner prays that he may be admitted to become a citizen of the United States of America according to the forms of the Statutes in such cases made and provided.

And the said Benjamin Gilfix petitioner further represents that Maurice Gilfix, residing at the building situated and numbered 61 in Clinton street, in the city of Newton, and Joseph Hoffman residing at the building situated and numbered 59 in Craft street, in the said city of Newton, are the persons whom he said petitioner intends to summon as witnesses at the final hearing on this application.

Benjaman Gelfex

Citizenship paper for Benjamin Gilfix

	Name						
	Kovachowskaja, Chada & ch	5	27	1	1	"	tel $
7	Gorachowa, Sora	6	14		1	"	cousin
8	Laitinen, Ida & ch	9	1		2	"	tel $
9	Campion, Mary	1	6		1	"	aunt
10	Kosumus, Jan	4	12		1	"	tel $
11	Gurin, Chane 2 ch and						
12	Brande, Chone	4	1		5	"	tel $
13	Budgar, Feige	4	6		1	"	uncle
14	Fitzpatrick, Mary & 3 ch	1	11		4	"	husband
15	Kernonen, Lydia	7	1		1	"	sister
16	Selmi, Elsa	7	3		1	"	friend
17	Mc Gerry, John	1	9		1	"	sister
18	Kalishowskaja, Maja Stefania	6	4		1	"	cousin
19							
20							

New York Passenger List or Manifest for Gurin, Jakis

This list illustrates the difficulty people might have in searching the records for their ancestors.

The first four names listed are Gurin, Chane, Ziwie, Getral and Jakis. The actual names are Gorin, Chana, Tzvi, Getral(?) in English called Celia, and Y'hudis (in English called Julia or Judith)

The number recorded next to Jakis' name on the Passenger Manifest is on the Certificate of Arrival.

The Certificate of Arrival was not issued on arrival in the United States. It would be issued by the U.S. Department of Labor, Immigration Service, after one filed the Declaration of Intent. In order to obtain the information necessary to complete the Certificate, a government employee had to hand-search the List or Manifest of Alien Passengers for that ship, so you had to remember the name of your ship and the date of arrival. The federal employee annotated the Manifest with the certificate number of the Declaration of Intent. In 1920-1921, some one million immigrants came to the United States. Imagine the time and effort required to provide the Certificate of Arrival for each passenger!

When you filed your "first papers," formally called the Declaration of Intent, the Immigration Service created the Certificate of Arrival by going back and hand searching the passenger arrival records. In reviewing these documents, keep in mind that all this paperwork was generated before computers so all records had to be searched and annotated by hand.

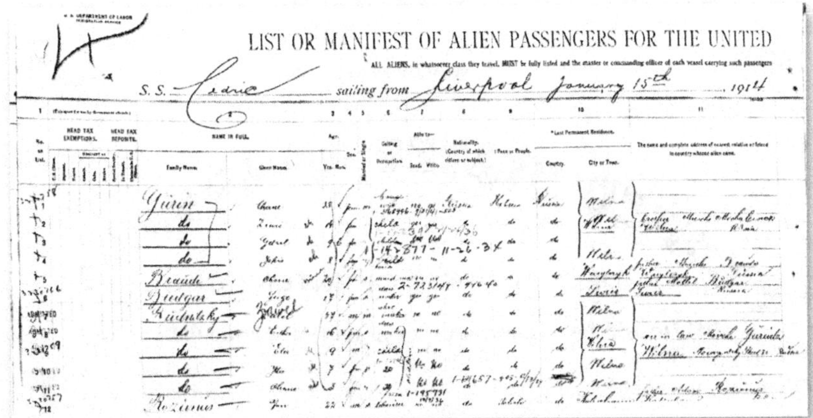

LIST OR MANIFEST OF ALIEN PASSENGERS FOR THE UNITED

ALL ALIENS, in whatsoever class they travel, MUST be fully listed and the master or commanding officer of each vessel carrying such passengers

S. S. Cedric sailing from Liverpool January 15th, 1914

Record of Detained Aliens

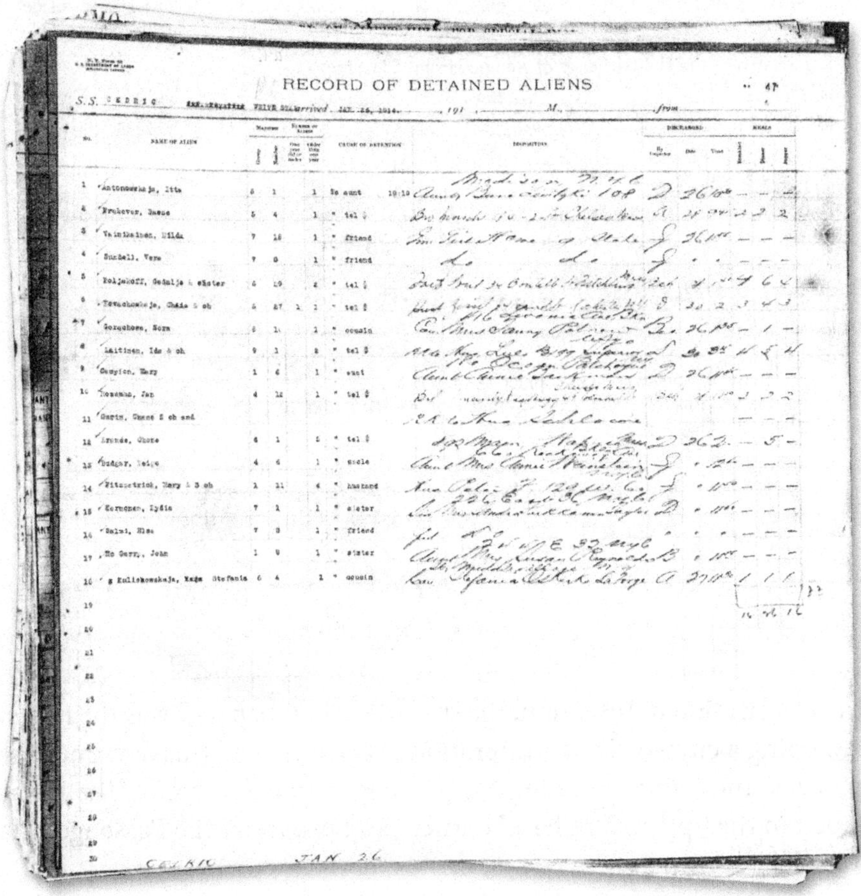

#11 on this list is the Gurin family. They were "detained" because no one met them at the boat. The record states that they will take the RR to meet husband Shloime

RECORD OF DETAINED ALIENS

S.S. CEDRIC arrived JAN. 26, 1914.

No.	Name of Alien					Cause of Detention
1	Antonowskaja, Itta	6	1		1	To aunt
2	Prokover, Dasse	5	4		1	" tel $
3	Vainikainen, Hilda	7	16		1	" friend
4	Sundell, Vera	7	0		1	" friend
5	Poljakoff, Gedalje & sister	6	19		2	" tel $
6	Tovachowskaja, Chaie & ch	6	27	1	1	" tel $
7	Goregkowa, Sora	6	16		1	" cousin
8	Laitinen, Ida & ch	9	1		2	" tel $
9	Campion, Mary	1	6		1	" aunt
10	Roseman, Jan	4	12		1	" tel $
11	Gurin, Chane & ch and					
12	Brande, Chone	6	1		1	" tel $
13	Budgar, Leige	4	6		1	" uncle
14	Fitzpatrick, Mary & 3 ch	1	11		4	" husband
15	Koruenen, Lydia	7	1		1	" sister
16	Salmi, Elsa	7	8		1	" friend
17	Mc Gerry, John	1	8		1	" sister
18	Kulishowskaja, Stefania	6	4		1	" cousin

CEDRIC JAN 26

1500

Form 2202.—L.
U. S. DEPARTMENT OF LABOR
NATURALIZATION SERVICE

TRIPLICATE
[To be given to the person making the Declaration]

209392

No. ....

1 112877

UNITED STATES OF AMERICA

DECLARATION OF INTENTION

☞ **Invalid for all purposes seven years after the date hereof**

District of Massachusetts, *ss:* In the District Court of the United States.

I, Judith Gorin, aged 21 years, occupation Secy. & Bookkeeper, do declare on oath that my personal description is: Color white, complexion light, height 5 feet 4 inches, weight 130 pounds, color of hair brown, color of eyes brown other visible distinctive marks none

I was born Vilna Lithuania Russia on the 8th day of March, anno Domini 1907; I now reside at 42 Hutchings St Roxbury, Massachusetts.
(Give number, street, and city or town.)

I emigrated to the United States of America from Liverpool England on the vessel Cedric; my last
(If the alien arrived otherwise than by vessel, the character of conveyance or name of transportation company should be given)
foreign residence was Vilna Lithuania; I am not married; the name of my {wife / husband} is ....; {she / he} was born at .... and now resides at ....

It is my bona fide intention to renounce forever all allegiance and fidelity to any foreign prince, potentate, state, or sovereignty, and particularly to The State of Russia and the Republic of Lithuania of whom I am now a subject; I arrived at the port of New York in the State of New York, on or about the -- day of December, anno Domini 1913; I am not an anarchist; I am not a polygamist nor a believer in the practice of polygamy; and it is my intention in good faith to become a citizen of the United States of America and to permanently reside therein: SO HELP ME GOD.

Judith Gorin
(Original signature of declarant)

Subscribed and sworn to before me in the office of the Clerk of said Court at Boston, Mass., this 28th day of June anno Domini 1928

[SEAL]

[signature]
Deputy Clerk of the District Court of the United States.

14-12

The Declaration of Intention, the so-called "first papers," was the first step in becoming a citizen. The Immigration Service created this document after going back and hand searching the passenger arrival records. The number stamped in the upper right hand corner can be seen on the Passenger Manifest itself.

U. S. DEPARTMENT OF LABOR
IMMIGRATION SERVICE

No. 1 142877

CERTIFICATE OF ARRIVAL

I HEREBY CERTIFY that the Immigration records show that the alien named below arrived at the port, on the date, and in the manner shown, and was lawfully admitted to the United States of America for permanent residence.

Port of entry: New York, N Y
Name: Gurin, Yakis
Date: January 24, 1914
Manner of arrival: SS Cedric

I FURTHER CERTIFY that this certificate of arrival is issued under authority of, and in conformity with, the provisions of the Act of June 29, 1906, as amended, solely for the use of the alien herein named and only for naturalization purposes.

IN WITNESS WHEREOF, this Certificate of Arrival is issued

December 6, 1934
(Date)

BYRON H. UHL
District Director
New York District

Form 160-Im. U. S. GOVERNMENT PRINTING OFFICE: 1930 14—2624a

This Certificate of Arrival serves as proof that you entered the country legally. The number in the upper right hand corner is recorded again on the Declaration of Intention.

OATH OF ALLEGIANCE

I hereby declare, on oath, that I absolutely and entirely renounce and abjure all allegiance and fidelity to any foreign prince, potentate, state, or sovereignty, and particularly to the Republic of Poland of whom (which) I have heretofore been a subject (or citizen); that I will support and defend the Constitution and laws of the United States of America against all enemies, foreign and domestic; that I will bear true faith and allegiance to the same; and that I take this obligation freely without any mental reservation or purpose of evasion: SO HELP ME GOD. In acknowledgment whereof I have hereunto affixed my signature.

Judith Gorin Gelfix
(Signature of petitioner)

Sworn to in open court, this 1st day of April, A. D. 1935

Frank H. Mason, Clerk.

By ...., Deputy Clerk.

NOTE.—In renunciation of title of nobility, add the following to the oath of allegiance before it is signed: "I further renounce the title of (give title or titles) an order of nobility, which I have heretofore held."

Petition granted: Line No. .... of List No. .... and Certificate No. 3883641 issued.

Petition denied: List No. ....

Petition continued from .... to .... Reason ....

14—2618

ORIGINAL
(To be retained by clerk)

UNITED STATES OF AMERICA

PETITION FOR CITIZENSHIP

No. 157816

GRANTED

To the Honorable the U. S. Dist. Court of Mass. Dist. at Boston

The petition of Judith Gorin Gilfix, hereby filed, respectfully shows:

(1) My place of residence is 154 Seaver St., Boston, Rox (2) My occupation is at home

(3) I was born in Vilna, Poland on March 8, 1907 My race is Hebrew

(4) I declared my intention to become a citizen of the United States on June 26, 1928 in the U. S. District Court of Mass. Dist., at Boston

(5) I am married. The name of my wife or husband is Jacob we were married on Sept 15, 1929 at Boston, Mass.; he was born at Newton, Mass on June 20, 1902; entered the United States at on for permanent residence therein, and now resides at with me I have 1 children, and the name, date, and place of birth, and place of residence of each of said children are as follows:

Yale M., March 29, 1932 at Boston, lives in Boston

(6) My last foreign residence was Vilna, Poland I emigrated to the United States of America from Liverpool, England My lawful entry for permanent residence in the United States was at New York, under the name of Gurin, Yakis on January 24, 1914, on the vessel Cedric as shown by the certificate of my arrival attached hereto.

(7) I am not a disbeliever in or opposed to organized government or a member of or affiliated with any organization or body of persons teaching disbelief in or opposed to organized government. I am not a polygamist nor a believer in the practice of polygamy. I am attached to the principles of the Constitution of the United States and well disposed to the good order and happiness of the United States. It is my intention to become a citizen of the United States and to renounce absolutely and forever all allegiance and fidelity to any foreign prince, potentate, state, or sovereignty, and particularly to

the Republic of Poland

of whom (which) at this time I am a subject (or citizen), and it is my intention to reside permanently in the United States. (8) I am able to speak the English language.
(9) I have resided continuously in the United States of America for the term of five years at least immediately preceding the date of this petition, to wit, since January 24, 1914 and in the County of Suffolk this State, continuously next preceding the date of this petition, since 1921, being a residence within said county of at least six months next preceding the date of this petition.

(10) I have not heretofore made petition for citizenship: Number, on at and such petition was denied by that Court for the following reasons and causes, to wit: and the cause of such denial has since been cured or removed.

Attached hereto and made a part of this, my petition for citizenship, are my declaration of intention to become a citizen of the United States, certificate from the Department of Labor of my said arrival, and the affidavits of the two verifying witnesses required by law.

Wherefore, I, your petitioner, pray that I may be admitted a citizen of the United States of America, and that my name be changed to

I, your aforesaid petitioner being duly sworn, depose and say that I have {read / heard read} this petition and know the contents thereof; that the same is true of my own knowledge except as to matters herein stated to be alleged upon information and belief, and that as to those matters I believe it to be true; and that this petition is signed by me with my full, true name.

Judith Gorin Gilfix
(Complete and true signature of petitioner)

AFFIDAVITS OF WITNESSES

Jacob L Gilfix, occupation salesman residing at 154 Seaver St., Boston, Rox, and Bertha Gorin, occupation pianist residing at 30 Colonial Ave., Boston, Dor each being severally, duly, and respectively sworn, deposes and says that he is a citizen of the United States of America; that he has personally known and has been acquainted in the United States with said Gilfix, the petitioner above mentioned, since 1927 and that to his personal knowledge the petitioner has resided in the United States continuously preceding the date of filing this petition, of which this affidavit is a part, to wit, since the date last mentioned, and at Boston, in the County of Suffolk this State, in which the above-entitled petition is made, continuously since 1927, and that he has personal knowledge that the petitioner is and during all such periods has been a person of good moral character, attached to the principles of the Constitution of the United States, and well disposed to the good order and happiness of the United States, and that in his opinion the petitioner is in every way qualified to be admitted a citizen of the United States.

Jacob Louis Gilfix (Signature of witness) Bertha Gorin (Signature of witness)

Subscribed and sworn to before me by the above-named petitioner and witnesses in the office of the Clerk of said Court at Boston this 24th day of December, Anno Domini 19 34 I hereby certify that certificate of arrival No. 1 142877 from the Department of Labor, showing the lawful entry for permanent residence of the petitioner above named, together with declaration of intention No. 209892 of such petitioner, has been by me filed with, attached to, and made a part of this petition on this date.

JAMES S. ALLEN, Clerk. (SEAL)

By Deputy Clerk.

No. 5980

14—2618

Form 2204—L-A
U. S. DEPARTMENT OF LABOR
IMMIGRATION AND NATURALIZATION SERVICE

Petition for Citizenship

The numbers on the Declaration of Intention and the Certificate of Arrival are repeated on the bottom of the first page of this document.

Form N-570 (REV. 12-24-52)

THE UNITED STATES OF AMERICA

No. 3883641

CERTIFICATE OF NATURALIZATION

Application No. 1500-P-157616

·ORIGINAL·

Personal description of holder as of date of issuance of this certificate: Age 51 years; sex Female; complexion Light; color of eyes Brown; color of hair Grey; height 5 feet 2 inches; weight 170 pounds; visible distinctive marks None

Marital status Married; former nationality Poland

(Complete and true signature of holder)

Be it known that -----JUDITH GORIN GILFIX----- residing at 933 Centre Street, Newton Centre, Massachusetts having applied to the Commissioner of Immigration and Naturalization for a certificate of Naturalization and having proved to the satisfaction of the commissioner that (s)he was naturalized by the United States District Court at Boston, Massachusetts on April 1, 1935.

Seal

Now Therefore, in pursuance of the authority contained in Section 343(b) of the Immigration and Nationality Act, this certificate of Naturalization is issued this 3rd day of April in the year of our Lord nineteen hundred and fifty-eight and of our Independence the one hundred and eighty-second and the seal of the Department of Justice affixed pursuant to statute.

IT IS A VIOLATION OF THE U. S. CODE (AND PUNISHABLE AS SUCH) TO COPY, PRINT, PHOTOGRAPH, OR OTHERWISE ILLEGALLY USE THIS CERTIFICATE.

197813

COMMISSIONER

DEPARTMENT OF JUSTICE

Certificate of Naturalization.

The number of the Petition for Citizenship is on the left hand side of this document. The record is retrospectively annotated by hand with the number of the Certificate of Citizenship on the Petition for Citizenship. The actual certificate was issued three days after the Petition.

מי שברך מי שמיחדים בתי כנסיות לתפלה
וכל מי שעוסקים בצרכי צבור באמונה
הקדוש ברוך הוא ישלח ברכה והצלחה בכל מעשה ידיהם

Bless those who dedicate synagogues for prayer
and bless those who are involved faithfully in the needs of the community.
May the Holy One, Blessed be He, send blessings and success to all their handiwork.

Community leadership card

EARLY SYNAGOGUE LEADERSHIP AT ADAMS STREET

Before everyone had a telephone and before telephone books, city directories were published every other year by private publishers. They identified every resident alphabetically by name and by street address. Copies of Newton's city directories are available on the Newton Free Library's web site.

Early Newton city directories also listed every congregation and the clergymen by name. That information was provided to the compilers of the directories by the congregation. The Adams Street Synagogue appears infrequently, probably because the men who were responsible for the synagogue neglected to provide the information. In the 1930's, the directory stopped listing names of clergy and officers and only listed institutions.

1912	Benjamin Gilfix, president, Joseph Mielman, clerk, Jacob Swartz, treasurer
1913	Louis Baker, president, J. Kaplan, secretary
1917	Rabbi Morris Roiter, Abraham Trachtman *(Possibly the compilers of the directory, in the absence of specific information, assumed that the head of the congregation must be a rabbi! Morris Roiter was not a rabbi but the president of the synagogue).*
1919-1921	Louis Baker, president, Morris Roiter, secretary, Hyman Meilman, treasurer
1922	S. J. Kaplan, president
1923	Elliot Gilfix, president
1924-1925	Abraham Trachtman, president, Morris Roiter, secretary, William Perlmutter, treasurer
1927-1928	Joseph Roiter, president, Max Berman, secretary, Benjamin Gilfix, treasurer
1929	Joseph Roiter, president, Jacob Hoffman, secretary, Hyman Meilman, treasurer
1930	Abraham Pass, president
1931	Hyman Meilman, treasurer
1932	Samuel J. Cohen, secretary
1933	Elliot Gilfix, president, Nathan Goodman, treasurer
1934	Samuel J. Cohen, secretary
	From 1930 to about 1960, we have almost no information about the synagogue leadership
1960- (?)	Abraham Pass, president, Harry Roiter, vice president, Elmer Lippin, treasurer, Louis Fried, secretary, Hyman Shrier, Chairman of trustees
1983-1985	Louis Fried
1985-1994	Bertram Grand, president, Harry Roiter, vice president, Elmer Lippin, secretary/treasurer
1994-2001	Leonard Berman
2001-2004	Aryeh Cheses
2004-2006	Beryl Gilfix
2006-2009	Ronny Drapkin
2009-2010	Steven Cantor
2010-2011	Michael Froimowitz Greenzeiger
2011-	Benyomin Fleischmann

RABBIS AT THE ADAMS STREET SYNAGOGUE

When you think about a synagogue, you always assume a rabbi at its head. But the Adams Street Synagogue did not have a rabbi until the 1980s. The small congregation could not afford to hire a rabbi. They would hire a cantor to lead the services on the High Holidays and occasionally a rabbi from Boston would come and stay with a local family for Shabbas. The rest of the year, members of the congregation conducted the services themselves.

The men were all well versed in the prayers and knew the rituals and customs that were traditional for this congregation. Nevertheless, the younger generations recalled arguments about the order of prayers, when to include or leave out certain prayers, etc. Sometimes the arguments could get quite heated but somehow were always resolved so the service could continue.

This system of lay-led prayer services continued at Adams Street until about 1987. The postwar generations who were moving to the neighborhood and helping to revive the congregation were accustomed to a synagogue with a rabbi, who led the services and answered questions and provided religious education and guidance. They felt lost without a rabbi to turn to. The problem of how to pay a rabbi still existed so the congregation began to search for ways to have the services of a rabbi at moderate expense.

The first solution was to engage a "rabbinic consultant." Rabbi Joseph Polak, a Hillel rabbi at Boston University, agreed to fill this role and to be "on call" to answer religious questions from members of the congregation. The congregation still did not have weekly religious services and the once per month services continued to be led by volunteers. This proved to be less successful at times, since the tradition of arguing about the order of services, customs, etc., survived from the earliest days of the congregation. In time, these discussion became arguments that threatened the survival of the fledgling congregation.

In 1995, a Hasidic rabbi, Zalman Gurkow, moved into the neighborhood and began to attend services at Adams Street. It was logical to turn to him to resolve the conflicts that had arisen and he became the first rabbi of the congregation in nearly one hundred years, in a part time position. Since he spoke Russian, he was able to work with the increasing number of newly arrived Russian immigrants who moved into the neighborhood and who were important contributors to the revival of the congregation. In 2005, he moved away to establish a Chabad Center in northeastern Massachusetts.

The congregation hired its next part time rabbi, Norbert Weinberg, who assumed the pulpit in November 2005. Rabbi Norbert Weinberg was born in Bad Nauheim Germany. He emigrated with his family to the United States in 1940. Raised in New York, he was educated at Yeshiva College, where he received his Bachelor of Arts degree. He continued his rabbinical studies for another three years, culminating in his ordination (semicha) from Yeshivat Yitzchak Elchanan–Yeshiva University, in New York in 1957. He also earned a Masters degree in Education from Rhode Island College.

Rabbi Norbert Weinberg

Rabbi Weinberg's pulpits include Congregation Beth Israel, Quebec City, Canada, (two years); Congregation Ahavath Achim, New Bedford, Massachusetts, director, Camp Tikvah, a children's summer day camp (eight years); Congregation Adas Israel, Fall River, Massachusetts (thirty years). At the same time, he was the Jewish chaplain at the Walpole State Prison, at a local Corrigan Health Center, and the Fall River Jewish Home for the Aged. After retiring from the Fall River Congregation, and before he came to Adams Street, he held a part-time position at Congregation Brothers of Joseph in Norwich, Connecticut.

The rabbi also served as sofer (scribe) for the Vaad HaRabbonim (The Rabbinical Court) of Massachusetts.

He retired from the Adams Street pulpit and the active rabbinate in 2015, after ten years in Newton.

Besides teaching and pursuing his rabbinic responsibilities, Rabbi Weinberg's main avocation is in the field of writing. To date, he has published the following four books:

The Essential Torah a review of the weekly Torah and Haftarah readings.

Beyond the Wall a compilation of fictional short stories, depicting how visits to the Western Wall in Jerusalem affected various individuals.

In the Footsteps a collection of Yahrzeit (memorial) lectures delivered by Rabbi Weinberg in memory of his father.

A Time to Tell autobiographical memoirs of the rabbi.

He has four daughters, three of whom live in Israel, 25 grandchildren and 32 great grandchildren in Israel as well. He and his wife Susan live in Newton.

The congregation, after more than one hundred years, still cannot afford a full-time rabbi.

Cantor Bertram/Beryl Barron

Although Cantor Barron was not a rabbi, his contribution to the life of the synagogue cannot be underestimated. His extraordinary voice and passionate leadership of the prayer services were memorable. The synagogue did not have a rabbi but he led the services and created an atmosphere of religious intensity and joy that uplifted the entire congregation. Despite severe physical limitations, he inspired the entire community to join with him in worship that has never been improved upon in the years since his death.

He was born October 13, 1924 and died January 31, 2002. He was raised in Roxbury and attended the Crawford Street Shul, where his father was the rabbi. He provided an example of truly Hasidic inspiration for everyone, even those who were not familiar with the liturgy. Before coming to Adams Street, he led services at Congregation Beth Israel in Malden, and then Congregation Ahavas Achim in Revere. His presence in the Adams Street Shul for seven years (about 1976 to 1983) brought both visitors and members and kept the shul alive in the early years of our restoration and revitalization. Only his failing health made it necessary for him to finally retire.

A plaque in the shul reads: "In memory of Cantor Bertram Beryl Barron, beloved cantor of the Adams Street Shul, Loyal and Devoted Friend."

Memorial by Bert Grand, president of the synagogue, March 2002

"Around 1985, Cantor Barron auditioned for the job of cantor for the High Holidays. Present at the audition was Elmer Lippin, Harry Roiter and myself. Cantor Barron's chanting of a few bars of a prayer convinced us to hire him immediately. His was not an operatic voice but rather one that expressed such feeling and understanding of the prayers and was very haimish. I think he could have davened the whole service by heart. And how loyal he was to us! I cannot remember his missing a single holiday service. Once, on the first evening of Pesach, it was getting late but in he walked, with his arm in a sling. He had been hit by a car and the hospital wanted to keep him overnight but he told them he had an obligation and bloody bandage and all, he showed up."

His good friend Maurice Aghion recalled that he first met Cantor Barron when he attended services at Kadimah Toras Moshe in Brighton. Since coming to America, it was the first time he had davened in an Ashkenazi synagogue and the ritual and melodies were unfamilar to him. "Cantor Barron's davening was very sweet," Mr. Aghion recalled. "While he davened, he was conducting himself, in a dialogue with G-d."

The two men became very friendly and Mr. Aghion visited Cantor Barron regularly until his death.

LAY LEADERSHIP AT THE ADAMS STREET SYNAGOGUE

Lloyd Cohen, Gabbai

Although not a president of the congregation, Lloyd's contributions to the growth of the shul was a notable one. Lloyd Cohen was the Gabbai for the synagogue for many years. (The word "gabbai" is Aramaic and, in Talmudic times, meant collector of taxes or charity, or treasurer). Today duties typically include ensuring that the services run smoothly. Currently at Adams Street, that role is filled by the chair of the Ritual Committee.

Lloyd and his wife Beth were living in Newtonville and attending a synagogue in Newton Centre when someone told him about the Adams Street Shul. They attended the High Holiday services around 1973 and met Elmer Lippin. Lloyd described an "inner attraction" to Adams Street," saying the services at Congregation Beth El which he had attended previously were "too modern."

He recalled Herbie Gerber's son-in-law davening before Cantor Barron. He knew Pacie Miehlman and Harry Roiter (sons of the immigrant families who maintained a lifelong connection to the synagogue).

He liked the fact that the atmosphere was casual and acceptance in the group did not depend on dress but upon manners. Also the shul was a little closer to his home, a benefit in the wintertime.

His late wife Beth, along with Helene Storch and Nechama Cheses, thought there was enough of a nucleus to hold Sabbath services on a regular basis. (Religious services in an Orthodox congregation require a quorum (minyan) of ten adult males). The women were the big pushers for this, Lloyd recalled. They also felt that they needed younger people coming in, otherwise the shul would die. After the sudden and unexpected death of Elmer Lippin in 1987, there was a push to build the congregation back up. "People saw life coming into the shul and responded," he said.

In the beginning, Lloyd recalled, "we needed minyan calls and minyan reminder postcards to keep the minyan numbers up, and with trial and error, we found the best way to increase the numbers of regulars. We wanted to keep the cozy feeling of the shul, and its informality." "What's with all this handshaking?"

He said "It was difficult to get people to know about us. We were not looking to be big mucky mucks. We are more like home style cooking. We raised money by many odd means, including collecting cans and bottles for the nickel deposits. It was a good time and I was sad to leave the area due to ill health."

Lloyd is now the gabbai at a Lubavitch shul in Albuquerque, NM.

Bertram Grand, President, 1985-1994, Chairman of the Board, 1995-present

Bert was raised in Dorchester. He was bar mitzvah at the Nightingale Street Shul in Dorchester, the so-called underground shul. (It was "underground" because the congregation dug the foundation for a new shul and then couldn't afford to build the building. They used what had been intended as the basement as a shul for years). He recalled people coming around the shul in Dorchester to offer snuff to the men during religious services.

Bert is a proud graduate of Boston Latin School. He spent 1943-1945 in the Army, studying engineering at Cornell and eventually graduated from Tufts University. He is also a graduate of Harvard Business School, class of 1949.

Watching workmen climbing on scaffolding led him to a career in insurance, beginning with disability insurance for construction workers. He was the only Jew in an agency of 25 people. In 1952 he married Polly and they moved to Newton. Although he belonged to Temple Emeth, he said kaddish at Temple Emanuel. "I first came to Adams Street in 1954 when a man at Temple Emanuel told me, "I'm going to take you to a real shul." He likes the Orthodox liturgy because it is "*geshmackt* (tasty)". He met Harry Roiter, Sam and Louis Fried, the Gilfix boys, Elmer Lippin, sons of the immigrant families and more recent arrivals like Al Landsman and Saul Aronow. He felt very shy among these older men whom he viewed as elders of the community. One day, Elmer told me, "you're the president pro tem," to cover for Louis Fried, who was ill.

From 1986 to 1995, he was deeply involved in every aspect of the shul's restoration and renovation. "Every year I wanted to do one thing that would set the year up right. One year I replaced the cyclone fence at the front of the building with a real fence. The non-Jewish contractor who put up the fence put a Jewish star on the gates without being asked. I was surprised and delighted. I had not even thought about it." Another contractor, working on the Elmer Lippin Social Hall and new bathrooms and kitchen, installed, at his own initiative, a hand washing station made of Jerusalem stone with a Jewish star, another innovation we had not considered. "We put up a notice board outside the shul which had never had one before, to show people that we are here and we are functioning. We planted a new tree in the front yard, with the financial assistance of Herbert and Suzanne Spatz, early supporters of our restoration efforts."

In 1954, the old school desks were still there. (There are disputes among respondents as to when the chairs from home were replaced by old school desks which were in turn replaced by the current benches). "We bought new benches for the womens' balcony, to replace the wooden folding chairs. With financial assistance from Ann Grand Burack, the new benches were custom made to match the benches downstairs in the men's section. We installed a screen to create a separate section for women (mechitza) on the main floor, as required by Orthodox custom, so that women who could not climb the stairs to the women's balcony could sit on the main floor in comfort. We installed new doors and air conditioning, half of the cost of which was paid by Harry Roiter. We put on a new roof, new carpeting and found donors to pay for historically correct new windows. We had the brass lighting fixtures repaired and shined at a shop in Newton Highlands that specialized in brass and copper ware."

Bertram Grand

Photo courtesy Newton Tab

"I determined that we need to start acting like an organization or a corporation. With the minyan, we knew we had to make a move; we couldn't go on piecemeal forever. There were several people who worked with me on the restoration, including the Spatz family, Lester Goldston, a local advertising executive who helped create a series of fundraising brochures, Beryl Gilfix, who helped with dozens of mailings, the Cheses family who led the laborious process of minyan calls and minyan postcards, and Jerry Swartz from the hardware store. Jerry had been bar mitzvah in the shul and although he was not a shul goer, he was a quiet and generous supporter of the shul behind the scenes and he made a major donation to the restoration project."

"There were so many things I wanted to do with the shul but they all required money and we didn't have any money so fundraising was a real priority. We were able to raise about $250,000 for the restoration, which included gutting the sanctuary, installing new wiring and insulation, new windows, air conditioning, refinishing the floors. We put it back the way it had been, PLUS. The only regret I have is that we were not able to restore the stenciling on the walls. We also found stenciling on the ceiling which had been painted over and I would have liked to restore that as well."

"My wife Polly suggested that we develop a mailing list. She wrote a letter and several of the shul members, including Mrs. Spatz and Beryl Gilfix, sat in the shul night after night pulling labels from the city's voter registration rolls to mail to people in Newton Centre, where we knew there was a large Jewish population. The historic exhibit at the Jackson Homestead in 1986 got our name out to the public and their visitor book formed our first mailing list. Being placed on the National Register of Historic Places (with the help of the Jackson Homestead), added to our prestige."

His wife Polly recalls that he was completely devoted to the shul and the restoration project, which became a full time job for him for at least four years. It was a labor of love, to modernize but to retain the old environment, the old aura.

"I thought to be the president of a shul you had to be rich or something. I saw my election to the presidency of the shul as the biggest honor of my life, and to be trusted to be president of an Orthodox shul when I was not so observant, even more so."

Leonard Berman, President, 1994-2001

Leonard is a native of Crown Heights in Brooklyn, New York. Richard Tucker was the cantor of his family's synagogue. Tucker famously went on to a distinguished career in opera.

Leonard and his wife Audrey attended Temple Emanuel in Newton but he was dissatisfied. "That temple was too big and impersonal and there was no way for members to participate in any meaningful way. One day, I was driving down Adams Street and saw the synagogue. Bert Grand was president at the time and Al Kalman, Aryeh Cheses and Lloyd Cohen were the backbone of the congregation. I felt shy when I first arrived but was drawn into synagogue life by being elected to the board and the by-laws committee."

When Leonard became involved in the synagogue, he suggested that his wife Audrey could offer ESL classes to the Russian members of the congregation. Audrey, who was an ESL teacher at Hebrew College, applied for and received grants from Combined Jewish Philanthropies to teach ESL to a group of ten to twelve Russian Jewish immigrant women every week at Adams Street. They were a friendly group and enjoyed being part of the congregation. They brought the male members of their families into the shul as well. Without the Russians, the synagogue would have struggled to find a minyan every Shabbas.

Leonard volunteered to be president in the 1990s and served as president for seven years. At the same time, he was chair of the pathology department at the Veterans Adminstration Hospital and on the faculty at Boston University Medical School.

What he valued most, he said, was the ability to get things done, interacting with people who were friendly and eager to help. "We had a good board. The more voices we had on the board, the better the shul would function."

Leonard Berman

At the beginning of my presidency, there was no rabbi. The congregation was run entirely by the membership, including leading services and planning social and religious events. But during my tenure, there were several incidents that caused serious divisions in the small congregation. The acrimony of some of these incidents made it necessary to bring in a rabbinic consultant who could serve as sounding board and halachic authority when necessary. I knew Rabbi Joseph Polak, a Hillel rabbi at Boston University and he agreed to serve as a rabbinic consultant for issues concerning the congregation. He was known and respected by the membership also. He had experience and knew how to handle difficult situations and difficult personalities."

While Leonard was president, there were isolated incidents of vandalism to the synagogue every year. However, after the swastika incident in 1997, when Father Walter Cuenin brought the synagogue to the attention of the wider Catholic community, the incidents stopped.

Aryeh Cheses, President 2001-2004

Aryeh and his wife Nechama were living in Brighton and wanted to move to Newton. Their current home was the first house they looked at and they bought it right away. That same weekend, the Jackson Homestead (now Historic Newton) hosted the exhibit on the history of the Jewish community in Newton. "So that told us that there was a shul in the neighborhood and we went to see it. That was around Pesach in 1986. Cantor Barron read the Torah and davened (led the prayers)."

In August 1986 the shul had its first Shabbas minyan in many years. Cantor Barron davened. To get a minyan, the women, Helene Storch, Nechama Cheses, and Beth Cohen set up a phone chain. Norman Jaffe davened once a month also.

Aryeh Cheses

Elmer Lippin met with the group in the Cheses home. "He was very suspicious of us and our motivations, since he had been approached by others to try to rebuild the shul. He had to be convinced to let the group try to have a minyan once a month. We seemed more sincere to him since we had bought a house in the neighborhood. While we were upstairs having services in the shul, Elmer would be downstairs preparing the kiddush. Elmer died suddenly around Purim in 1987. That was a very strong impetus to get things moving. We went from once a month minyans to every two weeks to every week."

Rabbi Zalman Gurkow arrived in the neighborhood. Since he spoke Russian, for ten years he was a major help in involving Russians in the shul, especially with ESL classes and teaching Jewish materials for the newcomers, many of whom had little or no Jewish education and only knew what they remembered from their grandparents.

The little group expanded. "Our vision, and the hope that more families would move into the neighborhood, helped build the new congregation. Even now, there are not quite enough people to satisfy us. We see Adams Street as an unusual opportunity for children to take part in shul life and to both see the leadership up close and to be leaders themselves, for example, with the boys' choir started by Beryl Gilfix when she was president."

"This shul has had a major impact on the lives of our children. They learned about organization and responsibility, that you have to step up, that you cannot leave it to someone else. We feel that everyone can make a difference at Adams Street and feel good about their participation. People have learned the value of a small community and their place in it." Aryeh is very proud that their oldest son, who grew up in the shul, is now a rabbi.

Beryl Gilfix, President, 2004-2006

"As a granddaughter of one of the founders of the Adams Street Shul, I felt a unique connection to the building and the community, both to the founding community and the current membership. Because I grew up attending the shul with my father on the few holidays per year when it was open, it formed an indelible image in my mind of what a shul should be. And that image was very different from the large, impersonal, sterile environments of the other congregations in the city."

Elmer Lippin had taken care of the shul in every way by himself for over 35 years, with financial help from the children of founding families. None of them were allowed to "interfere" to help in other ways, so he was able to fulfill the promise he had made to his father to "take care of the shul." At the same time, he was very possessive of the building and actively discouraged others from helping him.

Fortunately three families (Cheses, Storch and Cohen) moved into the neighborhood in the 1980s. The fact that they bought houses locally persuaded Elmer that they would not try to change the way he liked to do things. Slowly they began to rebuild the congregation by gradually instituting weekly services.

"I became president with grand plans to build the congregation, fix the building and create an atmosphere of respect and cooperation within the congregation. Our greatest issues were money and manpower, both of which remain central issues for the future of the congregation. We continue to struggle financially and struggle to attract and keep new families. In an all-volunteer congregation such as ours, there is the benefit of belonging to a congregation where your participation is critical to the functioning of the institution. Here every member really makes a difference."

The demographic of the membership has changed considerably since I was president. The families who were active in the 1980s and 1990s were elderly and they have been superceded by young families with young children.

Beryl Gilfix

"One of the innovations I introduced was the creation of a "boy's choir," because there were now several young boys in the congregation. The tradition of a male choir had a long history in Jewish synagogues but now we had the "boy power" to make it a reality. It gave me great satisfaction to see those little boys on the bimah every week, surely the face of the future of the shul. And now I see a new generation of young men, just bar mitzvah like Elazar Cramer, coming forward. I feel very confident about the future of the shul when I see the young families and young children in the shul every week and young members actively involved in running the shul."

Ronny Drapkin, President, 2006-2009

Ronny and his wife Beth moved to Newton from New Jersey when he graduated from medical school. They were looking for an affordable place near an Orthodox shul to accommodate Beth's family, which was observant. They found a place near Adams Street that they could afford.

Ronny Drapkin

Beth was actually the one who got involved at first, joining several committees and serving on the board. Because Ronny had not been raised Orthodox, it took him a while to feel comfortable at Adams Street, but everyone was so welcoming and didn't seem to notice what the family was doing or not doing.

As he became more involved in the shul, it drew him into Orthodox practice more deeply. He and his family began to appreciate the tranquility and peace and family orientation of Shabbas, so they gradually stopped driving on Shabbas.

Ronny valued the impact that he and other volunteers could have on the shul. "If you want something done, you have to be willing to roll up your sleeves and do it. You couldn't expect some anonymous employee of the shul to do it for you. You could really see the results of your efforts."

He regrets that his professional life has consumed more and more of his time and left less time for shul administration. One idea he had that was never put into action was to form a locally based president's council of Orthodox shul presidents to meet together regularly to keep in touch and to build a wider community for Adams Street as well.

In their new life in Philadelphia, they have joined a large Orthodox shul where his wife and daughter are very happy but Ronny finds himself drawn to a smaller Chabad congregation where he and his son often attend. He misses the intimacy of Adams Street and the impact that he could have on this small congregation. He regrets that professional demands will make it difficult for him to take such a leadership role again for years to come.

Steven Cantor, President, 2009-2010

Steve's grandfather had been principal of many Conservative synagogue Hebrew School programs. When he moved to Framingham, he took Steve to a small Orthodox synagogue that met in a private home. When Steve first came to Adams Street, he felt as though he was back in that little synagogue with his grandfather.

Steven Cantor

Steve was raised in Framingham. When he and his wife Zhanna moved to Newton, they joined Temple Emanuel, where they were members for fifteen years. But they felt very isolated and disconnected at Emanuel. When it came time for their son Max to be bar mitzvah, they decided that they would visit every synagogue in Newton, to give their son a sense of the variety of Jewish worship and practice that existed. Steve had been to Adams Street a few times in the past and so they began that Jewish journey at Adams Street. They never made it to any other synagogue. He remembers vividly that the first time they came to Adams Street as a family, someone invited them home for lunch. No one at Temple Emanuel had ever invited them anywhere. The atmosphere was so warm and welcoming and accepting that they stayed.

Steve had never thought about being an officer of any synagogue but he somehow found himself first as vice president and then as president. The warmth and character of the congregation impressed him and continues to impress him. "The members are people who are finding their own ways to express their Judaism, and the paths that they are on are in their search for a Jewish way of life are varied and interesting, as opposed to a congregation where everyone is frum (observant) from birth or all doing the same thing. And the rabbi is so warm and welcoming that he draws people who are made to feel comfortable as they continue on their paths toward their varied practices and beliefs."

Michael Froimowitz Greenzeiger, President, 2010-2011

Michael was born and raised in Newton and was educated at UMass Amherst (BA) and Brandeis University (MA). His family was religious and he has relations who were Haredi. However, he and his wife Linnea were not religious in the beginning but wanted to live in Newton and Nonantum was the only part of the city they could afford. But as they became more religious, they were attracted to the Adams Street Shul. "We liked the small intimate atmosphere and the wider mix of different types of people than what we saw in other synagogues. People at Adams Street were not judgmental and were very welcoming. I could really grow in my Judaism. The shul and Rabbi Weinberg helped us to make a lifestyle transition."

Michael Froimowitz Greenzeiger

Michael's involvement in the management of the shul began with work on the web site and then he became treasurer. He updated the accounting system. He then joined the bylaws committee and understood the need to follow the bylaws in the shul's functioning. As president, he worked to get people to be civil to each other. "If I see something and I don't like the way it is going, I want to change it. At each step, I felt I had to do more."

The family moved to California for work, and they have joined a Sephardi shul, which davens Nusach S'fard, which feels very familiar. "Although my wife and I moved to Silicon Valley in California in 2011, we feel like we are still members of the Adams Street family. We continue to pay our dues, even after moving to California!"

Benyomin Fleischmann, President, 2012-2017

Benyomin and his wife Nechama moved around a lot, from Philadelphia to Brookline to Worcester and ultimately to Newton, when their older daughter Shoshana entered Gann Academy. They had planned to move to Newton Centre but heard about Adams Street from their younger daughter Yoki, who had met Rabbi Weinberg, whom she really liked. The family came to visit Adams Street and were invited to join by Len Berman. "Michael Froimowitz became a good friend and Michael appointed me to be chair of Facilities Committee. I like to joke that I started by taking out the trash and the next thing I knew, I was vice president and then president of the shul."

Benyomin Fleischmann

He and his family felt and continue to feel very accepted in the congregation because they do not have to fit any mold of behavior or practice. "This rich history and open doors accept all Jews. We are a traditional shul that's eclectic," he says.

"I enjoy the old world atmosphere and a community who lets you be who you want to be." As Len Berman told me, "here, you make a difference. Len was right. We count here."

Newton Hebrew Ladies Aid Society

This local organization was founded in 1903, before the establishment of the synagogue. It was of great significance to the women of the community, and a source of prestige, and several of the women were recalled as either the founder or first president of the organization. It was founded to provide financial and material aid (primarily food and coal) to poor Jewish families in Nonantum. The group would meet at the homes of its members to discuss who in the community needed their help. Members would contribute small amounts (perhaps 10 cents or 25 cents) at each meeting. The members would present information on needy families and decide to spend their modest treasury on coal for a family in the winter, or to buy shoes for the children in a family so the children could go to school, or to provide baskets of food. Every attempt was made to provide assistance anonymously, so that the recipient families would not feel beholden to their neighbors or embarrassed by their need for charity.

Jane Shriberg: "The purpose of the Newton Hebrew Ladies Aid was to help the poor and underprivileged. I remember they used to buy coal and wood. It was non -sectarian but very few non-Jews came. They would have been helped if they had come, because that's what [the Society] was there for."

Rose Gilfix Schribman recalled that it was Dora Goodman who suggested to the ladies of the Jewish community that they form a social club, saying "now that our children are a little older, let's get out more and do something for our own enjoyment." She was a very friendly and outgoing woman who loved people. And she was very modern for her time, more so than most of the other women. Dora was president for the first two years. As a gift after the first year, the ladies gave her a pair of panties. When she wore them to the next meeting, she lifted up her skirt so they could all admire the present they had given her. It broke them all up with laughter! And after the second year, another woman wanted to be president, so she graciously stepped down.

The organization also served as a method of Americanization for immigrant women, teaching them how to "entertain" by setting a nice table, the kinds of refreshments that were considered appropriate and offering programs of edifying and educational information.

The Society found it unnecessary to provide financial aid for Jewish families by the 1940s and so donated their monthly treasury to various Jewish organizations instead.

Rose Silverman: The Newton Hebrew Ladies Aid was founded so that no Jewish person should have to ask for charity. And everything was given anonymously. There were a number of people who needed coal and this was one of the ways the money was spent. And then before Passover they had to make sure that everybody had the necessities for the seder. When I became active, the way charity was dispensed was that we had an emergency committee. There were three people, the president, the chairman of the emergency committee and possibly the vice president. If you had a need, you would go to one of those people and they would relay it to the emergency committeee.

D-86-4-6

Newton Hebrew Ladies' Aid Society

TEMPLE EMANUEL 385 Ward Street, Newton Centre, Mass. 02159

A ~~special~~ regular meeting will take place in the Vestry on

Monday, June 14, 1976 Coffee Hour 12:30 to 1:00

Election of officers. Discussion and establishment of new committees and guidelines for the future of our organization. Very important meeting.

Please make every effort to attend.

Cordially yours,

MILDRED SHELMAN, *Sec.*
Tel. 244-5820

ROSE QUINT, *Pres.*
Tel. 244-6377

She recalled that Rose Schribman was very involved with the Ladies Aid, very, very caring and charitable in the quiet way. We had a certain amount of money that we could allocate and Rose said, "well, I will give $10 too." This happened very often when she was called and I think she was almost always on the committee and it was not an unusual thing for her to supplement whatever money was given. The person who made us aware of the need would be given a check and would cash it and give the cash to the needy family so we didn't know who it was. That was done to protect their privacy. The feeling has always been in Judaism that if a person asked, they must need it and they wouldn't take it for themselves unless they needed it. A person would stand up at the meeting and a check would be given to them and they either cashed it or bought Passover goods for the person for whom they were asking. Organized meetings ended in June 1971. They had been meeting at Temple Emanuel for a number of years before that.

To raise money in the 1950's, the group created a "Golden Book, " which was financed by Sadie Hellman in honor of her 25th wedding anniversary. Women could make special donations to have a message elaborately inscribed in the book in calligraphy with illuminated capitals, as was the custom for such books at the time. The Book is now in the Collection of Historic Newton.

Golden Book
of the
Hebrew Ladies Aid Society
Newton, Massachusetts

Presented by
Mr. & Mrs. Louis G. Hellmann
in honor of their
25th Wedding Anniversary

Mrs. Nathan O. Goodman
Mrs. Jacob Pass
Mrs. Samuel J. Stone
Rose Feldberg Silverman
Mrs. Celia Wasserman
Mrs. William Shriberg
Anna F. Bergstein
Mrs. Julia Perlmutter
Mrs. Joseph Kotler

Pages from the Golden Book

Photo courtesy of Sarah Goldberg, Historic Newton

Jane Shriberg: The Association applied for a state charter in 1903. Nathan Goodman's mother founded the organization and was the first president for about ten years and Marion Fried was president for about ten years and I followed and I was president for at least four years. Rose Silverman was also president of Newton Hebrew Ladies Aid for many years. She was assisted by Celia Fried. Then there was Mrs. Louis Levine, of Carlton Street. There was also a Gertrude Lichtman who was president. Beryl Gilfix and then Esther Levenson, the doctor's wife, were the last presidents. Jane Shriberg served as secretary for the group from 1933 to about 1943.

In the 1950s or 1960s, Gertrude Lichtman was the one who invited Rabbi Samuel Chiel from Temple Emanuel to visit the synagogue and become acquainted with the community and their work. Rabbi Chiel then invited the ladies to use the vestry at Temple Emanuel for their meetings. The Newton Hebrew Ladies Aid Society moved to Temple Emanuel when there was no longer a functioning Jewish community in Nonantum. There, they heard lectures by members of the group, book reviews, discussions of current events and even Yiddish poetry readings (one such poetry reading was given by Beryl Gilfix in the 1970s).

K'lal Yisrael Award

In 1992, the congregation was honored to receive the *K'lal Yisrael Award.* It reads:

"May G-d who blessed our ancestors, Abraham, Isaac, Jacob, Sarah, Rebecca, Rachel and Leah, bless those who faithfully devote themselves to the needs of the community and to Eretz Yisrael in all their worthy endeavors grant successes to them and to all Israel"

K'lal Yisrael Award

Presented to Agudas Achim Anshei Sfard, Newton
for outstanding service in strengthening our community
and promoting the unity of the Jewish People

April 9, 1992
6 Nisan 5752
Synagogue Council of MA."

Michael Partensky

Michael came to the US from Russia in 1989. "I was fortunate to find a job very quickly at Brandeis University and determined that I would do everything for my fellow emigres, helping them find jobs and housing and to establish themselves in the community."

When he first arrived in the US, he stayed with friends in Newton Centre and attended Congregation Beth El.

"I was looking for a synagogue to affiliate with, one which would welcome my initiative for a Russian Centre but after canvassing several synagogues in Newton, I was unable to find anyone willing to host this informal Centre. I then met Al Landsman, a long time member of the Adams Street Synagogue, who invited me to come and see a synagogue I had never heard of. At around the same time, we moved to Newton Corner, much closer to the Adams Street Synagogue."

"My first meeting with the members of the congregation was in the basement, due to construction going on upstairs. Jordan Wagner, Matt Kramer and Beryl Gilfix were at the meeting. There was a very friendly atmosphere, very welcoming and very responsive."

Michael Partensky

At the time of this meeting, the economy was down and there were no networking programs in place to help newly arrived Russians find jobs. Adams Street offered a place for networking for younger immigrants looking for jobs, and a welcoming home for older Russians, many of whom were settled in senior citizen housing at JFK Circle within walking distance of the synagogue. The synagogue purchased prayer books with Russian/Hebrew translations, and were delighted when so many Russians helped to make the minyan (prayer quorum) at the struggling little shul. They even announced page numbers in Russian in the Russian prayer books so the newcomers could follow the service and occasionally had sermons in Russian as well.

Adams Street, he recalled, was very welcoming, cozy and warm. The shul also importantly provided a location for a Russian chessmaster, Valery Frenklach, to start a chess club for adults and children, which brought the newcomers and old timers together. They even had annual chess tournaments! Other innovations were a children's theatre group, ESL classes led by Audrey Berman and the all important networking for young adult job seekers.

In 1992, The Synagogue Council of MA presented the shul with the K'lal Yisrael Award to honor the work being done in the shul to integrate New Americans into our congregation and the Jewish community.

In 1993, Dr. Michael Partensky, Chair of our New Americans Committee, accepted the prestigious Keter Torah Award on behalf of the Adams Street Shul. The award was given by the Board of the Bureau of Jewish Education to honor our efforts to provide Jewish education for the New Americans in our community.

Michael observed that before 1990, emigrants were running away from Russia and all it represented. After about 1992, times in Russia were not so difficult and so many of the later immigrants did not part from Russia forever. Many of them went back and forth and some of them did not stay here.

Suzanne Spatz

We are happy to have the opportunity to honor a long time activist member of the congregation, Mrs. Suzanne Spatz. Many of her singular accomplishments and contributions to the shul began as long as twenty-five years ago, before many of you came to Adams Street, but we are proud of our history and the people who contributed in so many vital ways to the success we enjoy today.

CONGREGATION
AGUDAS ACHIM ANSHEI SFARD
THE ADAMS STREET SYNAGOGUE
HONORS
SUZANNE SPATZ
FOR TWENTY FIVE YEARS
OF OUTSTANDING DEDICATED VOLUNTEER SERVICE
IN RECOGNITION OF HER SIGNIFICANT CONTRIBUTIONS
TO THE RESTORATION AND REVITALIZATION OF
NEWTON'S FIRST AND OLDEST SYNAGOGUE
JUNE 24, 2009

I'd like to describe some of Mrs. Spatz's contributions. We all take pride in our shul's registration on the National Register of Historic Places. Did you know that Mrs. Spatz is responsible for that listing? She was the person who approached the city and spearheaded our listing on the National Register and followed through with city, state and federal officials until we received our designation.

All of you are aware of the special membership categories, like supporting and sustaining memberships, which we offer. These non-voting memberships bring in significant amounts of money to the shul each year and are vital to balancing our budget. The idea for these special memberships came from Mrs. Spatz and the late Elmer Lippin, who used their contacts at Temple Emanuel to invite members of Temple Emanuel to support the shul by making contributions each year and to join with us in restoring the synagogue. Without these sustaining and supporting memberships, the shul would never have been able to complete the restoration process.

You have seen the little drawing of the shul on our letterhead. Did you know that Mrs. Spatz commissioned a local artist to draw the sketch which adorns our letterhead?

You have all enjoyed the beautiful tree in the front of the shul. Its beautiful pink blossoms are a welcome sign of spring each year. Did you know that Mrs. Spatz and her husband Herbert donated the tree to the shul, to replace a dead tree which stood on that spot? They even tried to plant the tree themselves, until they realized that they were not up to digging a hole that deep and then hired a landscaper to plant the tree properly.

Almost none of you present today recall our early fundraising efforts. We were lucky to have the City of Newton provide us with name and address labels for every zip code in the city, listing all registered voters. Of course, many of the names on the labels were of non-Jewish voters. We spent hours and hours and hours peeling off the non-Jewish labels, and there were thousands and thousands and thousands of labels to peel. Then we attached the labels which remained to envelopes with letters asking the community to support our restoration efforts. We were amply rewarded for the time-consuming and very boring task by generous donations from many people. Interestingly, some of the mailings inadvertently went to non-Jewish households and some of those households actually sent donations as well!

And at the risk of embarrassing the Spatzes, I will tell you that they were as generous with their personal resources as they were with their time and efforts, being among the very first to contribute to our Endowment Fund.

Our shul is unique in many ways but one of its special characteristics is the devotion it inspires in our members. The Spatzes are shining examples of what volunteers can contribute and their activism continues to adorn the shul they love. Mrs. Spatz's health makes it difficult for her to attend services here but her presence is evident in ways both great and small. We are very grateful for her contributions to our community over the years and are pleased to present her with this token of our appreciation.

Albert Kalman Honored in 2001
for Twenty Years of Dedicated Service

Albert Kalman was born and raised in Boston. A graduate of Boston Latin School, he earned his BA at Northeastern University. He met Vivienne while they were saying kaddish for family members and they married to build a blended family of six adult children and sixteen grandchildren.

Albert Kalman joined the Adams Street Shul family in the early 1980's. In his volunteer roles, he was deeply involved in the renovation and restoration of the synagogue along with Bert Grand. He and his wife supervised the design and construction of the new kitchen and bathrooms. He was responsible for the renovation and furnishing of the synagogue office. He headed the Kitchen Committee that prepared and served the kiddish every Shabbat. More memorably, he is remembered as the chef who once prepared two hundred and fifty potato latkes for the annual Chanuka party.

He was elected to serve as treasurer of the congregation and served as chairman of the Finance Committee, where he used his financial acumen to husband the synagogue's hard won assets to provide a stable financial base for the synagogue for the future. He served on the Bylaws Committee.

He is remembered as a gentle, humble man with a dignified demeanor. His financial expertise, his years of service to the synagogue, and his tireless dedication to the work of restoring the building and rebuilding the congregation remains an inspiration to everyone.

Vivienne Kalman and Saul Aronow
Adams Street Shul Honors
Two Lifelong Shul Activists with Gala Weekend

Saturday and Sunday, the 18th and 19th of November 2006, were very special days in the life of the Adams Street Shul. We had the opportunity to honor two shul members who have contributed to the life of the our community for over twenty five years.

The Adams Street Shul is honored by the presence and activities of these two unique and dedicated individuals. Their lives and the work of their hands should inspire each of us to dedicate ourselves to the shul and the wider community as our guests of honor have done. Their example is a humbling illustration of what can be accomplished by individuals for the greater good.

Vivienne Kalman and Saul Aronow have been ative in the shul on many levels, some of which are obvious and some of which are "behind the scenes." From serving on the Board of Directors to changing light bulbs, from chairing committees to cleaning the shul after a kiddush or other event, from planning programs to erecting the sukkah, these two dynamos have been involved in every aspect of the shul's existence for over a quarter of a century. The list of their accomplishments and contributions to the shul included chairing or membership on virtually every committee in the shul. Chairman of the Board of Directors Bert Grand commented that only at Adams Street would a Harvard PhD be changing light bulbs and cutting the grass! And the community was also privileged to learn about the lives of these two activists outside the shul as well. How they found the time to contribute so much to the shul, while contributing so much to the Jewish community and the wider community as well, is a fine response to anyone who says they are too busy to volunteer.

On Sunday, a record crowd of eighty five family members, friends and shul members gathered in the Elmer Lippin Social Hall to honor these two activists. How appropriate that the event should have been held in the Elmer

Lippin Social Hall, named for another "unsung hero" of the shul's existence. Guests were treated to a breakfast catered by Ora Catering, and heard tributes to the two guests of honor by family members, other shul members, visiting rabbis and the mayor of Newton.

Tribute Weekend Chair Beryl Gilfix welcomed guests and explained to visitors about the necessity of active volunteers in a shul with no paid staff. "Without our volunteers," she said, "we wouldn't have a shul at all. When we honor a volunteer at Adams Street, we are honoring our most vital resource." Following her introduction, the shul heard from Ronny Drapkin, shul president, who recounted anecdotes about the two honorees, referring to Saul Aranow as MacGuyver, from an old TV series. He also recounted how he visited Vivienne in the hospital when she was critically ill, to be greeted by Vivienne's question, "So how was the board meeting?" Al Landsman, who has worked closely with Al on the Facilities Committee, delivered a very entertaining summary of the life and work of the Facilities Committee. After hearing his speech, everyone incorporated his reference to the "FC" into their own remarks. Mayor David Cohen honored the two volunteers by declaring Sunday and Monday to be Vivienne Kalman and Saul Aronow Days in Newton and presented them each with a citation from the city.

Vivienne Kalman, Honorable David Cohen, Saul Aronow

The assembled guests also heard comments by Rabbi Norbert Weinberg, Rabbi Zalman Gurkow, former rabbi of the congregation and Rabbi Victor Reinstein, a family friend of the Aronow family. Moving and tender tributes by Jamie Stolper and Jessie Aronow Kravette about their parents gave the audience insights into the character and personality of the guests of honor. There was also a brief speech by one of the young members of the congregation, Miriam Kramer, reflecting on her experiences helping Vivienne in the kitchen.

Family members came to the event from Canada, California and Arizona to participate in honoring their parents.

In their responses to the tributes, Vivienne spoke about her desire to pass on Judaism to her children, l'dor v'dor and how her work at the shul is the public face of her Jewish life, as her home is the private face. Saul took the opportunity to deliver a d'var Torah on the meaning of "building the ark" in Jewish life today.

St. Jean L'Evangeliste

The French community's first building was located on Dalby Street. Known as Lafayette Hall, it served as a community center for the French community. In 1911, Lafayette Hall became the site of the church, St. Jean L'Evangeliste. The church was founded by Reverend Father Joseph-E. Robichaud. It was one of dozens of French speaking churches in the diocese, mostly built for French-Canadian immigrants. The church later built a modern building on Watertown Street, which survived as a congregation until 1997 when it was closed and the congregation merged with Our Lady's. The French language parochial school in Nonantum lasted until 1982.

People recalled Father Robichaud from St. Jean L'Evangeliste greeting Jewish families on the High Holidays by saying, "Gut Yontif," a phrase he had been taught by his friend and community member Sam Fried.

Jean Birnbaum recalled an amusing story about Father Robichaud. One day, coming from the playground, she was wearing slacks. The priest called her over and told her very kindly that girls should wear dresses, not slacks. Jean was very amused by this episode, since, she recalled, the priest was wearing a dress! [Catholic priests sometimes wore long robes instead of trousers].

Before 1911, the French community made the building available to the Jewish community for services on the Jewish High Holy Days, when the numbers of attendees far exceeded the space available at 97 Dalby Street. As a church, the old Lafayette Hall was no longer an appropriate venue for the Jewish community's religious services. The conversion from French community center to church may have been the impetus for the Jewish community to build its own building.

"The French-American parishioners had great difficulties but after a number of problems, they revived to found a pretty small parish. The church which they built cost around $19,000 and the presbytery about $40,000. The land to build a school was bought for the price of $11,000."

Population 1000, 67 soldiers took part in the Grand War (World War I) and one was killed.

La paroisse Saint-Jean-l'Evangéliste a été fondée par le Rév. Père Joseph-E. Robichaud. Les paroissiens Franco-Américains ont eu de grandes difficultés, mais- après de nombreuses démarches, ils réussissirent à fonder leur jolie petite paroisse;; inutile d'entrer dans tous les détails, car ce serait une répétition des troubles qui- se sont produits ailleurs. L'église qui a été bâtie a coûté environ $19 000, et le- presbytère $40 000. Le terrain pour bâtir une école a été acheté au prix de $11000; il est à espérer que les travaux seront bientôt commencés. Cette paroisse a été fondée il y a environ 10 ans.

Population, 1,000. Soixante-sept soldats prirent part à la Grande Guerre, dont 1 est mort.[53]

Lafayette Hall, later St. Jean L'Evangeliste

Father Walter Cuenin

In June 2012, as part of our Centennial Celebration, the synagogue hosted an event honoring Father Walter Cuenin, S.T.D., who had been pastor of Our Lady Help of Christians Church a few blocks away from Adams Street. Father Cuenin received the synagogue's Cornerstone Award for Community Building. This event in our Centennial year was a unique opportunity to emphasize our relationships with the wider Nonantum community and the common bonds that unite us. His twelve year pastorate at the largest parish in the diocese embraced the multi-cultural, multi-ethnic and multi-religious character of the neighborhood.

Father Walter Cuenin, S.T.D.

Photo credit: Drew Hayman and Jennifer Nourse Rodman, Inspirational Families Photography

Father Cuenin related how his experiences in Newton had given him a deeper appreciation for Judaism, Jewish spirituality and the meaning of being a Jew. "For the first time in my life, I came to appreciate and value the spiritual heritage of the Jewish faith."

Following a swastika-smearing attack on the synagogue in 1997, Father Cuenin led about three hundred of his parishioners out of the church during Sunday Mass and down the street to the synagogue. Standing on the steps of the synagogue, he spoke to them about the Jewish origins of Jesus and the responsibility that church members had to respect and protect the synagogue as if it was their own. Those who participated on that Sunday were deeply moved by this experience and Father Cuenin states to this day that it was one of the most important days in his religious life. Now retired, Father Cuenin was the Catholic chaplain at Brandeis University, where he was the coordinator of the Interfaith Chaplaincy of five religious leaders. The students at Brandeis referred to him at the Chief Rabbi! Father Cuenin was ordained a priest at St. Peter's Basilica in 1970. He received a doctorate in sacred theology from Gregorian University in 1977. He speaks Latin, French, Italian, Spanish and English.

The photographer who took this photo was photographing important Newton families. Since as a Catholic priest, he has no wife and children, the photographer assumed that Father Cuenin would choose to be photographed in front of his church, Our Lady Help of Christians, the largest Catholic Church in the diocese. Instead, Father Cuenin asked to be photographed in front of the Adams Street Shul.

Ark

When the community finished building the synagogue, there was no money left for a fancy or elaborate Ark for the Torahs. The members of the congregation came mostly from Ukraine and from small villages with limited resources. They were very proud of the accomplishment of having built this wonderful building and could not afford and probably did not want a fancy Ark.

Having no money for anything more elaborate, they made an Ark from the same wood that is used for the wainscotting in the sanctuary and they used a bedsheet for a curtain. This is the original ark. It was used as the ark for twelve years, until 1924, when the second generation began to demand a more appropriate Ark. The women in the congregation raised the money to start a fund to acquire a more formal Ark.

Dimensions: Height 73 inches, Width 29 ½ inches, Depth 18 inches

Photo: Zara Tzanev, zaraphoto@gmail.com, Boston MA

Torah Crown

This crown was donated to the synagogue in memory of Avrahom Yehuda and Faige Rivka Shrier.

It is 20 inches high and measures 40 inches around at its widest point. There are seven medallions, twelve bells in all on the top of the crown and seven bells on the bottom of the crown. There are seven rosettes around the crown.

The inscription reads:

Bais HaKnesset
Agudas Achim Anshei Sfard
5700 [1940]
L'zachar Nishmas (in memory of) Zichronon Liv
Reb Avrahom Yehudah bar Yechiel
his wife Faige Rivka
dau Reb Sholom Shrier

The Rules

Photo courtesy Zara Tzanev, zaraphoto@gmail.com, Boston, MA

It is not allowed to go up
to the platform to daven without the
permission of the President.

It is forbidden to converse or
to smoke during the time of prayer.

Every Yahrzeit one must give
no less than 50 cent

---

per order President
One should know that
every cantor and every
Master Preacher will not
receive from the shul
more than one dollar

translation courtesy of Rabbi S. D. Yaffe

Desk

Desk measurements: 35 inches high, 35 inches long, 24 inches wide. The seat is 18 inches off the floor. Not very comfortable for an adult male.

Photo: Zara Tzanev, zaraphoto@gmail.com, Boston MA

Seating and Pews

When the congregation finished building and dedicating the building, they had spent all the money they had raised and had no money for seating. Therefore, each member brought a chair from his or her home and left it in the synagogue as their permanent seat. After several years, the synagogue had the opportunity to acquire some old school desks from a local school (maybe Lasell Seminary for Young Women, now Lasell College) and those desks were placed in the sanctuary. They were convenient because the desk had a space underneath that was useful for storing the tallis bag, siddurim and snuff box of the member. But they must have been rather cramped for the adult men, as the desks were sized for elementary school children.

The benches which are currently in the building were not there when Marshall Schribman moved away in 1938. They were still using the old school desks. There are several different dates given by informants as to when the desks and benches arrived. Some respondents remembered the old desks in place until as late as the 1950s.

The benches in the synagogue now came from Congregation Kehillath Israel in Brookline when they were remodeling their chapel and thought these benches were too plain and old fashioned. They are of the period when the Adams Street Synagogue was built.

Even if the actual seats were just a chair from home, the members of the congregation had individual property deeds drawn up and recorded, showing which seats in the building belonged to each member and stating that the seats could be passed down from one generation to the next.

This ownership of seats was customary in Europe and adapted to American custom by having the deeds to the seats recorded in Mortgages of Personal Property in the Clerk's Office of the City of Newton. It has been suggested that paying for High Holiday seats, which is customary in some synagogues, is derived from this custom of deeding seats. The Adams Street Synagogue has never charged for seats at the High Holidays and always welcomed visitors, as this was a community synagogue and open to everyone, member or not, at all times.

Deed to seats in shul for Benjamin and Sarah Gilfix

Know all men by these presents, that the Congregation Agudas Achim Anshai Sfard, a religious corporation, duly organized under the laws of the Commonwealth of Massachusetts, town of Newton and County of Norfolk, in consideration of one dollar and other valuable considerations to it paid by Benjamin Gilfix and Sarah Gilfix also of Newton aforesaid, the receipt whereof is hereby acknowledged, do hereby grant, sell, transfer and deliver unto the said Benjamin and Sarah Gilfix to wit:- two seats respectively numbered 7 and 1 in the said synagogue according to the numbering of said seats in said synagogue.

It is also agreed that said seats are not to be sold or transferred to any one without the consent of the Board of Directors of said corporation, first having been obtained.

To have and to hold said seats, and to be used as prescribed by the rules of the Board of Directors governing seatholders rights, to the said Benjamin and Sarah Gilfix and their heirs and assigns, to their own use and behoof forever.

And the said Congregation, Agudas Achim Anshai Sfard, hereby covenants with the grantee, that it is the lawful owner of said seats, and that it has a right to sell same as passed by the Board of Directors at a meeting duly called for that purpose, and that there will be no further charges on said seats to the said Benjamin and Sarah Gilfix that said Congregation has a good right and title to sell the same as aforesaid and will warrant and defend the same against the lawful claims and demands of all persons.

In witness whereof the said Congregation Agudas Achim Anshai Sfard hereunto set its corporate seal by its duly authorized officers, this ninth day of March, A. D. 1913.

Congregation Agudas Achim Anshai Sfard

Louis Baker President

I. Kaplan Secretary

Received Apr. 17 1913
11 H. 57 M. A. M. and entered in Records of Mortgages of Personal Property in the Clerk's office of the City of Newton Lib. K. Folio 18.

Frank M. Grant
City Clerk.

The *Pushkie*

In our synagogue there is a *pushkie*, a *tzedakah* box, a charity box, made of brass. It is very plain, with a slot on the top to insert money into the box. It has been in the synagogue since the building was built. Because it is so plain and unadorned, I assumed that it had been made by a local workman for the synagogue. This opinion was reinforced by the fact that there are no markings on the box to identify its maker.

But now I have seen identical *tzedakah* boxes in two other places. One is in a photograph in a book called *Mornings at the Stanton Street Shul*. The Stanton Street Shul was built on the Lower East Side of New York in 1913 and shares many characteristics with our synagogue, including periods of prosperity and adversity. On page 156 of the book is a photo of their *tzedkah* box, identical to our tzedakah box.

Measurements: 6 1/2 inches high, 13 inches circumference, 4 inches diameter

Photo: Zara Tzanev, zaraphoto@gmail.com, Boston MA

Another location that has an identical *tzedakah* box is Havurat Shalom in Somerville MA. Founded in 1968, Havurat Shalom is an egalitarian Jewish community. No one knows where their *tzedakah* box came from.

It is clear that all three boxes are made by the same manufacturer. My original supposition that this box was a treasure unique to our synagogue is clearly wrong. I am sure there are other surviving examples out there as well. But why are there no markings on the boxes to indicate who made them, or where they were made? I would expect even so simple an item to be "branded" in some way to identify the maker. I hope that someone will see this photograph and be able to help solve the mystery of the origins of this artifact.

Snuff boxes

Snuff is a smokeless tobacco made from ground or pulverized tobacco leaves. It is inhaled or "snuffed" into each nostril, delivering a swift 'hit' of nicotine and a lasting flavored scent (especially if flavoring has been blended with the tobacco). A pinch of snuff is placed onto the back surface of the hand, held pinched between thumb and index finger, or held by a specially made "snuffing" device or small spoon. The nicotine in snuff is absorbed through the mucus membrane in the nose. [55]

Snuff was routinely used by synagogue members to keep themselves alert and awake and was especially popular on fast days or times when worshippers felt sleepy in the heat of summer.

Round snuff box: 1 3/4" high, 3 1/2 " diameter
Oval snuff box: 2 1/2" high, 3 1/2 " diameter

Photo: Zara Tzanev, zaraphoto@gmail.com, Boston MA

These snuff boxes were donated to the synagogue by Harry Standel and were owned by his grandfather, Max.

Both snuff boxes are made of a segment cut from a shofar (ram's horn blown in the synagogue on the Jewish High Holidays). They have a wooden bottom and a wooden lid.

Original decorations

At the time that the synagogue was built, it was the custom to decorate the walls. columns and ceiling with colorful stencils and faux marbre (fake marble) painting. At some point, the ceiling stencils in our synagogue were painted over and were lost to memory, only to be rediscovered during the physical restoration of the building in the early 1990s. The wall stencils and column decorations remained intact until the restoration project, when the walls were dismantled in order to add insulation, air conditioning and new wiring.

The cost of restoring the stenciling was prohibitive so only these photos give an idea of what they looked like. The original colors when first uncovered were vibrant red, yellow, green and blue. The faux marbre painting was done in white, green and black. The walls were medium green color. The wall stencils were dark brown. The stencils can be seen in the photos on the following pages.

376 South Avenue
Weston, MA 02193

Re: Stencil Work
Newton Synagogue
Estimate No. 4896

Gentlemen:

We are pleased to submit our price of $28,000.00 for duplicating the stencils on the above referenced project.

Our price includes an artist to work with you to match color and design (allowance $1,000.00), all scaffolding, labor and materials for installation of our transfer system.

Should you have any questions, please do not hesitate to contact us.

Very truly yours,

SOEP PAINTING CORPORATION

Photos courtesy of Steve Rosenthal

George Washington

The famous Gilbert Stuart portrait of George Washington has pride of place in the synagogue's Elmer Lippin Social Hall. School children of the first half of the twentieth century would have seen two portraits in their public school classrooms, Washington and Abraham Lincoln. Why is this portrait to be found in our synagogue?

The reason for the portrait's presence in the shul actually begins in the Jewish community of Newport, Rhode Island, which was one of the largest and most prosperous Jewish communities in the colonies and was a generous supporter of the American Revolutionary. (However, Newport as a successful commercial port declined after the Revolution).

Newport's synagogue, known today as the Touro Synagogue, was founded in 1658 by the descendants of Jewish families who had fled the Inquisition in Spain and Portugal, going first to Recife in Brazil and then to Curacao in the Caribbean. They left the Caribbean seeking the greater religious tolerance that Rhode Island offered.

Immediately following the success of the Revolution, the community wondered if they would be allowed to remain in the newly established country, or if they should in fact prepare to leave. The opportunity to raise the issue came with a visit by President Washington.

Gilbert Stuart, Portrait of George Washington

Photo for this book: Zara Tzanev, zaraphoto@gmail.com, Boston MA

In August 1790, George Washington visited Newport to rally support for the new Bill of Rights. As part of the welcoming ceremonies for the President of the United States, Moses Mendes Seixas, then president of Congregation Yeshuat Israel, was one of the community leaders given the honor of addressing Washington. In his letter of welcome, Seixas raised the issues of religious liberties and the separation of church and state. Washington's response, quoting Seixas' thoughts, has come down to us as a key policy statement of the new government in support of First Amendment rights. [56]

In his response, Washington put his personal prestige on the line. There was no guarantee that the newly created United States would ratify the so-called Bill of Rights. (The Bill of Rights was not ratified until over a year later, in December 1791.) The immigrants at the Adams Street Shul, taught by their children about Washington's action, chose to honor George Washington, affirming their Americanism and their Jewish heritage at the same time.

When reading the letters, please note that the famous quote, "to bigotry no sanction, to persecution no assistance" is quoting from Seixas' letter and was not Washington's original words.

Moses Seixas, Letter to George Washington, August 17, 1790

Sir:

Permit the children of the stock of Abraham to approach you with the most cordial affection and esteem for your person and merits — and to join with our fellow citizens in welcoming you to Newport.

With pleasure we reflect on those days — those days of difficulty, and danger, when the God of Israel, who delivered David from the peril of the sword — shielded Your head in the day of battle: and we rejoice to think, that the same Spirit, who rested in the Bosom of the greatly beloved Daniel enabling him to preside over the Provinces of the Babylonish Empire, rests and ever will rest, upon you, enabling you to discharge the arduous duties of Chief Magistrate in these States.

Deprived as we heretofore have been of the invaluable rights of free Citizens, we now with a deep sense of gratitude to the Almighty disposer of all events behold a Government, erected by the Majesty of the People — a Government, which to bigotry gives no sanction, to persecution no assistance — but generously affording to all Liberty of conscience, and immunities of Citizenship: deeming every one, of whatever Nation, tongue, or language equal parts of the great governmental Machine:

This so ample and extensive Federal Union whose basis is Philanthropy, Mutual confidence and Public Virtue, we cannot but acknowledge to be the work of the Great God, who ruleth in the Armies of Heaven, and among the Inhabitants of the Earth, doing whatever seemeth him good.

For all these Blessings of civil and religious liberty which we enjoy under an equal benign administration, we desire to send up our thanks to the Ancient of Days, the great preserver of Men beseeching him, that the Angel who conducted our forefathers through the wilderness into the promised Land, may graciously conduct you through all the difficulties and dangers of this mortal life: And, when, like Joshua full of days and full of honour, you are gathered to your Fathers, may you be admitted into the Heavenly Paradise to partake of the water of life, and the tree of immortality.

Done and Signed by order of the Hebrew Congregation in NewPort, Rhode Island August 17th 1790.

Moses Seixas, Warden

George Washington's Response

To the Hebrew Congregation in New Port, Rhode Island, August 21, 1790

Gentlemen:

While I receive with much satisfaction your address replete with expressions of affection and esteem: I rejoice in the opportunity of assuring you that I shall always retain a grateful remembrance of the cordial welcome I experienced in my visit to New Port from all classes of Citizens.

The reflection on the days of difficulty and danger which are past is rendered the more sweet from a consciousness that they are succeeded by days of uncommon prosperity and security. If we have wisdom to make the best use of the advantages with which we are now favored, we cannot fail, under the just administration of a good government to become a great and happy people.

The Citizens of the United States of America have a right to applaud themselves for having given to mankind examples of an enlarged and liberal policy, a policy worthy of imitation.

All possess alike liberty of conscience and immunities of citizenship. It is now no more that toleration is spoken of, as if it was by the indulgence of one class of people, that another enjoyed the exercise of their inherent natural rights. For happily the government of the United States, which gives to bigotry no sanction, to persecution no assistance, requires only that they who live under its protection should demean themselves as good citizens, in giving it on all occasions their effectual support.

It would be inconsistent with the frankness of my character not to avow that I am pleased with your favorable opinion of my administration, and fervent wishes for my felicity.

May the children of the Stock of Abraham, who dwell in this land, continue to merit and enjoy the good will of the other inhabitants, while every one shall sit in safety under his own vine and fig-tree, and there shall be none to make him afraid.

G. Washington

The Synagogue Here and There

Michael Weingarten

History of the Boston Synagogue, 1888-2013

"To the early settlers the synagogue meant much more than just a place of worship. Before and after the services, worshipers discussed all matters that were vital to them in the new world....In these discussions, they exchanged experiences gained in peddling, gave advice and encouragement to newcomers and received news about the old country and about landsleit who lived in other communities.

"The synagogue was for a long time the only place where the immigrants cultural needs could be satisfied. For the learned this was the place where their knowledge would be recognized and appreciated. Small auxiliary groups could be formed to satisfy specific religious or educational needs." [57]

On the other hand, while the shul was a transplanted version of the world they were accustomed to, Jews in America were also increasingly interacting with the secular world. This tended to lessen religious observance, even within Orthodox shuls.

"The Orthodox were submerged in the mass which constituted the majority of the American Jewish community.... There were those who were nominally Orthodox but who had to or chose to work on the Sabbath and holidays. There were those who left religious practice entirely out of lack of faith. There were those who were politically active, usually Socialists, who rejected religious faith in favor of internationalism. And there were Zionists whose focus was on Palestine and not religion." [58]

"To all outward appearances, my first days in Boston, when I was able to live as I had in Slutzk, were only a matter of change of locale: the synagogue where I prayed daily was always packed; the congregants gathered after the morning prayers to study the Mishna, etc; everything was just as it had been in Slutzk. But in Slutzk, the learned and pious had been the vast majority; here in Boston, they were a small minority, so I felt like an alien in Boston. [59]

Kiddish, a Taste of Home

Tabletmag.org, October 29, 2012

In early 20th-century America, *Kiddush* with a capital "K" (the blessing) gave rise to kiddush with a lowercase "k" (the social hour). Community leaders began to understand the importance of the synagogue as a place for congregants to rest and form relationships—especially for hardworking immigrants in a new and unfamiliar country. Meanwhile, "people were becoming more ignorant of certain traditions," so synagogues responded by institutionalizing some rituals once designated for the home. One man remembers his rebbetzin mother "doing her best to make a nice sit-down kiddush to give congregants the Shabbat experience they would not have at home."

From a gastro-sociological level, the development of kiddush makes perfect sense: Whenever Jews and socializing meet, a little nosh is likely to follow. But the specific nosh that emerged (herring, *kichel*, and schnapps) was no accident. "Early 20th-century synagogues rarely had kitchens, let alone iceboxes or refrigeration," Marks said. So, foods that traveled well and kept for long periods of time, like pickled fish, were ideal.

Because *Kiddush* is supposed to be said in association with a meal, that nosh also had to be substantial. Hence the *kichel*, an egg cookie sprinkled with sugar that, like other cookies, cakes, and other nonbread grain foods, requires one to say a *mizonot* blessing, bumping up its status to a near-meal. In a move that might horrify some contemporary taste buds, kiddush-goers would top the *kichel* with a juicy bite of fish and eat them together as a sweet, briny sandwich. And then there was the schnapps. Brought over from Eastern Europe, where it was regarded as *chemer hamedinah*, schnapps and whiskey were considered suitable ritual substitutes for wine. Never mind the whole issue about drinking early in the day; these drinks tasted like home. [60]

What Goes Into A Glass of Wine

Laurie Gwen Shapiro, The Forward

"The syrupy tale of how Jews invited Kedem and modern America"

The Concord grape is a robust and aromatic grape whose ancestors were wild native species found growing in the rugged New England soil. The hardy Concord grape thrives where European cuttings had failed to survive.

In the middle 1840s, on an eastern-facing slope, good for grape-growing, Concord resident Ephraim Wales Bull obsessively bred grapes, looking for a prolific vine with notable flavor that would be resilient in the icy-cold New England wind. Bull estimated that he planted 22,000 seedlings before he produced the ideal grape in 1849, early ripening to escape the killing northern frosts. His grapes have a heavy sweet scent, what winemakers call "foxy." It is named after the Massachusetts village of Concord where the first of its variety was grown.

In August 28, 1853, Henry Thoreau wrote in his journal: "I detect my neighbor's ripening grapes by the scent twenty rods off, though they are concealed behind his house. Every passer knows of them. Perhaps he takes me to his back door a week afterward and shows me with an air of mystery his clusters concealed under the leaves, which he thinks will be ripe in a day or two—as if it were a secret. He little thinks that I smelled them before he did."

The ancestral vine of all of Lower East Side sugary sweet kosher wine is still growing at Grapevine Cottage, 491 Lexington Road, Concord, Massachusetts.

Schapiro's, the original mass-market Concord grape wine has the most memorable advertising slogan in the history of wine and it says: "So Thick You Can Almost Cut It With a Knife!" [61]

Adams Street in Poetry and Song

Robert Pinsky is the Warren Distinguished Professor at Boston University. He is the author of nineteen books. He was the Poet Laureate of the United States from 1997-2000, the only person to serve three terms in that position. As a Newton resident, he visited the Adams Street Shul and the Vilna Shul, both of which have Sam Katz arks. Poem reprinted with the kind permission of the author

Obscure as That Heaven of the Jews

Robert Pinsky

In the rabbi's parable a lame one climbs
  Onto a blind one's shoulders and together
  They take the fruit of the garden of the Lord.

O body the blind one, O soul the lame one.
  Soul that is never purely the soul, thank God.
  The body purely the body only in Death.

Barney Katz, Puritan mullah in the sixth grade,
  Scowled at me O Little Town when I sang
  The carols, and Robert you won't go to Heaven.

O Barney, where did you get that idea?
  When we were in our twenties I heard he died,
  In a strange accident involving LSD.

Body that trembled on the shoulders of the soul,
  How still we see thee lie. Above thy deep
  And dreamless sleep the silent stars go by.

Or do I misremember, and was it Barney
  Whose body was attracted by the carol?
  Was mine the priggish soul that scolded him

Away from those traif hymns, thy dark streets shineth?
  Purity of Sheohl, dappled impurity of life–
  The ancient Jewish community included

Many who were not Jewish, the ger toshav.
  In the pre-Christian Empire, Greek-speaking gentiles
  Joined the synagogue body without conversion.

Is anyone ever entirely in the synagogue,
  O Little Town? Or ever entirely outside it?
  When the great Maimonides temporizes upon

The nature of the Jewish resurrection,
  A whirring of subtle wings, a storied shadow.
  And if we lack a heaven shall we construct one–

With bannisters of pearl, six-pointed stars
  And cartoon harps? Or Milton's eternal shampoo?
  "With nectar pure his oozy locks he laves."

A generation named their children Milton
    And Sidney and Herbert: names of a past and a future:
    The old world on the shoulders of the new,

The new world on the shoulders of the old.
    The convert Hopkins thanks God for dappled things.
    Barney I wish I could take you onto my shoulders

Into the Vilna Shul on Adams Street
    Where an immigrant master carver from Ukraine,
    Sam Katz, who specialized in merry-go-rounds

Has made a Holy Ark adorned with light bulbs
    And shapes like manes and tails. How silently
    The wondrous gifts are given, the freckled-forth,

Obscure inventions. Blessed is the dotted
    And spotted tabernacle. O lame and blind–
    O mottled town, that harbors our hopes and fears.

"Nonanatum Bulgar" by Hankus Netsky

"I wrote The Nonantum Bulgar in response to a request for a klezmer-style piece for middle school band. Since my local middle school (F. A. Day) is located in close proximity to Nonantum, the oldest area of Newton, MA, I decided to imagine the dedication of the Adams St. Shul, our city's oldest synagogue, which took place around a hundred years ago (December 15, 1912). According to the Yiddish and English poster announcing the dedication, the event featured a prominent Boston cantor and choir and a klezmer orchestra leading a 'Grand March' down Adams St.

When the Adams Street Synagogue celebrated its centennial , the local newspaper described part of the original dedication of the synagogue in the following terms: "When the synagogue opened in 1912, an orchestra led a parade down Adams Street while playing a grand march." [62]

Netsky said, "There is an old Russian style of dance called a bulgar. So this piece is a kind of combination of a bulgar and a grand march, trying to imagine what it was like a hundred years ago in that parade."

"A Bulgar is a Romanian Jewish Dance that was very popular among Jewish immigrants at the beginning of the twentieth century. The trumpet solo that opens the piece is a typical rubato prelude, with the trumpet playing 'cantorial-style' Jewish ornaments, and phrasing in the manner of Eastern-European Jewish prayer leaders. Once the dance starts, the piece is underscored with a Romanian Jewish 'Bulgaresca' rhythm, heard in the trombone, snare drum, and tympani. The 'bulgar' section of the piece begins with a typical klezmer band orchestration of the time, featuring solo clarinet (played with a somewhat nasal tone), trumpet (or, even more ideally, cornet) trombone, saxophone, tuba and percussion. The percussion section is prominently featured in the third strain. In the final round of the opening melody the band slows down in the manner of a Russian 'Grand March,' bringing the piece to a proud and majestic conclusion."[63]

Hankus Netsky is a major influence in the revival of klezmer music. He is a resident of Newton.

Music and the Second Generation

Musical knowledge and especially the ability to play the piano, was seen as a marker of middle class respectability and Americanization. Owning a piano was a status symbol.

The Baker family bought a piano for their daughter Minnie. Benjamin Gilfix bought an upright piano for his youngest child, daughter Isabel, which is still in the family. The Hoffman family owned a piano, which was kept in the "music room." And Joseph Hoffman, the family patriarch, played the organ or the accordian.

Three male members of the second generation were married to classically trained musicians. Elliot Gilfix's wife Ruth was a classical cellist, with a degree from Radcliffe College. She also had a beautiful singing voice and sang with the Boston Cecelia, a musical ensemble founded in 1876. The Cecelia had an historic relationship with the Boston Symphony Orchestra and Ruth was very proud of this association.

Another classical musician was Pauline Shrier, married to the first Jewish doctor the community produced, Dr. Hyman Shrier. Pauline was a graduate of Boston University School of Music.

Jane Shriberg, married to Will Shriberg, was trained as a singer and gave vocal concerts in the Newton area.

Norma Fried, daughter of Sam Fried, was trained as a classical pianist at Framingham State Teacher's College.

In the accompanying ad from the Newton Times, the local Jewish owned furniture store was advertising "talking machines" and records, an indication that the entire community, although composed primarily of immigrants, was prosperous and Americanized enough to buy record players and records as well.

Jackson Homestead exhibit

In 1986, the Jackson Homestead (now Historic Newton) mounted an exhibit on the history of the Jewish community in Newton and its historic synagogue. The exhibit drew the largest crowds in the history of the Homestead. After the exhibit was taken down, a booklet was written by Thelma Fleischman, a curator at the Homestead and a member of the synagogue, to preserve photos of the artifacts and some information about the synagogue and the community. The research done by the Homestead staff and the interviews they conducted have proven to be an invaluable resource in reconstructing the history of the building and the community which supported it. The members of the staff of the Homestead who worked on every aspect of the exhibit included the director of the Homestead, Duscha Scott Weisskopf, archivist Susan Abele and curator Malinda Blustain.

The Board of Trustees and the Director of the Jackson Homestead
and the Executive Board of the Newton Historical Society
cordially invite you
to the opening of an exhibition,

AGUDAS ACHIM: The First Synagogue in Newton

on Sunday, April 6, 1986 from 2 to 5 P.M.
at the Jackson Homestead
527 Washington Street
Newton Corner

R.S.V.P. 552-7238

The synagogue would never have made the strides it did in reconstructing the building and rebuilding the congregation without the impetus of this exhibit. The exhibit put the synagogue on the map of the city's consciousness, especially that of the Jewish community, which previously had hardly known of its existence.

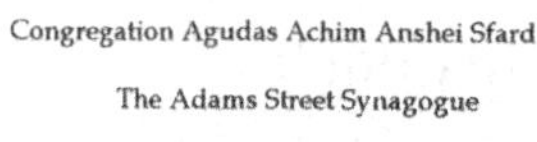

Congregation Agudas Achim Anshei Sfard

The Adams Street Synagogue

Dedication
National Register of Historic Places

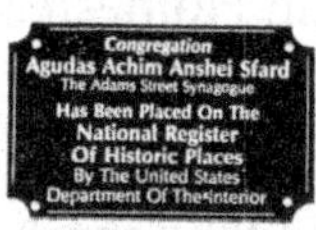

Sunday May 3, 1992
Newton, Massachusetts

Program

Invocation — Rabbi Gershon Segal
Congregation Beth El
Atereth Israel

Speakers

The Honorable Barney Frank
U.S. House of Representatives
MA 4th Congressional District

The Honorable Theodore D. Mann
Mayor, Newton, Massachusetts

The Honorable Lois Pines
Massachusetts Senate

The Honorable Anthony Mandile
Massachusetts General Court

Duscha Weisskopf
Director, The Jackson Homestead

Alan Edelstein
American Jewish Historical Society

National Register Marker Unveiling
Ruth and Sam Pass

Master of Ceremonies
Bertram Grand

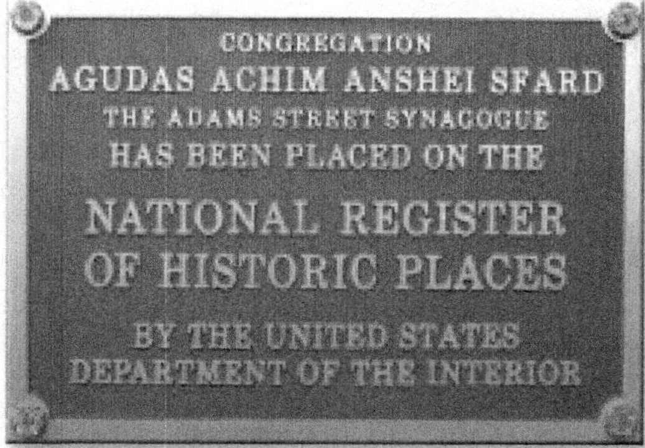

Heritage of Faith

In the year 2000, Beryl Gilfix, a member of the synagogue and a member of the board of the Jackson Homestead, developed a public education program for Historic Newton called "Celebrating Our Heritage of Faith: Newton's oldest houses of worship from an historical perspective." The event, which took place on four Sundays in March of that year, highlighted the history of four diverse congregations, St. Mary's Episcopal Church (1814), Myrtle Baptist Church (1874), Our Lady Help of Christians Church (1873) and Congregation Agudas Achim Anshei Sfard (1912). Of the four institutions featured in the lecture series, all had existed before 1900 except the synagogue.

The variety of religious experience described in the series, as well as the mixture of ethnic and racial groups in the city's history, proved to be a valuable addition to Newton residents' knowledge of the city and its citizens. The program highlighted a classical American Protestant (Episcopal) church, built in 1814, an African-American church whose roots predate the Civil War, a Catholic church built in 1878 and an Orthodox Jewish synagogue, the most recent addition to the city's many religious buildings. Each institution presented its own history, which added a depth of knowledge, information and love of the institution that made the presentations rich and varied. The lectures included music of the period for each congregation.

Learning about the history of each congregation, the struggles they had and the issues they confronted, emphasized the commonality of religious institutions and experience, and exposed visitors to the rich and varied tapestry of the city's inhabitants. Newton is a very diverse community and as this lecture series illustrated, has always been so.

The series was awarded the New TV Red Carpet Award of Excellence for Overall Excellence in Field Production in 2005. (New TV is the local public access cable station). DVDs of the series are available at Historic Newton.

Newton Free Library

As part of the synagogue's Centennial Celebration, in January 2012, the three exhibit cases on the first floor of the Newton Free Library were home to an exhibit about the Adams Street Synagogue and the Jewish community of Newton in the early years of the twentieth century. The display cases made it possible to include physical artifacts as well as letters, newspaper articles and historic photographs. The first case contained historic artifacts, the second case emphasized the multi-ethnic and multi-religious community that lived in Nonantum and the third case illustrated the contemporary life of the synagogue and community. The exhibit reached a wide audience in one of Massachusetts' most visited public libraries and made it possible to tell our synagogue's story and history in a venue that reached far beyond the confines of our building and the Jewish community.

The design and production of the exhibit was under the direction of synagogue member Zhanna Cantor, with the assistance of Beryl Gilfix.

Newton Salutes

Continuing our Centennial Celebration, and searching out ways to reach beyond the synagogue and the Jewish community, Historic Newton (better known to Newton residents as the Jackson Homestead) hosted an exhibit about the Shul from January to June 2012. This exhibit space did not contain display cases so the exhibit could only show photographs of the synagogue and community. We were able to highlight the same historic subjects presented in the Library exhibit described above, even with the limitations of space and lack of display cases. The exhibit included material about Nonantum's mixture of diverse ethnic and religious groups, making it an interesting subject for all visitors who came to see the exhibit.

The design and production of the exhibit was under the direction of synagogue member Zhanna Cantor, with the assistance of Beryl Gilfix.

Nonantum Walking Tour

As part of the Centennial Celebration, Beryl Gilfix produced and led a walking tour of Nonantum in June 2012, which concluded with a visit to the Adams Street Synagogue.

The tour began with a visit to the last surviving wetland of what was called Silver Lake, the lake that gave the neighborhood its nickname, The Lake. That portion of the tour was given by Lucy Stairs, a board member of Historic Newton and an expert on water issues in Newton.

Research was presented on the Jewish immigrant families and their contribution to Nonantum's business life, along with a brief history of the French Canadian community that shared space with Italian and Irish immigrant communities in the early years of the twentieth century.

Most of the participants knew little or nothing about the variety of ethnic and religious groups in the area, so this was an opportunity for them to learn that the neighborhood was not always predominantly Italian. Learning about the existence of a French Catholic church and French speaking parochial school was a revelation to the attendees. Learning about the animosity between Irish and Italian immigrants was also a story that had not been told before. Having the opportunity to visit the synagogue brought forth stories about families whose ancestors lit stoves and turned on lights on the Sabbath for Jewish residents.

This tour offered the residents of Newton and visitors from other communities as well a chance to deepen their knowledge of immigrant history, which is a fascinating and often poorly understood aspect of American history.

Adams Street Stars!

In 1989, the Adams Street Synagogue made its debut as a movie star at the Boston Jewish Film Festival! Boston College Professor Pamela Berger used our synagogue as the setting for her movie, "The Imported Bridegroom." Not only our building was featured. Members of the congregation also appeared in the movie as extras. Many of the scenes were filmed in the sanctuary and the Elmer Lippin Social Hall. A review of the movie noted "the attention to details of architecture and furnishings of the time is constant and exact."

Among the actors was Reb Moshe Waldoks, currently rabbi of Temple Beth Zion in Brookline, MA and co-editor of The Big Book of Jewish Humor.

The movie is available on Amazon. A review of it said, "This is Fiddler on the Roof without music. I saw this in 1991 in a theater and have been waiting all these years for it to be released for home use. One of the best Jewish stories ever written. A Must see."

The shul was the inspiration for a musical piece called "Nonantum Bulgar" by Hankus Netsky, a pioneer in the revival of klezmer music. Netsky, a Newton resident, composed piece after reading about the one hundredth anniversary of the Adams Street Synagogue. The piece, a march, commemorates the opening of the synagogue, which was celebrated by a parade with a band marching down Adams Street in 1912.

HAPPY BIRTHDAY TO ALL OF US

We share our one hundredth birthday with other notable institutions. One hundred years and we are all still going strong!

Fenway Park

Fenway Park, home ballpark of the Boston Red Sox baseball club since it opened in 1912. It is the oldest Major League baseball stadium currently in use.

Hadassah

Hadassah, the Women's Zionist Organization of America, was founded in 1912 by Henrietta Szold.

Oreo Cookie

Since its introduction in 1912, the Oreo cookie has become the best selling cookie in the United States. The first Oreo cookie looked very similar to the Oreo cookie of today, with only a slight difference in the design on the chocolate disks.

Oreos became kosher in 1998 and have an O-U-D certification.

Fig Newtons

This may not be a hundredth anniversary but we should be proud that our city gave its name to one of the oldest cookies in the country. The cookie is named for the City of Newton. Fig Newtons were first produced in 1891 by the National Biscuit Company, now known as Nabisco. Fig Newtons are O-U-D certified.

The City of Newton

The City of Newton celebrated the 100th anniversary of Fig Newtons April 10th, 1991: "The 100th anniversary of a cookie may not be considered a milestone for the history books, but residents of Newton believe the Fig Newton's first century is something to celebrate. Newton is an all-American city, and the Fig Newton is an all-American cookie."

APPENDIX A

All the documents referring to Keneses Israel Anshei Sfard are included in this Appendix. All documents are located in the South Middlesex Country Registry of Deeds, Cambridge MA.

---

1. Commonwealth of MA, Incorporation of Keneses Israel Anshei Sfard, pages 1-2, 14 April 1909

233

FEE, $ 5.00

The Commonwealth of Massachusetts:

Be it known That whereas Morris Fried, William Perlmutter, Maurice S. Perlmutter, Reuben Slesinger, Morris Pactovis, Able Goodman, Sam Swartz, Herman Perlmutter and Charles James

have associated themselves with the intention of forming a corporation under the name of the Keneses Israel Anshe Sephard,

for the purpose of holding religious services, in accordance with the teachings and traditions of the Hebrew faith; and in transacting business appertaining thereto, and to establish a ~~with a capital of~~ place of meeting;

and have complied with the provisions of the Statutes of this Commonwealth in such case made and provided, as appears from the certificate of the President, Treasurer, Secretary and Trustees of said corporation, duly approved by the Commissioner of Corporations, and recorded in this office:

Now, Therefore, I, WILLIAM M. OLIN, Secretary of the Commonwealth of Massachusetts, DO HEREBY CERTIFY that said Morris Fried, William Perlmutter, Maurice S. Perlmutter, Reuben Slesinger, Morris Pactovis, Able Goodman, Sam Swartz, Herman Perlmutter and Charles James,

their associates and successors, are legally organized and established as and are hereby made an existing corporation under the name of the Keneses Israel Anshe Sephard,

with the powers, rights and privileges, and subject to the limitations, duties and restrictions which by law appertain thereto.

Witness my official signature hereunto subscribed, and the Great Seal of the Commonwealth of Massachusetts hereunto affixed this fourteenth day of April in the year of our Lord one thousand nine hundred and nine.

(Signed) Wm. M. Olin
Secretary of the Commonwealth.

[L. S.]

2. Commonwealth of MA, Charter of Keneses Israel Anshei Sfard, 12 March 1909

× 423

Keneses Israel Anshe Sephard.

We, Morris Fried President, William Perlmutter Treasurer, ~~and~~ Maurice S. Perlmutter Secretary, and Reuben Slesinger, Morris Pactovis and Able Goodman, Directors

being a majority of the ~~directors of~~ Trustees (having the powers of directors), of Keneses Israel Anshe Sephard, Corporation in compliance with the requirements of the sixth section of chapter one hundred and twenty-five of the Revised Laws, do hereby certify that the following is a true copy of the agreement of association to constitute said Corporation, with the names of the subscribers thereto:—

Certificate of Organization.

Filed April 14, 1909.

Fee, $ 5.00 Paid.

"We, whose names are hereto subscribed, do, by this agreement associate ourselves with the intention to constitute a Corporation according to the provisions of the one hundred and twenty-fifth chapter of the Revised Laws of the Commonwealth of Massachusetts, and the Acts in amendment thereof and in addition thereto.

The name by which the Corporation shall be known is Keneses Israel Anshe Sephard

The Corporation is constituted for the purpose of holding religious services, in accordance with the teachings and traditions of the Hebrew Faith, and in transacting business appertaining thereto, and to establish a place of meeting.

The place within which the Corporation is established or located is the City of Newton within said Commonwealth.

The amount of its capital stock is none dollars. The par value of its shares is none dollars. The number of its shares is none

We hereby waive all requirements of the statutes of Massachusetts for notice of the first meeting for organization, and appoint the nineteenth day of March, 1909, at eight o'clock P. M., at 308 Watertown Street, Newton as the time and place of holding said first meeting.

In Witness Whereof, we have hereunto set our hands this twelfth day of March in the year nineteen hundred and nine

Morris Fried
William Perlmutter
Maurice S. Perlmutter.
Reuben Slesinger
Sam Swartz
Herman Perlmutter
Charles James
Morris Pactovis
Able Goodman

That the first meeting of the subscribers to said agreement was held on the nineteenth day of March in the year nineteen hundred and nine.

In Witness Whereof, [w]e have hereunto signed our names, this nineteenth day of March in the year nineteen hundred and nine.

Morris Fried, President
Maurice S Perlmutter, Secretary
William Perlmutter, Treasurer
Reuben Slesinger 1st Trustee
Morris Pactovis 2nd Trustee
Able Goodman 3rd Trustee

Commonwealth of Massachusetts, Middlesex ss. Newton March 19th 1909.

Then personally appeared the above-named Morris Fried, President; Maurice S Perlmutter, Secretary; William Perlmutter, Treasurer; Reuben Slesinger 1st Trustee; Morris Pactovis, 2nd Trustee; Able Goodman 3rd Trustee

and severally made oath that the foregoing certificate, by them subscribed, is true, to the best of their knowledge and belief. Before me, Reuben Forknall

Justice of the Peace.

I hereby certify that it appears, upon an examination of the within written certificate and the records of the corporation duly submitted to my inspection, that the requirements of sections one, two and three of chapter one hundred and twenty-five, and sections fifteen to twenty, inclusive, of chapter one hundred and ten of the Revised Laws have been complied with, and I hereby approve said certificate, this twenty-third day of March A.D. nineteen hundred and nine.

William D. T. Trefry Commissioner of Corporations.

Charter issued April 14, 1909, to Keneseo Israel Anshe Sephard as a new Corporation, ~~No.~~

a copy of which charter, or certificate of incorporation, is recorded in Charter Book, No. 227, Page 233.

Fee, $, paid.

3. Registry of Deeds, Book 3521, pages 385-386, Deed to Plot #40 (Watertown Street), Kenny to Slesinger, 19 May 1910

Company at the point of beginning. Albert H. Flagg. Elmar A. Flagg. Middlesex ss. June 2, 1910. 10 h. 34 m. A. M. Recd & Recorded.

Kenny et al. Trs. to Slesinger et al. Trs.

Know all men by these Presents that we, Thomas J. Kenny of Boston in the County of Suffolk and Elihu G. Loomis of Bedford in the County of Middlesex in the Commonwealth of Massachusetts surviving trustees under the last will of George W. Morse late of Newton in the County of Middlesex and Commonwealth aforesaid deceased which will was duly proved and allowed by the Probate Court for said County on twenty sixth day of April A.D. 1905, do by virtue and in execution of the power to us given in and by said will, and of every other power and authority us hereto enabling and in consideration of the sum of one dollar

3521
386

and other valuable considerations to us paid by Reuben Slesinger, Julius Pass and Abraham Shreir Trustees of Keneseth Israel Anshe Sephard a religious corporation organized under the laws of the Commonwealth of Massachusetts and located at said Newton, the receipt whereof is hereby acknowledged hereby grant, bargain, sell and convey unto the said Reuben Slesinger, Julius Pass and Abraham Shreir trustees as aforesaid, their successors and assigns, a certain tract or parcel of land situated in that part of said Newton called "Nonantum" and being lot numbered forty (40) as shown on a "Plan of land in Nonantum Park Newton belonging to the American Land Company" dated May 5, 1903 and recorded with Middlesex South District Deeds, Book of plans 143 plan 6. For a more specific description see said plan. Said parcel containing five thousand six hundred one (5601) square feet more or less. This conveyance is made subject to any and all unpaid assessments, taxes and liens. To have and to hold the granted premises with all the privileges and appurtenances thereto belonging to the said Reuben Slesinger, Julius Pass and Abraham Shreir trustees as aforesaid and their successors and assigns, to their own use and behoof forever. In witness whereof we the said Thomas J. Kenny and Elihu G. Loomis surviving trustees as aforesaid hereunto set our hands and seals this first day of March in the year one thousand nine hundred and ten. Thomas J. Kenny (seal) Elihu G. Loomis (seal) Surviving Trustees as aforesaid. Commonwealth of Massachusetts. Suffolk ss. Boston April 25, 1910. Then personally appeared the above named Thomas J. Kenny and Elihu G. Loomis and acknowledged the foregoing instrument to be their free act and deed before me, Forrest Hillam Justice of the Peace.

Middlesex ss. May 19, 1910. 4 h. 15 m. P.M. Recd & Recorded

4. Registry of Deeds, Book 3521, pages 387-389, Slesinger to Kenny, 19 May 1910

Slesinger val. Trs.
to
Kenny val. Trs.

Know all men by these Presents
that we, Reuben Slesinger, Julius Pass and Abraham Shrein
trustees of the Kenesee Israel Anshe Sephard, a religious
corporation organized under the laws of the Commonwealth of Massachusetts and located at Newton in the
County of Middlesex and said Commonwealth, in consideration of five hundred seventy-two and 12/100 ($572.12)
dollars paid by Thomas J. Kenny of Boston in the County
of Suffolk and said Commonwealth and Elihu G. Loomis

3521
387

of Bedford in said County of Middlesex surviving trustees
under the will of George W. Morse late of said Newton the
receipt whereof is hereby acknowledged, do hereby give, grant,
bargain sell and convey unto the said Thomas J. Kenny
and Elihu G. Loomis surviving trustees as aforesaid, their
successors and assigns a certain tract or parcel of land
situated in that part of said Newton called "Nonantum"
and being lot numbered forty (40) as shown on a "Plan
of land in Nonantum Park Newton, belonging to the American Land Company" dated May 5, 1903 and recorded with
Middlesex South District Deeds book of plans 143 plan 6. For
a more specific description see said plan. Said parcel containing five thousand six hundred one (5601) square feet
more or less and being the same premises conveyed to
us by deed of the grantees dated March 1, 1910 and to be
recorded herewith. This mortgage is given to secure a
portion of the purchase money. To have and to hold
the granted premises with all the privileges and appurtenances thereto belonging to the said Thomas J. Kenny
and Elihu G. Loomis Trustees as aforesaid and their successors and assigns to their own use and behoof forever.
And we hereby for ourselves and our successors and assigns covenant with the grantees and their successors
and assigns that we are lawfully seized in fee simple
of the granted premises, that they are free from all incumbrances, that we have good right to sell and convey
the same as aforesaid, and that we will and our successors and assigns shall Warrant and defend the same
to the grantees and their successors and assigns forever
against the lawful claims and demands of all persons.
Provided nevertheless that if we or our successors or assigns shall pay unto the grantees or their successors
or assigns the sum of five hundred seventy two and 12/100
($572.12) dollars in five yearly installments of one hundred
dollars payable on the first day of March in each year
beginning March 1, 1911, the last payment of seventy two
and 12/100 ($72.12), being due in six years from this date
with interest semi annually at the rate of six per cent per
annum, on the first days of March and September of each
year and until such payment shall pay all taxes and assessments to whomsoever laid or assessed whether on
the granted premises or on any interest therein or on this
mortgage, or on the debt secured hereby shall keep the

3521
388

buildings on said premises insured against fire in a sum not less than dollars for the benefit of the grantees and their successors and assigns in such form and at such insurance offices as they shall approve and at least two days before the expiration of any policy on said premises shall deliver to or them a new and sufficient policy to take the place of the one so expiring, and shall not commit or suffer any strip or waste of the granted premises or any breach of any covenant herein contained then this deed as also a note of even date herewith signed by us whereby we promise to pay to the grantees or order the said principal sum and instalments of interest at the times aforesaid shall be void. But upon any default in the performance or observance of the foregoing condition the grantees or their successors or assigns may sell the granted premises or such portion thereof as may remain subject to this mortgage in case of any partial release hereof, together with all improvements that may be thereon by public auction in said Newton first publishing a notice of the time and place of sale once each week for three successive weeks in some one newspaper published in said Newton the first publication of such notice to be not less than twenty one days before the day of sale and may convey the premises so sold by proper deed or deeds to the purchaser or purchasers absolutely and in fee simple and such sale shall forever bar us and all persons claiming under us from all right and interest in the granted premises whether at law or in equity. And out of money arising from such sale the grantees or their representatives shall be entitled to retain all sums then secured by this deed whether then or thereafter payable including all costs, charges and expenses incurred or sustained by them by reason of any default in the performance or observance of the said condition rendering the surplus if any to us or our successors or assigns, and we hereby for ourselves and our successors and assigns covenant with the grantees and their successors and assigns that in case a sale shall be made under the foregoing power, we or they will upon request execute, acknowledge and deliver to the purchaser or purchasers a deed or deeds of release confirming such sale and said grantees and their successors, assigns are hereby appointed and constituted the attorney or attorneys, irrevocable of the said grantors to execute and deliver to the said purchaser a full transfer of all policies of insurance on the buildings upon the land covered by this mortgage at the time of such sale. And it is agreed that the grantees or their successors or assigns or any person or persons in their behalf may purchase at any sale made as aforesaid, and that no other purchaser shall be answerable for the application of the purchase money, and that until default in the performance or observance of the condition of this deed the grantors and their successors and assigns may hold and enjoy the granted premises and receive the rents and profits thereof. In witness whereof we the said Reuben Slesinger, Julius Pass and Abraham Shreir trustees as aforesaid hereunto set our hands and seals this first day of March in the year one thousand nine hundred ten. Reuben Slesinger (seal) Julius Pass (seal) Abraham Shreir (seal) Trustees as aforesaid. Signed and sealed in presence of Reuben Forknall witness to all three. Commonwealth of Massachusetts. Middlesex ss. Newton May 14th 1910. Then personally appeared the above named Reuben Slesinger, Julius Pass, and Abraham Shreir and acknowledged the foregoing instrument to be their free act and deed before me, Reuben Forknall Justice of the Peace.

Middlesex ss. May 19, 1910. 4h. 15m. P.M. Rec'd & Recorded.

5. Plot Plan for Plot #40, Watertown Street

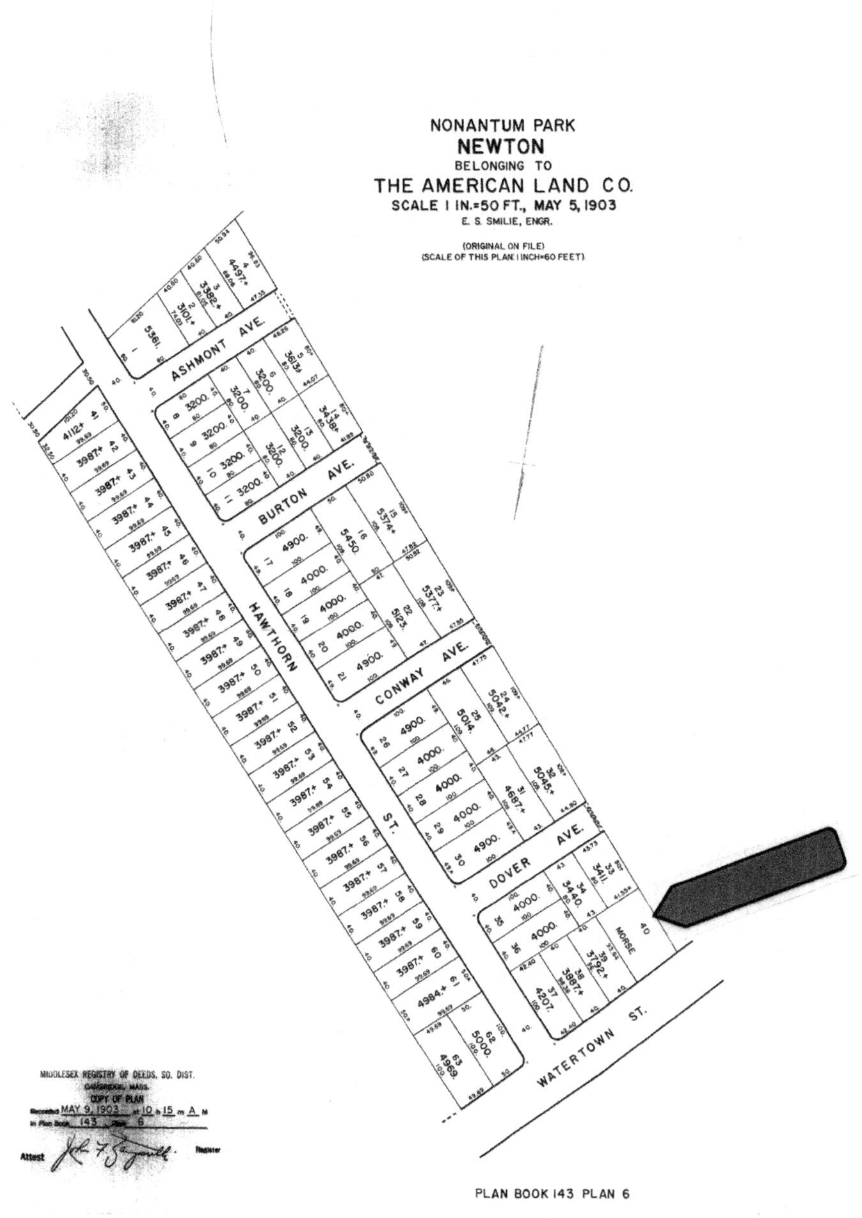

6. Registry of Deeds, Book 3601, page 300, Dalby Street deed, Murphy to Fried, 9 May 1911

3601 194
300
Murphy
to
Fried

Know all men by these presents

that I, Richard H. Murphy of Newton in the County of Middlesex and Commonwealth of Massachusetts

in consideration of one dollar and other valuable considerations
paid by Morris Fried of Newton in said County

the receipt whereof is hereby acknowledged, do hereby give, grant, bargain, sell and convey unto the said Morris Fried his heirs and assigns forever a certain lot of land with the buildings thereon, situated on the westerly side of Dalby Street in said Newton lot numbered nine on a plan of lots owned by Josiah Rutter & J. Moore in Newton, drawn by Jos. H. Curtis and dated Aug. 1869 and recorded in Middlesex Registry of Deeds Book of Plans No. 17, Plan 61 and bounded and described as follows: Beginning at the southeasterly corner of the granted premises and thence running northerly, bounded easterly on Dalby Street, sixty feet, more or less to land of one Canfield; thence westerly, bounded northerly on said Canfield's land, one hundred eleven and nine tenths (111.9) feet (more or less) to land now or formerly of the Dalby Mills Co., thence southerly, bounded westerly by said Company's land sixty and twenty-six one hundredths (60.26) feet to other land of grantor known as lot No. 7; thence easterly, bounded southerly on said other land of grantor one hundred and seventeen and six tenths (117.6) feet to the point of beginning at Dalby Street containing about 6882 square feet, more or less. Being the same premises conveyed to me by deed of John M. Moore dated November 1st, 1887 and recorded in South Middlesex Registry of Deeds, Book 1824, Page 45[illegible]

To have and to hold the granted premises, with all the privileges and appurtenances thereto to the said Morris Fried his heirs and assigns, to their own use and behoof forever. And I do hereby for myself my heirs, executors and administrators, **covenant** with the said grantee and his heirs and assigns I am lawfully seized in fee-simple of the granted premises, that they are free from all incumbrances that I have good right to sell and convey the same as aforesaid; and that I will and my heirs, executors, administrators shall **warrant and defend** the same to the said grantee and his heirs and assigns forever against lawful claims and demands of all persons by and thro' me but none other.

And for the consideration aforesaid, I, Margaret A. Murphy wife of said Richard H. Murphy

do hereby release unto the said grantee and his heirs and assigns all right of or to both **dower** and **homestead** in the granted premises and all rights by statute therein and all other rights and interests therein.

In witness whereof we the said Richard H. Murphy and Margaret A. Murphy hereunto set our hands and seals this ninth day of May in the year one thousand nine hundred and eleven

Signed sealed and delivered
in presence of
James S. Cannon to both.

Richard H. Murphy
Margaret A. Murphy

Commonwealth of Massachusetts, Middlesex ss. May 9th 1911. Then personally appeared the above named Richard H. Murphy and acknowledged the foregoing instrument to be his free act and deed, before me:— James S. Cannon Justice of the Peace.

Middlesex, ss., May 9. 1911. At 1 h. 25 m. P. M., received and recorded.

7. Registry of Deeds, Book 3614, pages 188-189, Plot #40, Keneses Israel Anshei Sfard to Fried, 21 June 1911

3614
188

Whereof the said Watertown Co-operative Bank ha
its corporate seal to be hereunto affixed and thes
to be signed, acknowledged, and delivered in i
and behalf by Samuel S. Gleason its Treasurer
day of June A.D. 1911. Watertown Co-operative Bank By S
Gleason Treasurer (Corporate Seal) Approved Fred
Director. Commonwealth of Massachusetts, M.
Watertown June 16. 1911. Then personally appeare
above-named Samuel S. Gleason and acknow
foregoing instrument to be the free act and d
Watertown Co-operative Bank, before me, Frederic
Notary Public (Notarial Seal)
Middlesex s.s. June 21. 1911, 10h. a.m. Rec'd & Recorded

Newton, Mass., June 11, 19

Vote

special meeting of the Keneses Israel Anshe Sephar
duly called for the purpose, and held at sai
on the eleventh day of June, 1911, the follow
was passed - Voted - that the trustees, Abram
Max Canter, and Joseph Hoffman, are hereby au
and instructed to make, execute acknowledge a
in the name and behalf of said corporation, a o
veying to Morris Fried, a certain lot of land on Watert
in said Newton, being lot numbered Forty (40) as c
said corporation by deed dated March 1st 1910, an
in Middlesex (South District) Deeds book 3521 page .
A true copy from the records. Attest - David Rosenthal S

Keneses Israel Anshe Sephard's Tre. to Fried

Know all men by these
That we, Abram Shreir, Max Canter and Joseph Ho
Newton in the County of Middlesex, Trustees of Kene
Anshe Sephard a corporation duly established un
of the Commonwealth of Massachusetts, in conside
Dollar and other valuable considerations to it paid
Fried of said Newton, the receipt whereof is hereby
edged, hereby remises, releases and forever quitclai
the said Morris Fried a certain tract or parcel
situated in that part of said Newton called "No
and being lot numbered forty (40) as shown on
Land in Nonantum Park Newton belonging to the
Land Company" dated May 5th 1903 and recorded
Middlesex South District Deeds, Book of Plans 14
Being the same premises conveyed to it by deed
1st 1910 and recorded with Middlesex So. Dist. Deeds

1920 See Book 4342 Page 130

3614
189

page 385. This conveyance is made subject to a mortgage to the surviving Trustees under the last will of George W. Morse late of Newton and all unpaid assessments, taxes and liens, which mortgage, unpaid assessments, taxes and liens the grantee hereby assumes and agrees to pay. To Have and To Hold the granted premises, with all the privileges and appurtenances thereto belonging to the said Morris Fried and his heirs and assigns, to their own use and behoof forever. And said corporation hereby covenants with the grantee and his heirs and assigns that the granted premises are free from all incumbrances made or suffered by it except as aforesaid and that it will Warrant and Defend the same to the grantee and his heirs and assigns forever against the lawful claims and demands of all persons claiming by, through, or under it, except as aforesaid but against none other. In Witness Whereof the said Keneses Israel Anshe Sephard having no corporate seal have caused these presents to be signed in its name and behalf by its Trustees this fourteenth day of June in the year one thousand nine hundred and eleven. Abram Shreir (seal) Max Canter (seal) Joseph Hoffman (seal) As trustees as within stated. Commonwealth of Massachusetts. Middlesex ss. Newton June 14th 1911. Then personally appeared the above named Abram Shreir, Max Canter & Joseph Hoffman and acknowledged the foregoing instrument to be the free act and deed of the Keneses Israel Anshe Sephard Corp: Before me Reuben Forknall Justice of the Peace. Middlesex ss. June 21. 1911. 10 h. a.m. Rec'd & Recorded

8. Registry of Deeds, Book 3698, page 365, Dalby Street deed, Fried to Keneses Israel Anshei Sfard, 5 June 1912

Know all men by these presents

[Th]at I Morris Fried of Newton in the County of Middlesex and Commonwealth of Massachusetts

[in con]sideration of one dollar and other valuable considerations to me [pa]id by Keneses Israel Anshe Sephard, a corporation duly established by law and having a usual place of business in said Newton in the County of Middlesex [the] receipt whereof is hereby acknowledged, do hereby give, grant, bargain, sell and convey unto the said Keneses Israel Anshe Sephard, its successors and assigns, a certain parcel of land with the buildings thereon situated on the Westerly side of Dalby Street in said Newton being lot 9 on a plan of lots owned by Josiah Rutten and John Moore in Newton drawn by ... Curtis and dated August 1869 and recorded in Middlesex South District Deeds book of Plans 17 Plan 61 and bounded and described as follows:- Beginning at the southeasterly corner of the granted premises and thence running northerly bounded easterly on Dalby Street sixty (60) feet more or less to land now or late of ... Canfield; thence Westerly bounded Northerly on said Canfield's land one hundred eleven and 9/10 (111.9) feet more or less to land now or formerly of the Dalby Mills Company; thence Southerly bounded westerly by said company's land sixty and 26/100 (60.26) feet to land now or formerly of one Murphy known as lot No 7; thence Easterly bounded southerly on said Murphy's land one hundred seventeen and 6/10 (117.6) feet to the point of beginning at Dalby Street, containing 6882 square feet more or less and being the same premises conveyed to me by deed of Richard H. Murphy recorded with said deeds in book 3661, page 300.

3698
365

Fried
to
Keneses Israel
Anshe Sephard

To have and to hold the granted premises, with all the privileges and appurtenances thereto belonging to the said Corporation and its successors ~~heirs~~ and assigns, to their own use and behoof forever. And I hereby for myself my heirs, executors and administrators, **covenant** with the grantee and its successors ~~heirs~~ and assigns that, I am lawfully seized in fee-simple of the granted premises, that they are free from all incumbrances

that I have good right to sell and convey the same as aforesaid; and that I will and my heirs, executors, and administrators shall **warrant and defend** the same to the grantee and its successors ~~heirs~~ and assigns forever against the lawful claims and demands of all persons

And for the consideration aforesaid I, Cilia Fried, wife of said Morris Fried, hereby release unto the said grantee and its successors and assigns all right of or to both dower and homestead in the granted premises, and all other rights and interests therein

In witness whereof we the said Morris Fried and Cilia Fried hereunto set our hands and seals this fifth day of June in the year one thousand nine hundred and twelve.

Morris Fried (seal)
Cilia Fried (seal)

Commonwealth of Massachusetts, Suffolk ss. June 5 1912. Then personally appeared the above named Morris Fried and acknowledged the foregoing instrument to be his free act and deed, before me:— Samuel [illegible]urwitz, Notary Public

Middlesex, ss. June 5 1912. At 3 h. 20 m. P. M., received and recorded.

One word over erasure; four stricken out; two interlined.

...—W.B.P.T.K. & M. For Dower and No Dower.

9. Registry of Deeds, Book 3721, pages 76-79, Dalby Street deed, Keneses Israel Anshei Sfard to Fried, 26 August 1912

3721
76

sideration aforesaid I, Anna P. Smith, wife of the sa[id]
Bryant G. Smith do hereby release unto the grantee
its successors and assigns all right of or to both
dower and homestead in the granted premises, In Witness Whereof we, the said Bryant G. Smith and Anna
P. Smith hereunto set our hands and seals this fifth
day of August in the year nineteen hundred and twelve
Bryant G. Smith (seal) Anna P. Smith (seal) Signed, sealed and
delivered in presence of D. Chester Parsons to B. G. S. & A. P. S.
Commonwealth of Massachusetts. Middlesex ss. August
1912. Then personally appeared the above-named Bryant
G. Smith and acknowledged the foregoing instrument
to be his free act and deed, before me, D. Chester Parsons
Justice of the Peace. Middlesex ss. August 21, 1912. 4 h. 45 m. P. M. Rec'd & Rec[orded]

Keneses Israel Anshe Sephard to Fried

Know all Men by these Present[s]
That we, the Keneses Israel Anshe Sephard, a corporat[ion]
duly established by law and having a usual pla[ce]
of business in Newton, in the County of Middlese[x]
and Commonwealth of Massachusetts, in consideratio[n]
of seven hundred and eighty dollars to it paid b[y]
Morris Fried of said Newton, the receipt whereof i[s]
hereby acknowledged, do hereby give, grant, bargain,
and convey unto the said Morris Fried, his heirs a[nd]
assigns, a certain lot of land with the building[s]
thereon situated on the westerly side of Dalby Str[eet]
in said Newton being lot No. 9 on a plan of lot[s]
owned by Josiah Rutter & John Moore in Newton, dra[wn]
by Jos. H. Curtis and dated August 1869 and recorde[d]
Middlesex So. Dist. Deeds, Book of Plans 17, Plan
bounded and described as follows:- beginning at t[he]
southeasterly corner of the granted premises and
thence running northerly bounded easterly on Dal[by]
Street sixty (60) feet more or less to land now [or]
late of one Canfield; thence westerly bounded nort[herly]
on said Canfield's land one hundred eleven and 1/10
feet more or less to land now or formerly of th[e]
Dalby Mills Co., thence southerly bounded westerly by
company's land sixty and 26/100 (60.26) feet to land
or formerly of one Murphy known as lot No. 7, th[ence]
easterly bounded southerly on said Murphy's land
hundred seventeen and 6/10 (117.6) feet to the point
beginning at Dalby Street, containing 6882 square

3720 418

ore or less and being the same premises conveyed said Fried by deed of Richard H. Murphy recorded ith said deeds in book 3601 Page 300. Said premises e conveyed subject to two mortgages aggregating $1300, nd accrued interest thereon and unpaid taxes. To ave and To Hold the granted premises, with all the ivileges and appurtenances thereto belonging, to the aid Morris Fried and his heirs and assigns, to their wn use and behoof forever. And the said corpora- tion for itself, its successors and assigns covenant, with the grantee and his heirs and assigns that it is awfully seized in fee simple of the granted prem- es, that they are free from all incumbrances, ex- pt as aforesaid; that it has good right to sell and nvey the same as aforesaid; and that it will and s successors and assigns shall warrant and defend the same to the grantee and his heirs and as- igns forever against the lawful claims and demands f all persons. Provided nevertheless that if grantor r its successors or assigns, shall pay unto the gran- ee or his executors, administrators, or assigns, the um of seven hundred and eighty dollars ($780) in two years and six months from this date, with interest emi-annually at the rate of six per centum per an- num, and until such payment shall pay all taxes nd assessments, to whomsoever laid or assessed, wheth er on the granted premises or on any interest therein, r on the debt secured hereby, shall keep the build- ngs on said premises insured against fire, in a sum not less than seven hundred and eighty dollars for the benefit of the grantee and his executors, ad- ministrators, and assigns, in such form and at such nsurance offices as they shall approve, and at least two days before the expiration of any policy on said premises, shall deliver to him or them, a new and sufficient policy to take the place of the one so ex- piring; and shall not commit or suffer any strip r waste of the granted premises, or any breach of any covenant herein contained, or any default in the erformance or observance of the condition of said prior mortgage, then this deed, as also one note of even date herewith, signed by grantor whereby it promises to pay to the grantee or order the said

78

principal sum and instalments of interest at the times aforesaid, shall be void. But upon any default in the performance or observance of the foregoing condition, the grantee, or his executors, administrators or assigns, may sell the granted premises, or such portion thereof as may remain subject to this mortgage in case of any partial release hereof, together with all improvements that may be thereon, by public auction in said Newton first publishing a notice of the time and place of sale once each week for three successive weeks in some one newspaper published in said Newton the first publication of such notice to be not less than twenty-one days before the day of sale, and may convey the same by proper deed or deeds to the purchaser or purchasers absolutely and in fee simple; and such sale shall forever bar grantor and all persons claiming under it from all right and interest in the granted premises, whether at law or in equity. And out of money arising from such sale the grantee or his representatives shall be entitled to retain all sums then secured by this deed, whether then or thereafter payable, including all costs, charges and expenses incurred or sustained by them by reason of any default in the performance or observance of the said condition, rendering the surplus, if any, to grantor or its successors or assigns; and grantor hereby, for itself and its successors or assigns, covenants with the grantee and his heirs, executors, administrators and assigns that in case a sale shall be made under the foregoing power, it or they will upon request, execute, acknowledge and deliver to the purchaser or purchasers a deed or deeds of release confirming such sale, and said grantee and his assigns are hereby appointed and constituted the attorney or attorneys irrevocable of the said grantor to execute and deliver to the said purchaser a full transfer of all policies of insurance on the buildings upon the land covered by this mortgage at the time of such sale. And it is agreed that the grantee or his executors, administrators or assigns, or any person or persons in their behalf, may purchase at any sale made as aforesaid, and that no other

79

urchaser shall be answerable for the application of
he purchase money; and that, until default in
he performance or observance of the condition of this
ed, grantor and its successors and assigns may hold
nd enjoy the granted premises and receive the rents
d profits thereof. And for the consideration afore-
aid, do hereby release unto the said grantee
nd, heirs and assigns all right of or to both
ower and homestead in the granted premises and
ll other rights and interests therein. In Witness
hereof the said corporation by Fredrick R. Denning,
orris Greenwald, William Perlmutter, its Trustees hereun-
duly authorized hereunto set its hand and corporate
al this fifth day of June in the year one thou-
and nine hundred and twelve. Keneses Israel Anshe
phard by Fredrick R. Denning, Morris Greenwald, William
lmutter, Trustees. (Corporate Seal). Commonwealth of Mas-
chusetts. Suffolk ss. June 5th, 1912. Then personally ap-
ared the above-named Fredrick R. Denning and ac-
nowledged the foregoing instrument to be the free
t and deed of said corporation, before me, Samuel Hurwitz
tary Public Middlesex ss, August 26, 1912. 9h. 19m. A.M. Rec'd, & Recorded.

10. Plot plan 97 Dalby Street

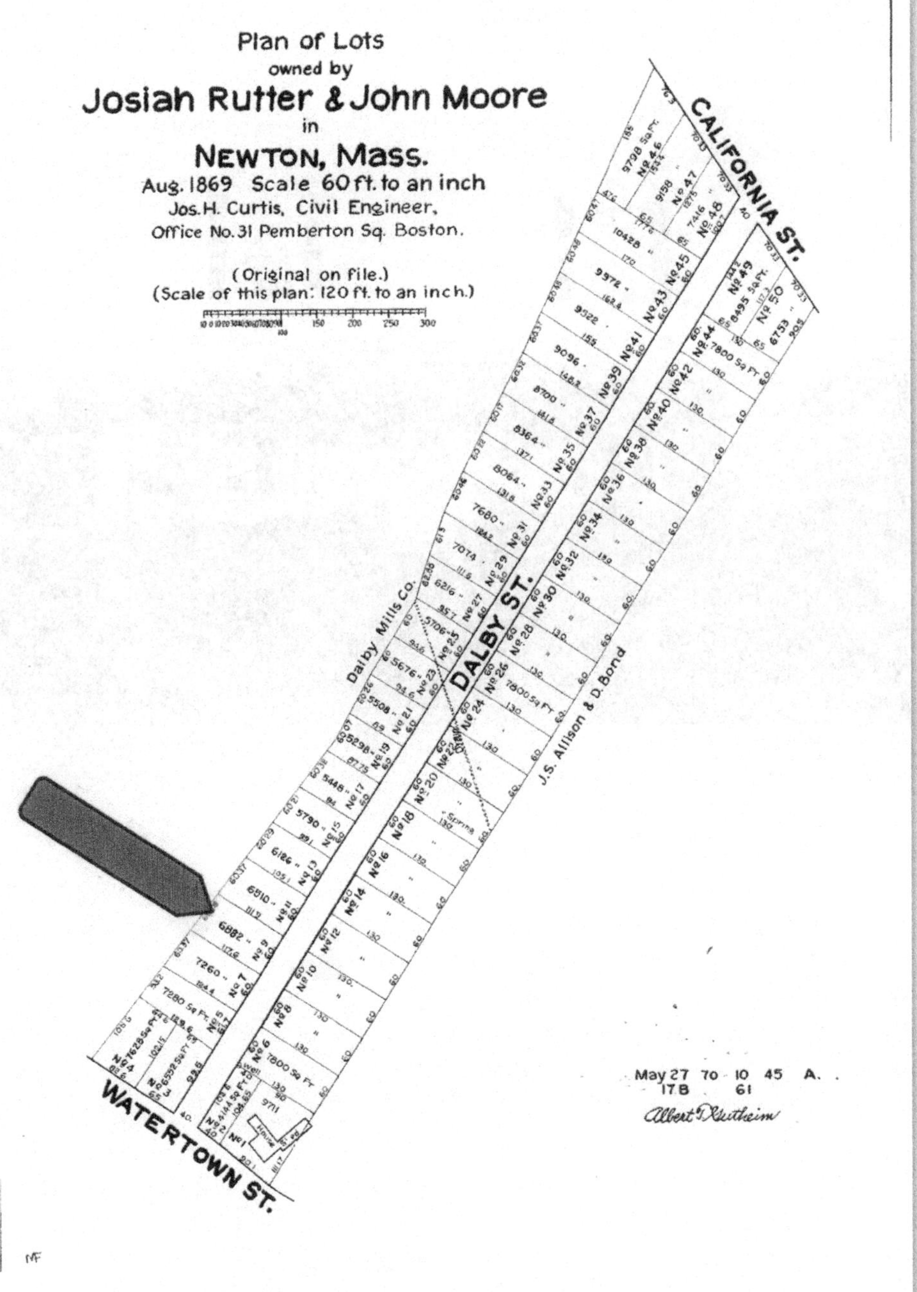

11. Photo 97 Dalby Street

12. City of Newton, building permit, 97 Dalby Street, 31 July 1911

Location, ownership, and detail must be complete and legible.
Separate application required for every building. No. 5057

APPLICATION FOR PERMIT FOR ALTERATIONS, ETC.

Newton, Mass., July 31 1911

TO THE
INSPECTOR OF BUILDINGS:

The undersigned applies for a permit to make addition to the following described

Building, Church

Location, 97 Dalby St. Ward 1

Name of owner, Morris Fishel Name of occupant, Jewish Congregation

Name of mechanic, Name of architect, none

Malden, Mass. Material, wood

Size of building, No. feet front, ; feet rear, ; feet deep, ; No. of stories,

Size of L feet long; feet wide; feet high; No. of stories; Roof,

No. of feet in height from land to highest point of roof,

Style of roof, Material of roofing,

Material of foundation, Distance from line of street,

Thickness of external walls, inches. Thickness of party walls, inches.

How is the building occupied? For what purpose built?

If a dwelling, by how many families? No. of stores in the lower story?

Hoistways and elevators? How protected?

DETAIL OF PROPOSED ALTERATIONS, ETC.

addition of one room 15 × 16 ft.

Estimated cost? $200.

IF EXTENDED ON ANY SIDE.

Size of extension, No. of feet long, 15' ; No. of feet wide, 16 ; No. of feet high above land, 13

No. of stories high, one ; Style of roof, flat ; Material of roofing, tar & gravel

Of what material will the extension be built? wood Foundation? stone piers

If of brick, what will be the thickness of external walls? inches; and party walls inches.

Will the extension be placed within 30 feet of the present or proposed street line?

How will the extension be occupied? religious services Connection with main building? yes

Distance from surrounding buildings:—

Front, feet; side, feet; side, feet; rear, feet.

What distance from the lines of the adjoining lots will be placed?

IF MOVED, RAISED OR BUILT UPON.

Malden, Mass. Material, *wood*

Size of building, No. feet front, ; feet rear, ; feet deep, ; No. of stories,

Size of L feet long; feet wide; feet high; No. of stories; Roof,

No. of feet in height from land to highest point of roof,

Style of roof, Material of roofing,

Material of foundation, Distance from line of street,

Thickness of external walls, inches. Thickness of party walls, inches.

How is the building occupied? For what purpose built?

If a dwelling, by how many families? No. of stores in the lower story?

Hoistways and elevators? How protected?

DETAIL OF PROPOSED ALTERATIONS, ETC.

addition of one room 15 x 16 ft.

Estimated cost? *$200.*

IF EXTENDED ON ANY SIDE.

Size of extension, No. of feet long, *15'*; No. of feet wide, *16*; No. of feet high above land, *13*

No. of stories high, *one*; Style of roof, *flat*; Material of roofing, *tar & gravel*

Of what material will the extension be built? *wood* Foundation? *stone piers*

If of brick, what will be the thickness of external walls? inches; and party walls inches.

Will the extension be placed within 30 feet of the present or proposed street line?

How will the extension be occupied? *religious services* Connection with main building? *yes*

Distance from surrounding buildings:—

Front, feet; side, feet; side, feet; rear, feet.

What distance from the lines of the adjoining lots will be placed?

IF MOVED, RAISED OR BUILT UPON.

No. of stories high of when moved, raised or built upon, Proposed foundations?

No. of feet high from level of ground to highest part of roof,

Distance from surrounding buildings:—

Front, feet; side, feet; side, feet; rear, feet.

Distance back from line of street, Distance from nearest line of lot,

Will roof be flat, pitch, hip, or mansard? What will be the material of roofing?

How many feet will the external wall be increased in height?

How many feet will the party walls be increased in height?

How will the building be occupied after alterations?

IF ANY PORTION OF THE EXTERNAL OR PARTY WALLS ARE REMOVED

Will an opening be made in the party or external walls *yes* on *1st* story.

What will be the size of the opening? *12'* feet wide; *9* feet high.

How will the remaining portion of the wall be supported?

If by iron or stone lintels, give size,

If iron columns are used, give diameter, inches; and thickness of shell, inches.

If brick piers are used, give size,

[OVER.]

IF THE BUILDING IS TO BE OCCUPIED FOR A TENEMENT OR LODGING HOUSE

How many families will occupy each floor? .... Whole number ....

What is the distance from surrounding buildings? .... feet front; .... feet side; .... feet rear

Number of water-closets provided .... Where located? ....

Will all sleeping-rooms and water-closets open to the external air? ....

What will be the means of egress in case of fire? .... If by escape, where located? ....

Is the lower story to be used for business purposes? .... Will the hall partitions be built of brick? ....

Heights of each story in the clear—1st ....; 2d ....; 3d ....; 4th ....;

SIGNATURE, Morris Fried

ADDRESS, 13 Cooks St

NOTICE:—Present Permit at the office of Supt. of Streets, City Hall, for occupation of Sidewalk or Street.

No. 115

Book 2.

Building Permit.

#36291

CITY OF NEWTON,

City Hall, West Newton, Sept. 13, ~~189~~ 1911

Permission is hereby granted Morris Fried

to make alterations to wooden building

on 97 Dalby St Ward 1

to be used for place of public meeting, Jewish Congregation

By Order of the Mayor and Aldermen.

Frank M. Grant. *City Clerk.*

No. 5057

Application for Permit for Repairs, Alterations, Etc.

LOCATION.

No. Street, 97 Dalby Ward, 1

Owner, Morris Fried

Architect,

Builder, " "

PERMIT GRANTED.

Sept. 14, 1911 ~~190~~

13. Registry of Deeds, Book 3920, pages 418–422, 97 Dalby Street, Fried discharge of Mortgage, 13 October 1914

3920
418

... A. Pryor and acknowledged the foregoing instrument to be his free act and deed before me Herbert P. Sheldon Notary Public (Notarial seal)

Middlesex ss. Oct. 13, 1914. 9h.0m. A.M. Recd. & Recorded

Fried
Disc. Mort

Know all Men by these Presents. that I, Morris Fried owner and present holder of a certain mortgage given by Keneses Isreal Anshe Sephard F. H. Denning Morris Greenwald William Perlmutter Trustees to Morris Fried dated June 5 A.D. 1912 and recorded with the Middlesex So. Dist. Registry of Deeds, book 3721 page 76 do hereby acknowledge that I have received full payment and satisfaction of the debt thereby secured and of the conditions therein contained and in consideration thereof I do hereby cancel and discharge said mortgage. In witness whereof I hereunto set my hand and seal this 15th day of June A.D. 1914 Morris Fried (seal) Signed and sealed in the presence of Maurice S. Perlmutter Commonwealth of Massachusetts Middlesex ss. June 15th 1914 Then personally appeared the above-named Morris Fried and acknowledged the foregoing instrument to be his free act and deed, before me Maurice S. Perlmutter Justice

Middlesex, ss. Oct. 13, 1914. 9h. 17m. A.M. Recd. & Recorded

Keneses Israel
Anshe Sephard
Vote

Newton, Mass., June 15 1914.

At a meeting of the Members of Keneses Israel Anshe Sephard held this day a quorum being present on motion made and seconded, it was voted that the property at 17 Dalby Street shall be sold and that the trustees be and hereby are authorized and given full authority to sign and seal with the corporate seal, acknowledge and deliver in the name and behalf of said Corporation of the deed of said property, A true copy attest. Maurice S. Perlmutter Sec. Middlesex ss. October 10, 1914 Then personally appeared the above-named Maurice S. Perlmutter and acknowledged the foregoing instrument to be his free act and deed, before me Edwin O. Childs Jr. Justice of the Peace.

Keneses Israel Anshe
Sephards Trs.
to
Calingiri et ux

Know all Men by these Presents that Keneses Israel Anshe Sephard a corporation duly established by law and having a usual place of business in Newton in the County of Middlesex and Commonwealth of Massachusetts in consideration of one dollar and other valuable considerations paid by Dominick Calingiri and Rose Calingiri his wife of said Newton in the County and Commonwealth aforesaid the receipt whereof is hereby acknowledged, do here...

3920
419

by give, grant, bargain, sell and convey unto the said Dominick Calingiri and Rose Calingiri a certain parcel of land with the buildings thereon situated on the westerly side of Dalby Street in said Newton being lot No. 9 on a plan of lots owned by Josiah Rutter and John Moore in Newton drawn by Jos. H. Curtis and dated August 1869 and recorded with Middlesex South District Deeds Book of Plans 17 Plan 61 and bounded and described as follows: Beginning at the southeasterly corner of the granted premises and thence running northerly bounded easterly on Dalby Street sixty (60) feet more or less to land now or formerly of one Canfield; thence westerly bounded northerly on said Canfield's land one hundred eleven and 9/10 (111.9) feet more or less to land now or formerly of the Dalby Mills Company; thence southerly bounded westerly by said Company's land sixty and 20/100 (60.20) feet to land now or formerly of one Murphy known as lot No. 7 thence easterly bounded southerly on said Murphy's land one hundred seventeen and 0/10 (117.0) feet to the point of beginning at Dalby Street containing 6882 square feet more or less and being the same premises conveyed to Fried by Murphy by deed recorded with said Middlesex Deeds Book 3601 Page 300 Said premises are hereby conveyed subject to mortgages to Newton Savings Bank amounting to $1300. and subject also to taxes due the City of Newton for the current year To Have and to Hold the granted premises, with all the privileges and appurtenances thereto belonging to the said Dominick Calingiri and Rose Calingiri and their heirs and assigns to their own use and behoof forever. And said corporation does hereby, for itself and its successors and assigns covenant with the said grantees and their heirs and assigns that it is lawfully seized in fee simple of the granted premises, that they are free from all incumbrances except as aforesaid that it has good right to sell and convey the same as aforesaid; and that it will and its successors and assigns shall warrant and defend the same to the said grantees and their heirs and assigns forever against the lawful claims and demands of all persons except as aforesaid In witness whereof the said Corporation by its Trustees hereunto duly authorized hereunto sets its hand and corporate seal this first day of October in the year one thousand nine hundred and four

3920
420

tees Harry Perlmutter Chas. Russeck Frederick R. Denning Trustees Keneses Israel Anshe Sephard (Corporate seal) Signed sealed and delivered in presence of Maurice S. Perlmutter Commonwealth of Massachusetts Middlesex ss. October 3rd 1914 Then personally appeared the above named Harry Perlmutter Trustee and acknowledged the foregoing instrument to be his free act and deed before me, Maurice S Perlmutter Justice of the Peace. Middlesex ss. Oct. 13, 1914. 5h. 17m. A.M. Recd. + Recorded

One word stricken out + "61" over erasure.

Calingiri et ux to Fried.

Know all Men by these Presents that We Dominick Calingiri and Rose Calingiri his wife both of Newton in the County of Middlesex and Commonwealth of Massachusetts in consideration of five hundred dollars paid by Morris Fried of Newton in the County and Commonwealth aforesaid the receipt whereof is hereby acknowledged do hereby give, grant, bargain, sell and convey unto the said Morris Fried a certain parcel of land with the buildings thereon situated in said Newton on the westerly side of Dalby Street being lot numbered nine (9) on a plan of lots owned by Josiah Rutter and John Moore in Newton Mass. drawn by Jos. R. Curtis and dated August 1869 and recorded in Middlesex South District Deeds Book of Plans 17 plan 61 for a fuller description of which see deed of Murphy to Fried recorded with said deeds Book 3601 Page 300. Being the same premises conveyed to us by deed of Keneses Israel Anshe Sephard of even date herewith to be recorded. To Have and to Hold the granted premises, with all the privileges and appurtenances thereto belonging, to the said Morris Fried and his heirs and assigns to their own use and behoof forever. And we hereby for ourselves and our heirs, executors and administrators, covenant with the grantee and his heirs and assigns that we are lawfully seized in fee simple of the granted premises that they are free from all incumbrances, excepting mortgages upon which $1300 of principal remains unpaid given by Fried to Newton Savings Bank dated May 9th A.D. 1911 and recorded with Middlesex County Deeds Book 3602 Page 322 and Book 3657 Page 195 that we have good right to sell and convey the same as aforesaid; and that we will and our heirs, executors, and administrators shall warrant and defend the same to the grantee and his heirs and assigns forever against the lawful claims and demands of all persons. Provided

421

nevertheless that if we, or our heirs, executors, administrators or assigns, shall pay unto the grantee, or his executors, administrators or assigns, <u>the sum of five hundred dollars</u> in <u>one year from this date, with interest semi-annually</u> at <u>the rate of six per</u> cent per annum and until such payment shall pay all taxes and assessments, to whomsoever laid or assessed, whether on the granted premises or on any interest therein or on the debt secured hereby; shall keep the buildings on said premises insured against fire in a sum not less than, dollars, for the benefit of the grantee, and, executors, administrators, and assigns, in such from and at such insurance offices as they shall approve and, at least two days before the expiration of any policy on said premises, shall deliver to, or them a new and sufficient policy to take the place of the one so expiring and shall not commit or suffer any strip or waste of the granted premises, or any breach of any covenant or condition contained in said other mortgages or herein contained then this deed, as also our note of even date herewith, signed by us whereby we promise to pay to the grantee, or order, the said principal sum and instalments of interest at the time aforesaid, shall be void. But upon any default in the performance or observance of the fregoing condition or of the condition of said other mortgages the grantee, or his executors administrators, or assigns may sell the granted premises or such portion thereof as may remain subject to this mortgage in case of any partial release therefrom together with all improvements that may be thereon, by public auction in said Newton first publishing a notice of the time and place of sale once each week for three successive weeks in some one newspaper published in said Newton the first publication of such notice to be not less than twenty one days before the day of sale and may convey the same by proper deed or deeds to the purchaser or purchasers absolutely and in fee simple; and such sale shall forever bar us and all persons claiming under us from all right and interest in the granted premises, whether at law or in equity. And out of money arising from such sale the grantee or his representatives shall be entitled to retain all sums then secured by this deed whether then or thereafter payable, including all payments, costs charges, and expenses made

422

incurred or sustained by them by reason of any default in the performance or observance of the condition of this deed or of the said other mortgages rendering the surplus if any, to us or our heirs, or assigns; and we hereby, for ourselves and our heirs and assigns, covenant with the grantee and his heirs, executors administrators, and assigns that, in case a sale shall be made under the foregoing power we or they will upon request execute, acknowledge, and deliver to the purchaser or purchasers a deed or deeds of release confirming such sale and said grantee and his assigns are hereby appointed and constituted the attorney or attorneys irrevocable of the said grantor to execute and deliver to the said purchaser a full transfer of all policies of insurance on the buildings upon the land covered by this mortgage at the time of such sale. And it is agreed that the grantee, or his executors, administrators, or assigns, or any person or persons in their behalf, may purchase at any sale made as aforesaid, and that no other purchaser shall be answerable for the application of the purchase money; and that, until default in the performance or observance of the condition of this deed, we and our heirs and assigns may hold and enjoy the granted premises and receive the rents and profits thereof. In witness whereof we the said Dominick Calingiri and Rose Calingiri hereunto set our hands and seals this first day of October in the year one thousand nine hundred and fourteen. Dominick Calingiri (seal) Rose Calingiri (seal) Signed and sealed in presence of Maurice S. Perlmutter Commonwealth of Massachusetts Middlesex ss. October 3rd, 1914. Then personally appeared the above named Dominick Calingiri & Rose Calingiri and acknowledged the foregoing instrument to be their free act and deed, before me _ Maurice S Perlmutter Justice of the Peace. Middlesex, ss. Oct, 13, 1914. 5h. 17m. A.M. Rec'd. & Recorded

14. Registry of Deeds, Book 4342, pages 129-130, Confirmation of Deed from Keneses Israel Anshei Sfard to Fried, 15 April 1920

4342

129

strument to be his free act and deed, before me, Patrick J. Delaney, Notary Public. My commission expires Oct. 29, 1926. - - - - - - - - -

Middlesex ss. April 15, 1920. 1h. 23m. P.M. Rec'd & Recorded.

KNOW ALL MEN BY THESE PRESENTS that we, Reuben Slesinger, Julius Pass and Abraham Shrier, sometimes written Shreir, named as Trustees of Keneses Israel Anshe Sephard, a religious corporation organized under the laws of the Commonwealth of Massachusetts, and located at Newton, Massachusetts, in a deed by Thomas J. Kenny and Elihu G. Loomis surviving trustees under the will of George W. Morse, dated March first, 1910, and recorded with Middlesex South District Deeds, Book 3521, Page 385, conveying to us as Trustees as aforesaid the premises hereinafter described, do hereby certify and declare that the trust under which we acquired the premises thereby conveyed was for the sole benefit of said Keneses Israel Anshe Sephard Corporation. And we further certify and declare that Abram Shrier, Max Canter and Joseph Hoffman, the grantors, as Trustees of said Keneses Israel Anshe Sephard Corporation, in a deed of said premises, to Morris Fried, dated June 14, 1911, and recorded with said Deeds in Book 3614, Page 188, were the duly appointed and qualified successors of us as Trustees under said trust said deed being executed and delivered in conformance with a vote of the Keneses Israel Anshe Sephard Corporation appended to said deed, and Whereas it is desired to perfect and confirm the legal title of said premises conveyed by said last mentioned deed in said Morris Fried and those lawfully claiming title under him; Now, for consideration paid, we, the said Reuben Slesinger, Julius Pass and Abraham Shrier, Trustees as aforesaid, hereby remise, release and forever QUITCLAIM to the said Morris Fried and those lawfully claiming title under him, all that parcel of land with any buildings thereon, situated in that part of NEWTON Middlesex County, Massachusetts, called Nonantum, being lot number forty, as shown on a Plan of land in Nonantum Park, Newton, belonging to the American Land Company, dated May 5, 1903, and recorded with said Deeds, Book of Plans 143, Plan 6. TO HAVE AND TO HOLD the granted premises with all the privileges and appurtenances thereto belonging to the said Morris Fried and those lawfully claiming title under him according to their respective interests and estates therein, and to his and their respective heirs and assigns forever. IN WITNESS WHEREOF as Trustees as aforesaid we hereunto set our hands and seals this tenth day of April A.D. 1920. Julius Pass (seal) Abram. Shrier (seal) Reuben

KENESES ISRAEL ANSHE SEPHARD AT NEWTON'S TRS. to FRIED et al

Slesinger (seal) Trustees of Keneses Israel Anshe Sephard Corporation. COMMONWEALTH OF MASSACHUSETTS. Middlesex ss. Newton, Apl. 14, 1920. Then personally appeared the above named Julius Pass Abram Shrier & Reuben Slesinger and acknowledged the foregoing instrument to be his free act and deed as Trustee as aforesaid, before me, Reuben Forknall, Justice of the Peace. -

Middlesex ss. April 17, 1920. 12h. 47m. P.M. Rec'd & Recorded.

KENESES ISRAEL ANSHE SEPHARD AT NEWTON'S TRS.
to
FRIED et al
CONF.

KNOW ALL MEN BY THESE PRESENTS that we, Abram Shrier sometimes written Shreir, Max Canter and Joseph Hoffman as Trustees of the Keneses Israel Anshe Sephard, a corporation duly established under the laws of the Commonwealth of Massachusetts, successors in said trust of Reuben Slesinger, Julius Pass and Abraham Shrier, by power conferred by vote of said Corporation dated June 11, 1911, duly recorded with Middlesex South District Deeds, Book 3614, Page 188, and every other power for consideration paid, grant to Morris Fried and those lawfully claiming title under him according to their respective interests and estates therein, and to his and their respective heirs and assigns forever all that parcel of land with any buildings thereon situated in that part of NEWTON, Middlesex County, Massachusetts, called Nonantum, being lot number forty, as shown on a Plan of land in Nonantum Park, Newton, belonging to the American Land Company, dated May 5, 1903, and recorded with said Deeds, Book of Plans 143, Plan 6, hereby ratifying and confirming the deed made by us as Trustees as aforesaid and of said Keneses Israel Anshe Sephard Corporation to said Morris Fried dated June 14, 1911, duly recorded with said Deeds Book 3614, Page 188. IN WITNESS WHEREOF as Trustees as aforesaid we hereunto set our hands and seals this tenth day of April A.D. 1920. Abram. Shrier (seal) Max Canter (seal) Joseph Hoffman (seal) COMMONWEALTH OF MASSACHUSETTS. Middlesex ss. Newton Apl. 14, 1920. Then personally appeared the above named Abram Shrier, Max Canter & Joseph Hoffman and acknowledged the foregoing instrument to be his free act and deed as Trustee as aforesaid; before me, Reuben Forknall, Justice of the Peace. - - - - - - - - - - -

Middlesex ss. April 17, 1920. 12h. 47m. P.M. Rec'd & Recorded.

APPENDIX B

All the documents referring to Congregation Agudas Achim Anshei Sfard are included in this Appendix. All documents are located in the South Middlesex Country Registry of Deeds, Cambridge MA.

---

1. Commonwealth of MA, Charter of Congregation Agudas Achim Anshei Sfard, 6 October 1911

We, Benjamin Gilfix President, Jacob Swartz Treasurer, and Joseph Mielman Clerk, and Joseph Roiter, Jacob Kligman and Hyman Mielman

Congregation Agudas Achim Anshai Sfard of Newton

Certificate of Organization.

Filed Oct. 6, 1911.

Fee, $5.00 paid.

being a majority of the directors of Congregation Agudas Achim Anshai Sfard of Newton in compliance with the requirements of the sixth section of chapter one hundred and twenty five of the Revised Laws, do hereby certify that the following is a true copy of the agreement of association to constitute said Corporation, with the names of the subscribers thereto:—

"We, whose names are hereto subscribed, do, by this agreement, associate ourselves with the intention to constitute a Corporation according to the provisions of the one hundred and twenty-fifth chapter of the Revised Laws of the Commonwealth of Massachusetts, and the Acts in amendment thereof and in addition thereto.

The name by which the Corporation shall be known is Congregation Agudas Achim Anshai Sfard of Newton

The purpose for which the Corporation is constituted is conducting religious meetings and ceremonies

The place within which the Corporation is established or located, is the City of Newton within said Commonwealth.

The amount of its capital stock is ______ dollars. The par value of its shares is ______ dollars. The number of its shares is ______

We hereby waive all requirements of the statutes of Massachusetts for notice of the first meeting for organization, and appoint the twenty-second day of July 1911 at 8.30 o'clock p. M., at 93 West St., Newton, Mass. as the time and place of holding said first meeting.

In Witness Whereof, we have hereunto set our hands, this twenty-second day of July in the year nineteen hundred and eleven.

Benjamin Gilfix
Joseph Roiter
Hyman Mielman
Jacob Kligman
Morris Gilfix
Joseph Mielman
Jacob Swartz

That the first meeting of the subscribers to said agreement was held on the twenty-second, day of July in the year nineteen hundred and eleven.

In Witness Whereof, we have hereunto signed our names, this twenty-second day of July in the year nineteen hundred and eleven.

Benjamin Gilfix
Jacob Swartz
Joseph Roiter
Hyman Mielman
Jacob Kligman
Morris Gilfix
Joseph Mielman

The Commonwealth of Massachusetts, Middlesex ss. Newton, Mass., July 22, 1911.

Then personally appeared the above-named Benjamin Gilfix, Jacob Swartz, Joseph Roiter, Hyman Mielman, Jacob Kligman, Morris Gilfix and Joseph Mielman

and severally made oath that the foregoing certificate, by them subscribed, is true, to the best of their knowledge and belief. Before me, Abraham Leventall
Justice of the Peace.

I hereby certify that it appears, upon an examination of the within-written certificate and the records of the corporation duly submitted to my inspection, that the requirements of sections one, two and three of chapter one hundred and twenty-five, and sections fifteen to twenty, inclusive, of chapter one hundred and ten of the Revised Laws have been complied with, and I hereby approve said certificate this twenty-fourth day of July A.D. nineteen hundred and eleven.

William D. T. Trefry Commissioner of Corporations.

Charter issued Oct. 6, 1911, to Congregation Agudas Achim Anshai Sfard of Newton as a new Corporation, a copy of which charter, or certificate of incorporation, is recorded in Charter Book, No. 262, Page 254.

Fee, $5.00 paid.

Congregation Agudas Achim Anshai Sfard of Newton | Newton

Application withdrawn July 24, 1911.

Organization approved by Commissioner of Corporations, July 16, 1911.

Congregation Agudas Achim Anshai Sfard of Newton | Newton

DATE INCORP. Oct. 6, 1911.
CHARTER 262-254
ORGANIZATION 272-365
CHANGE OF NAME

DUNN & CO. INC. MFRS. 9790

2. Commonwealth of MA, Incorporation of Congregation Agudas Achim Anshei Sfard, pages 1-2, handwritten

254

The Commonwealth of Massachusetts

Be it Known *That whereas* Benjamin Gilfix, Jacob Swartz, Joseph Mielman, Joseph Roiter, Jacob Kligman, Hyman Mielman and Morris Gilfix

have associated themselves with the intention of forming a corporation under the name of the Congregation Agudas Achim Anshai Sfard of Newton,

for the purpose of conducting religious meetings and ceremonies,

and have complied with the provisions of the statutes of this Commonwealth in such case made and provided, as appears from the certificate of the President, Treasurer, Clerk and Directors *of said corporation, duly approved by the Commissioner of Corporations and recorded in this office:*

Now, Therefore, I, ~~WILLIAM M. OLIN,~~ Albert P. Langtry, *Secretary of The Commonwealth of Massachusetts,* DO HEREBY CERTIFY *that said* Benjamin Gilfix, Jacob Swartz, Joseph Mielman, Joseph Roiter, Jacob Kligman, Hyman Mielman and Morris Gilfix,

their associates and successors, are legally organized and established as, and are hereby made, an existing corporation under the name of the Congregation Agudas Achim Anshai Sfard of Newton, *with the powers, rights and privileges, and subject to the limitations, duties and restrictions, which by law appertain thereto.*

Witness *my official signature hereunto subscribed, and the Great Seal of The Commonwealth of Massachusetts hereunto affixed, this* sixth *day of* October *in the year of our Lord on thousand nine hundred and* eleven.

{ L.S. }

[Signed] Albert P. Langtry

3. Commonwealth of MA, Incorporation of Congregation Agudas Achim Anshei Sfard, pages 1-2, typed

The Commonwealth of Massachusetts

Be it Known That whereas Benjamin Gilfix, Jacob Swartz, Joseph Mielman, Joseph Roiter, Jacob Kligman, Hyman Mielman and Morris Gilfix have associated themselves with the intention of forming a corporation under the name of the Congregation Agudas Achim Anshai Sfard of Newton,

for the purpose of conducting religious meetings and ceremonies,

and have complied with the provisions of the statutes of this Commonwealth in such case made and provided, as appears from the certificate of the President, Treasurer, Clerk and Directors of said corporation, duly approved by the Commissioner of Corporations and recorded in this office:

Now, Therefore, I, ALBERT P. LANGTRY, Secretary of The Commonwealth of Massachusetts, DO HEREBY CERTIFY that said Benjamin Gilfix, Jacob Swartz, Joseph Mielman, Joseph Roiter, Jacob Kligman, Hyman Mielman and Morris Gilfix, their associates and successors, are legally organized and established as, and are hereby made, an existing corporation under the name of the Congregation Agudas Achim Anshai Sfard of Newton, with the powers, rights and privileges, and subject to the limitations, duties and restrictions, which by law appertain thereto.

Witness my official signature hereunto subscribed, and the Great Seal of The Commonwealth of Massachusetts hereunto affixed, this sixth day of October in the year of our Lord one thousand nine hundred and eleven.

Albert P. Langtry
Secretary of the Commonwealth.

4. Registry of Deeds, Book 3670, page 556, Deed to Adams Street, Stanton to Swartz, 15 February 1912

3670
556

Stanton et al.
to
Swartz

Know all men by these presents

that we, Louis C. Stanton and S. Emma Stanton, his wife, in her right, both of Newton, in the County of Middlesex and Commonwealth of Massachusetts

in consideration of One dollar and other valuable considerations

paid by Jacob Swartz of said Newton,

the receipt whereof is hereby acknowledged, do hereby remise, release, and forever **quitclaim** unto the said Jacob Swartz, his heirs and assigns, A certain parcel of land situated on the Northeasterly side of Adams Street in said Newton, and bounded as follows: Beginning at the Westerly corner of said premises and running Northeasterly on land of owners unknown one hundred feet to other land of the grantors, thence turning at a right angle and running Southeasterly on said other land of grantors sixty feet; thence turning at a right angle and running Southwesterly on a proposed court or private driveway one hundred feet to Adams Street, thence turning and running Northwesterly on Adams Street about sixty feet to the point of beginning. Containing about 6000 square feet of land, more or less. Being a portion of lot numbered nineteen on a plan recorded with Middlesex South District Deeds, Book of Plans 16, plan 60.

To have and to hold the granted premises, with all the privileges and appurtenances thereto belonging to the said Jacob Swartz and his heirs and assigns, to their own use and behoof forever. And we do hereby for ourselves and our heirs, executors and administrators, **covenant** with the said grantee and her heirs and assigns that the granted premises are free from all incumbrances made or suffered by us,

and that we will and our heirs, executors, and administrators shall **warrant and defend** the same to the said grantee and her heirs and assigns forever against the lawful claims and demands of all persons claiming by, through, or under us but against none other.

In witness whereof we the said Louis C. Stanton and S. Emma Stanton hereunto set our hands and seals this fifteenth day of February in the year one thousand nine hundred and twelve.

Signed and sealed in the presence of
John T. Burns
Justice of Peace

Louis C. Stanton (seal)
S. Emma Stanton (seal)

Commonwealth of Massachusetts, Middlesex ss. February 15th 1912. Then personally appeared the above named S. Emma Stanton and acknowledged the foregoing instrument to be her free act and deed, before me:— John T. Burns Justice of the Peace.

Middlesex, ss. March 1 1912. At 10 h 10 m. A. M., received and recorded.

5. Registry of Deeds, Book 3670, page 557, Deed to Adams Street, Swartz to Congregation Agudas Achim Anshei Sfard, 23 February 1912

557

Know all men by these presents

I, Jacob Swartz, of Newton, in the County of Middlesex and Commonwealth of Massachusetts

[con]sideration of One dollar and other valuable considerations
[paid] by Congregation Agudas Achim Anashai Sfard, of said Newton, in said County and [Com]monwealth, a religious corporation duly organized under the laws of this Commonwealth
[the r]eceipt whereof is hereby acknowledged, do hereby remise, release, and forever **quitclaim** unto the said Congregation [Ag]udas Achim Anashai Sfard, and its successors and assigns, a certain [par]cel of land situated on the northeasterly side of Adams Street in said [Ne]wton, and bounded as follows:- Beginning at the Westerly corner of said [pr]emises and running Northeasterly on land of owners unknown one [h]undred feet to other land of the grantors, thence turning at a right [a]ngle and running Southeasterly on said other land of grantors [si]xty feet; thence turning at a right angle and running Southwesterly on a proposed court or private driveway one hundred feet to Adams [S]treet; thence turning and running Northwesterly on Adams Street [a]bout sixty feet to the point of beginning. Containing about six thousand [(6]000) square feet of land, more or less. Being a portion of lot numbered [n]ineteen on a plan recorded with Middlesex South District Deeds, Book [of] Plans 16, plan 60. Being the same premises conveyed to me by deed of Emma Stanton, dated February 15, 1912.

Swartz
to
Congregation Agu[das]
Achim Anasha[i]
Sfard

To have and to hold the granted premises, with all the privileges and appurtenances thereto belonging [to] the said Congregation Agudas Achim Anashai Sfard and its successors and assigns, to their own use and behoof forever. And I do hereby for myself and my heirs, executors and administrators, **covenant** with the said grantee and its successors and assigns [th]at the granted premises are free from all incumbrances made or suffered by me

[an]d that I will and my heirs, executors, and administrators shall **warrant and defend** the same to the said grantee [an]d its successors and assigns forever against the lawful claims and demands of all persons claiming by, through, or under me but against none other.
[A]nd for the consideration aforesaid I, Julia Swartz wife of said Jacob Swartz [d]o hereby release unto the said grantee and its successors and assigns all right [of] or to both dower and homestead in the granted premises, and all other [r]ights and interests therein.

In witness whereof we the said Jacob Swartz and Julia Swartz [her]eunto set our hands and seals this twenty-third day of February [in] the year one thousand nine hundred and twelve.

Signed, sealed and delivered
in presence of
Reuben Forknall

Jacob Swartz (seal)
Julia Swartz (seal)

[Co]mmonwealth of Massachusetts, Middlesex ss. February 23d 1912. Then personally appeared [th]e above named Jacob Swartz and acknowledged the foregoing instrument to be his [fr]ee act and deed, before me:— Reuben Forknall Justice of the Peace.

[M]iddlesex, ss. March 1 1912. At 10 h. 10 m. a. M., received and recorded.

Three words stricken out & two interlined

6. Original quitclaim deed to Adams Street, Swartz to Congregation Agudas Achim Anshei Sfard, 1 March 1912

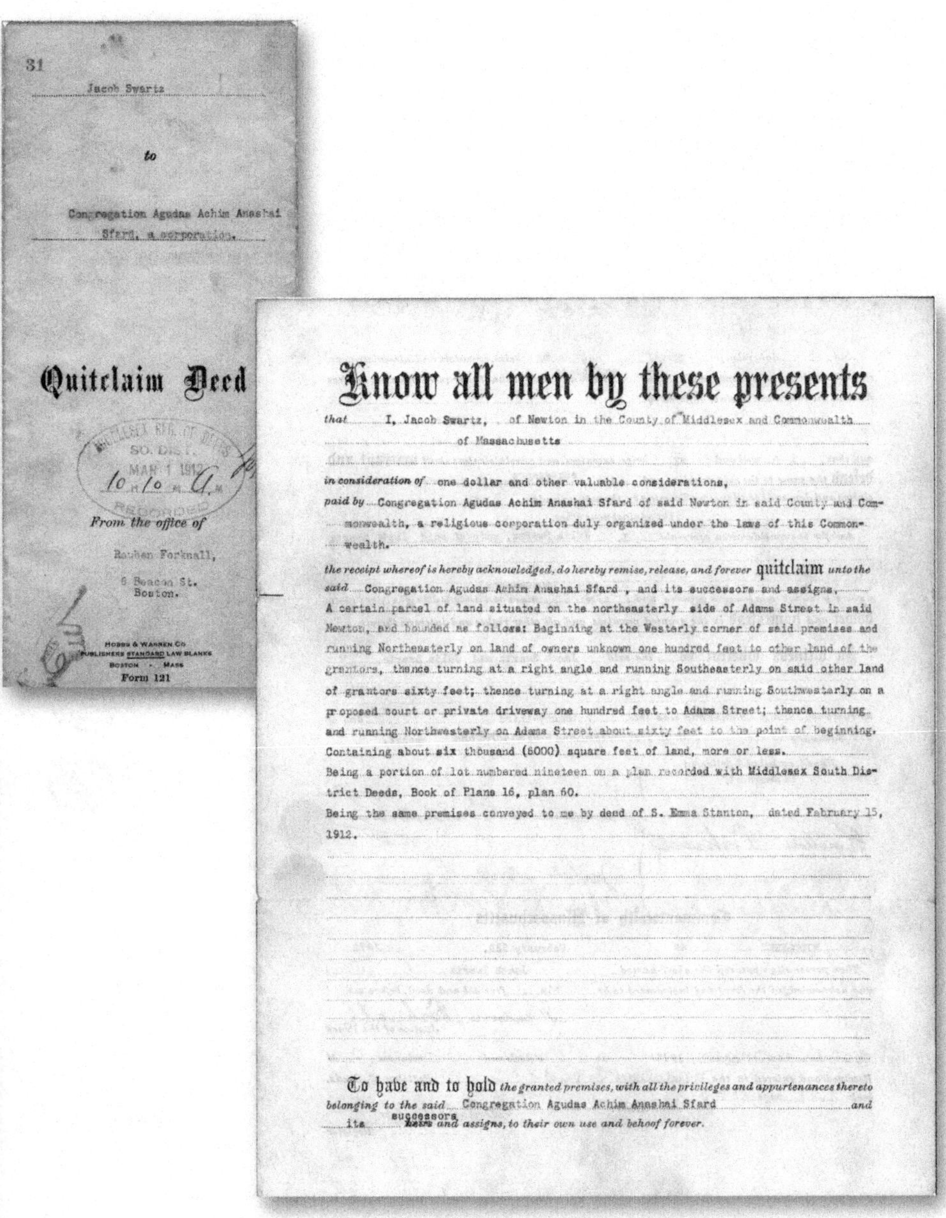

31

Jacob Swartz

to

Congregation Agudas Achim Anashai Sfard, a corporation.

Quitclaim Deed

MIDDLESEX REG. OF DEEDS SO. DIST. MAR 1 1912 10 H 10 M A.M RECORDED

From the office of

Reuben Forknall,

6 Beacon St. Boston.

Hobbs & Warren Co. Publishers Standard Law Blanks Boston Mass

Form 121

Know all men by these presents

that I, Jacob Swartz, of Newton in the County of Middlesex and Commonwealth of Massachusetts

in consideration of one dollar and other valuable considerations,

paid by Congregation Agudas Achim Anashai Sfard of said Newton in said County and Commonwealth, a religious corporation duly organized under the laws of this Commonwealth.

the receipt whereof is hereby acknowledged, do hereby remise, release, and forever **quitclaim** *unto the said* Congregation Agudas Achim Anashai Sfard, and its successors and assigns,

A certain parcel of land situated on the northeasterly side of Adams Street in said Newton, and bounded as follows: Beginning at the Westerly corner of said premises and running Northeasterly on land of owners unknown one hundred feet to other land of the grantors, thence turning at a right angle and running Southeasterly on said other land of grantors sixty feet; thence turning at a right angle and running Southwesterly on a proposed court or private driveway one hundred feet to Adams Street; thence turning and running Northwesterly on Adams Street about sixty feet to the point of beginning. Containing about six thousand (6000) square feet of land, more or less.

Being a portion of lot numbered nineteen on a plan recorded with Middlesex South District Deeds, Book of Plans 16, plan 60.

Being the same premises conveyed to me by deed of S. Emma Stanton, dated February 15, 1912.

To have and to hold *the granted premises, with all the privileges and appurtenances thereto belonging to the said* Congregation Agudas Achim Anashai Sfard *and* its successors *and assigns, to their own use and behoof forever.*

Documents courtesy of Cynthia Spitzer

And I *do hereby, for* myself *and* my *heirs, executors and administrators, covenant with the said grantee and* its successors *and assigns that the granted premises are free from all incumbrances made or suffered by* me

and that I *will and* my *heirs, executors, and administrators shall* **warrant and defend** *the same to the said grantee and* its successors *and assigns forever against the lawful claims and demands of all persons claiming by, through, or under* me

but against none other.

And for the consideration aforesaid I, Julia Swartz, wife of said Jacob Swartz

do hereby release unto the said grantee and its successors *and assigns all right of or to both* **dower** *and* **homestead** *in the granted premises, and all other rights and interests therein.*

In witness whereof We *the said* Jacob Swartz and Julia Swartz,

hereunto set our *hands and seals this* twenty-third *day of* February *in the year one thousand nine hundred and* twelve.

Signed, sealed and delivered in presence of

Reuben Foxknall

Jacob Swartz

Julia Swartz

Commonwealth of Massachusetts

MIDDLESEX ss. February 23d, 1912

Then personally appeared the above-named Jacob Swartz *and acknowledged the foregoing instrument to be* his *free act and deed, before me*

Reuben Foxknall
Justice of the Peace

Cambridge March 1, 1912 *at* 10 *o'clock and* 10 *minutes* A *M*
Received and entered in the Middlesex So. Dist. *Registry of Deeds, book* 3670 *page* 557

Attest: Edwin O. Childs
Register

7. Plot Plan, Adams Street

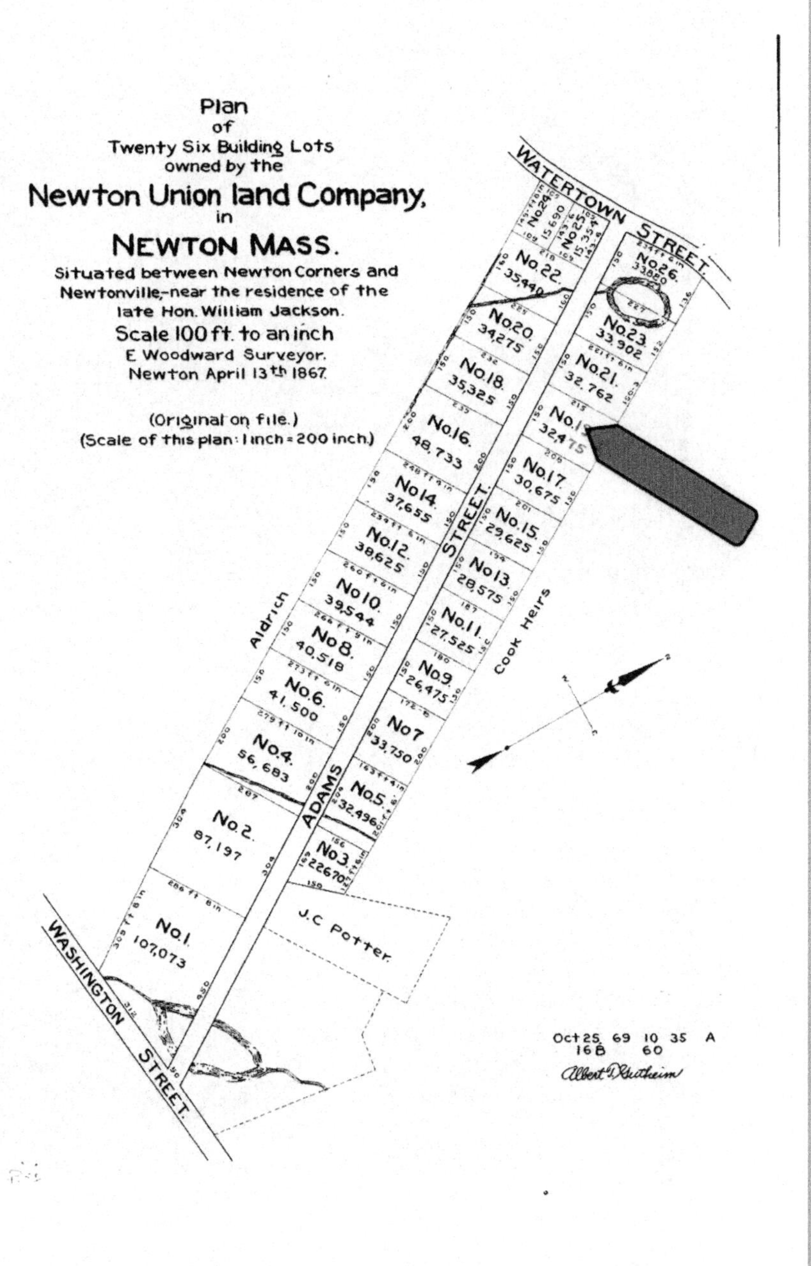

8. Cover of original donation record book

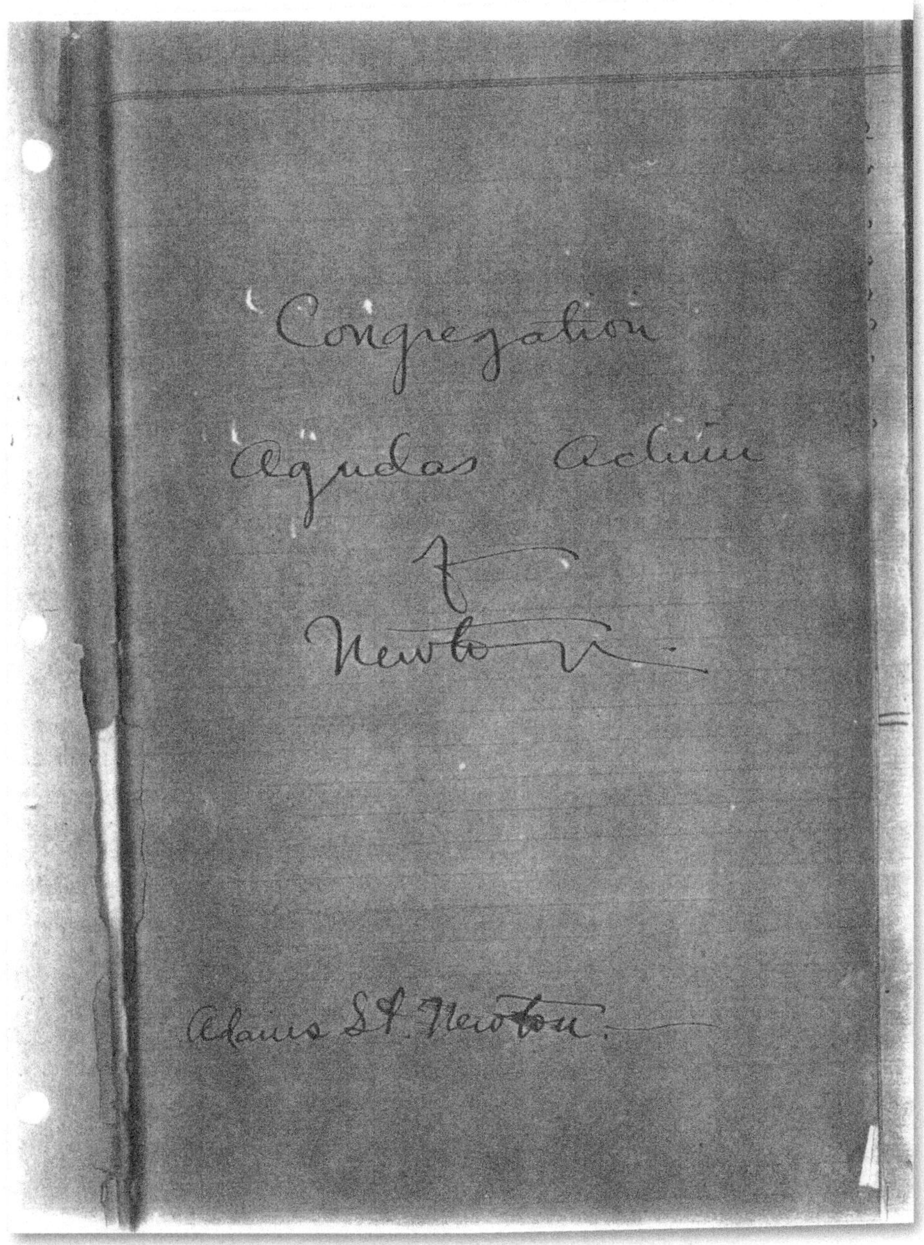

9. Original handwritten solicitation document (3 pages)

Whereas, — The almighty has endowed the said Hebrews of Newton with greater zeal and religious fervor than worldly goods, and—

Whereas, — What little could be spared by individual members of the faith, has been dedicated to the founding of a Jewish Synagogue and Talmud Torah (Sabbath School), — it has been

Resolved, — by the members of the Congregation Agudas Achim of Newton, Mass, to make known to their friends and wellwishers, their aims and aspirations

—— || ——

Ever since the Hebrews first began to settle in this community, some fifteen years ago, their potency as a religious factor has been smothered by the fact that lack of means and accommodations necessitated extremely hardy measures to be adopted. Their inherent nature and nurture demanded that the Sabbath continue to be observed and that their children receive the same religious training that their fathers had received in better circumstances and perhaps more congenial surroundings. To this end and according to the Mosaic Law, religious meetings were conducted every

Sabbath day and other Holy days, despite the antagonistic means and surroundings. Now here now there, the members of the Congregation, yet without a central place of worship, contributing occasionally the services of their homes, for religious uses.

Discouraging as such shifting methods of worship were, there was nevertheless enshrouded in this a blessing in disguise. Philosophy teaches us ~~that~~ the world progresses truly, only after the endurance of a pain economy. That is, the burden of trials and tribulations, however weighty, are the essentials which lead to the ultimate increase of human happiness. Thus it was with these few Hebrew endeavorers. Lacking in religious atmosphere, and immediate prospects very dim, they only hoped and prayed for the time when a temple would stand in their midst that might take its place among others as a token of real reverence to the Almighty, who is One.

After all these years, under the constant leadership of their guiding spirit, a mighty effort was made and the blossom of their hope began to bear fruit. Immediate plans for the erection of a Synagogue were drawn up, even before it was known whence the funds for this purpose were to come. Disregarding this, ~~the~~ work was pushed, all gave what might be easily spared without detriment to the welfare of their families and soon the realization of their highest aims was a fact. Attesting to this, there now stands in our midst, a House of Worship, simple and unostentatious though it be, a monument to those whose highest hopes and aspirations made the desire father to the fact.

Our message to our friends, well-wishers, benefactors, and all others interested is one of faith in mankind. We feel that you all as members of organized religion and society and every one believes in the Unity of God, will do all in your power to assist a movement of this kind that it may not fail of its ultimate success. Your beneficence will remain as a beacon-light to posterity, a veritable tower of fire in fact to guide the youth into the hallowed dominion of the Brotherhood of Man.

[The worthiness of this movement is attested to by the written acknowledgment of leading Rabbis of Boston, proof of which may be found in the back part of this volume. Rabbi Friedman and Rabbi Rabinovitz have here testified in their own hands to the sincerity of purpose of the Hebrews of Newton.]

10. Donors in original solicitation book (6 pages)

1

Contributors. —
[Order in point of time] —

		$
Isaac Heller,	of Boston —	50.00
Zoblatsky & Co,	" Chelsea —	5.00
Jacob Swartz,	" Newton —	25.00
H. Godfried,	" Melrose —	1.00
Benj. Gilfix,	" Newton —	25.00
S. Rosenbaum,	" Watertown —	20.00
Hyman Gilfix,	" Newton —	10.00
Louis Baker,	" " —	25.00
Joseph Berman,	" Waltham —	25.00
M. Bluestone,	" Watertown —	5.00
R. Zelenetsky,	" Waltham —	25.00
Louis Berman,	" " —	10.00
Abr. Pass,	" Newton —	5.00
H. Perry,	" " —	10.00
H. Shelman,	" " —	5.00
Max Standel,	" Watertown —	25.00
Abr. Luff,	" Wellesley —	5.00
M. Shafran,	" Boston —	5.00
A. Shreier,	" Newton —	10.00
S. Rabinovitz,	" Waltham —	3.00
H. Greenblatt,	" Waltham —	2.00
Sapovitz,	" " —	5.00
Katz,	" " —	3.00
Dubinsky,	" " —	3.00
Morris Gilfix,	" Newton —	25.00
H. Yanco,	" " —	1.00
D. Bronfman,	" " —	5.00
Hy. Meilman,	" " —	10.00
L. Tippin	" " —	3.00
M. Greenwald	" " —	1.00
J. H. Eustis	" " —	5.00
S. Moranis	" Boston —	1.00
Sam Bram,	" Newton —	5.00

Continued: —

Name		Town	$
Jos. Meilman,	of	Newton	2.00.
Jac. Neiberg	"	Watertown	5.00
M. Godfried	"	Melrose	5.00
Niedelman	"	Saxonville	1.00
M. Cohen	"	Watertown	3.00
S. Perry	"	Newton	2.00
Har. Meilman	"	Boston	1.00
P. Shriberg	"	Newton	5.00
J. Kligman	"	"	5.00
A. Frackman	"	"	10.00
Jac. Meilman	"	"	5.00
M. Silverman	"	"	5.00
J. Roiter	"	"	5.00
H. Frackman	"	"	1.00
J. Kligman	"	"	1.00
Max Meilman	"	"	5.00
Max Canter	"	"	3.00
S. Hurwitz, Rev.	"	Malden	1.00
W.J. Holmes,	"	Newton	1.00
Dr. Fucco	"	"	5.00
Mrs. Godfriend	"	Melrose	2.00
" Swartz	"	Newton	5.00
" Perry	"	"	3.00
" Zelenetzky	"	Waltham	10.00
" Frackman	"	Newton	5.00
" Baker	"	"	5.00
" Fuff	"	Wellesley	2.00
" Kligman	"	Newton	2.00
" M. Gilfix	"	"	1.00
" Shelman	"	"	1.00
" Standel	"	Watertown	1.00
" Silverman	"	Newton	1.00
" M. Milman	"	Newton	1.00
" S. Bram	"	"	1.00

Continued:—

		$
Mrs. Lippin	of Newton	10.00
" Niberg	" Watertown	1.00
" Yanco	" Newton	1.00
" Canter	" "	1.00
Miss L. Godfried	" "	5.00
Mrs. Bitman	" "	1.00
" S. Perry	" Newton	2.00
Miss R. Bulman	" "	1.00
" M. Baker	" "	1.00
" R. Shriberg	" "	1.00
" G. Swartz	" "	1.00
" M. Milman	" "	1.00
" Esth White	" "	2.00
" Roiter	" "	1.00
" G. Perry	" "	1.00
" M. Hoffman	" "	1.00
" R. Gilfix	" "	1.00
" P. Trackman	" "	1.00
Mrs. B. Gilfix	" "	5.00
" Shafran	" "	1.00
" Shreier	" "	1.00
American Grocery Co,	of Boston	10.00
H. Gussman	" "	5.00
M. Wyner	" "	5.00
Bay State Grocery Co	" "	5.00
S. Abramson	" "	1.00
Morris Oxman	" "	1.00
K. Kalman	" "	1.00
H. Slobodkin	" "	5.00
L. Shain	" Newton	2.00
C. Newcomb	" "	1.00
S. Fuller	" "	1.00
S.Y. Goldings	" Boston	1.00
Swenson Bros	" "	5.00

7

Continued:—

Ph. Swachman	of Boston Not Paid 2.00	3.00
Ch. Shafin	" "	3.00
I. Frost	" Newton	1.00
J. Shaffer	" Boston	1.00
Oppenheim Bros	" "	3.00
Knigle	" "	1.00
Hershman	" "	1.00
Jac. Bressler	" Maynard	10.00
S. Berman	" Boston	5.00
J. Fuff	" Waverley	1.00
M. Baker	" Waltham	1.00
J. Cohen	" "	1.00
M. Berman	" "	1.00
P. Levin	" "	1.00
H. Gilleson	" "	1.00
H. Sherzon	" "	1.00
Kaplan	" "	2.00
Alpert	" "	1.00
Rosenberg	" "	1.00
S. Cantor	" "	5.00
B. Rabovoy	" "	1.00
Alderman Lifton	of Waltham	5.00
H. Katz	" "	2.00
Allen	" "	1.00
Alpert	" "	1.00
Sohan	" "	1.00
L. Knijnik	" "	5.00
Knizik Bros	" "	1.00
Mason	" "	1.00
M. Baker	" "	2.00
S. Nissinow	" "	5.00
L. Grenspon	" Newton	2.00
Mrs. Brookman	" "	2.00
Greenberg	"	1.00

Continued:—

		$
Benj. Gilfix	of Newton	100.00
Louis Baker	" "	100.00
Morris Gilfix	" "	100.00
Jac. Swartz	" Newton	50.00
Phil. Steinberg	" Newton	50.00
Jos. Roiter	" "	25.00
H. Perry	" "	25.00
A. Frackman	" "	25.00
J. Kligman	" "	25.00
M. Silverman	" "	15.00
Max Michman	" "	15.00
H. Bronfman	" "	10.00
George F. Richardson	" Newton Centre	1.00
Hon. John W. Weeks	" West Newton	100.00
George E. Stuart	" Newtonville	2.00

Continued,—

Max Blatt	of	Boston	$1.00
Grasher		"	"2.00
Cohen	"	"	1.00
M. Gold	"	Brighton	2.00.
M. Mindik	"	"	2.00
" Gordon	"	"	1.00
" Sigel	"	Newton	2.00
A. Sigel	"	Brighton	1.00
J. M. Woodworth	"	Newton	1.00
H. W. Crowell	"	"	1.00
J. A. McQuinn	"	"	1.00
H. Brower	"	Newton	1.00
S. Shain	"	"	1.00
A. Saltz	"	"	1.00
Maklowitz Bros	"	Boston	5.00
D. Rosenthal	"	Newton	2.00
L. Katz	"	"	1.00
L. Golden	"	Boston	2.00
J. Golden	"	"	2.00
A. Garber	"	Boston	1.00
A. Shapiro	"	Chelsea	1.00
J. Sheinfeld	"	"	1.00
J. W. Gray	"	Newton	1.00
J. M. Gallagher M.D.	"	"	20.00.
J. Stuart	"	"	5.00
Jacob M. Schiff of New York City			$100.00
A. Brackett & Son of Newton			10.00
J. T. Bailey	"	"	2.00
P. Swartz	"	Boston	1.00
L. Rosenstein	"	"	1.00
James L. Richards	"	Newton	5.00
Middlesex & Boston St. Ry	"	"	5.00
George M. Cox	"	"	2.00
J. F. Flanagan	"	"	20.00
Riley	"	Newton	50.00

11. City of Newton, Building Permit, 6 May 1912

Location, ownership and detail must be complete and legible.
Separate application required for every building.

CITY OF NEWTON.

PUBLIC BUILDINGS DEPARTMENT.

Application for Permit to Build.

No. 7

(OTHER THAN FRAME.)

Newton, Mass., May 6 1912

To the
PUBLIC BUILDINGS COMMISSIONER:—

The undersigned hereby applies for a permit to build, according to the following specifications:

1. If in a block, how many buildings will be erected?
2. Material? Brick Purpose of building? Synagogue
3. Name of Owner? Agudas Achim Anshei Sfard Address 170 Adams St. Newton
4. Name of Architect? [illegible] 35 Court St. Boston
5. Name of Builder? Isaac Frost, "94 Essex St. Malden
6. Street 170 Adams St. Newton No. Ward?
7. What is the nearest cross street?
8. If a dwelling, for how many families? Number of stores in the lower story? —
9. Size of lot, No. of feet front, 65 ; No. of feet rear, 65' ; No. of feet deep, 100
10. Size of building, No. of feet front, 35' ; No. of feet rear, 35' ; No. of feet deep, 50'
11. Height of building 2'
12. Distance of the proposed structure from the adjoining lot line 15
13. Distance from adjoining buildings, front, feet; side, feet; side, feet; rear, feet
14. Distance back from line of street? 10'
15. Thickness of walls { Basement, 20" ; 1st floor 12" ; 2d floor, ; 3d floor, ; 4th floor, ; 5th floor, ; 6th floor, ;
16. Size of rafters? 2x6
17. Size of floor timber, 1st floor 2x12 ; 2d floor ; 3d floor ; 4th floor
18. Foundation on Filled Land? No
19. Foundation, material of? Stone height of 5' thickness of 2' Mortar. Cement Brick
20. Fire stops, 1st floor Brick ; 2d floor ; 3d floor ; 4th floor
21. Will the roof be flat, pitch, mansard, or hip? Flat Material of roofing Comp.
22. Heating? Furnace Are all the flues lined?
23. Plumbing? [illegible]
24. What is the height of the cellar? 8'
25. What will be the height of ceilings on first story? 16 2nd 3rd 4th 5th 6th
26. Is the cellar to be occupied for a dwelling? —
27. Will any old material be used? None What kind? —
28. If there is a building already on the front or rear of the lot, give height. —
29. State how many means of egress are to be provided, one
30. Kinds of egress, [illegible]
31. Estimated cost? [illegible]
32. Plans submitted? Yes.

Show location by diagram on back of this form, giving relative distances from adjoining buildings.

SIGNATURE OF OWNER LESSEE OR AGENT. [illegible]

ADDRESS, 35 Court St. Boston

Plans in duplicate must be submitted to and approved by this Department before a permit for erection will be granted.

CITY OF NEWTON.

PUBLIC BUILDINGS DEPARTMENT.

No. 7

Application for Permit to Build.

OTHER THAN FRAME

LOCATION.

Street, Adams St. No. 170 Ward, 2.

Owner, Agudus Hiem Ashes Svrach

Architect, Samuel S. Levy

Builder, Isaac Fox

PERMIT GRANTED.

May 13, 1912

12. City of Newton, Plumbing Permit, 27 August 1912

All work hereafter performed must be tested by water pressure, and the Inspector must be notified when soil, drain pipe and all connections therewith are placed in position.

No. 362

CITY OF NEWTON.

Application for Permit to do Plumbing.

Newton, Mass., Aug 27 1912.

SEPARATE APPLICATION REQUIRED FOR EVERY BUILDING.

To the Inspector of Buildings:—

The undersigned hereby applies for a permit to perform plumbing work according to the following specifications.

1. Old or New building? New
2. Location of building, No. 170 114 Adams St.
3. Nearest cross street, Watertown St.
4. Owner and address, Congregation Agudass Achime.
5. ~~How many families~~ No Farm Jacob Swartz treasurer
6. Plumber and address, J. F. Gunnan 308 Watertown St
7. Connected with sewer and cesspool Sewer
8. Description of trap and clean-out in main drain, G & Cleanout.
9. Main drain, diameter in cellar, 4 Inch Material, Iron
   Above or below cellar floor? Below
10. Waste pipes, diameter, 2 inch Material, iron

PROPOSED FIXTURES IN DETAIL.

		Size and Material of Trap	Size & Material of Ventilation Pipe to Trap	Ventilation Pipes Run
BASEMENT	Two comb closets	4 iron	4 inch	Direct
	One sink	4 inch lead	2 inch 2 inch iron	Direct
FIRST STORY				
SECOND STORY				
THIRD STORY				
FOURTH STORY				
FIFTH STORY				

Application must be filed and written permit obtained before work is commenced.

LOCATION, OWNERSHIP, AND DETAIL MUST BE COMPLETE AND LEGIBLE.

MAKE SKETCH ON THE OTHER SIDE

Name J. F. Gunnan

Address 308 Watertown St Newton

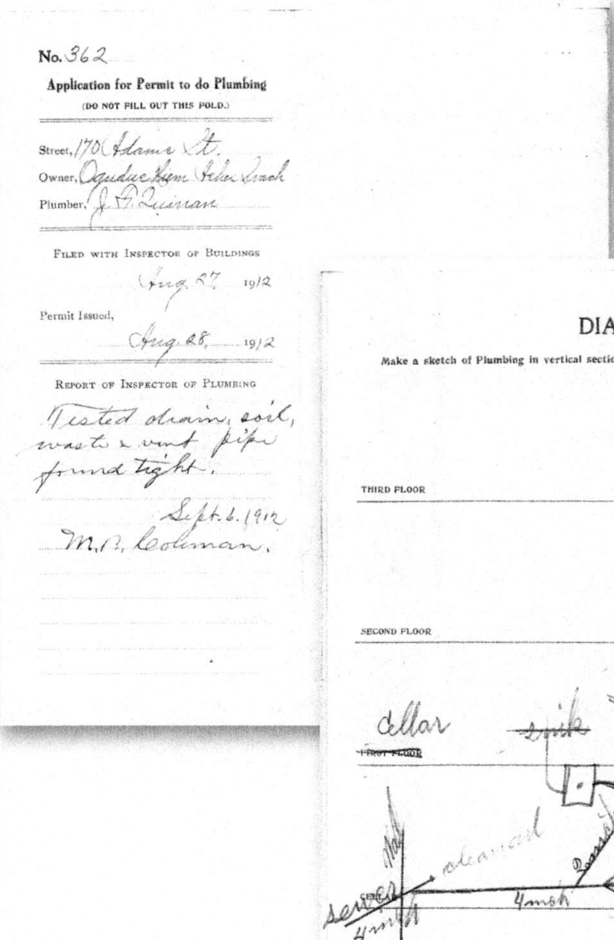

No. 362

Application for Permit to do Plumbing

(DO NOT FILL OUT THIS FOLD.)

Street, 170 Adams St.

Owner, Agudas Achim [illegible]

Plumber, J. F. Quinan

FILED WITH INSPECTOR OF BUILDINGS

Aug. 27, 1912

Permit Issued,

Aug. 28, 1912

REPORT OF INSPECTOR OF PLUMBING

Tested drain, soil, waste & vent pipe found tight.

Sept. 6. 1912

M. B. Colman.

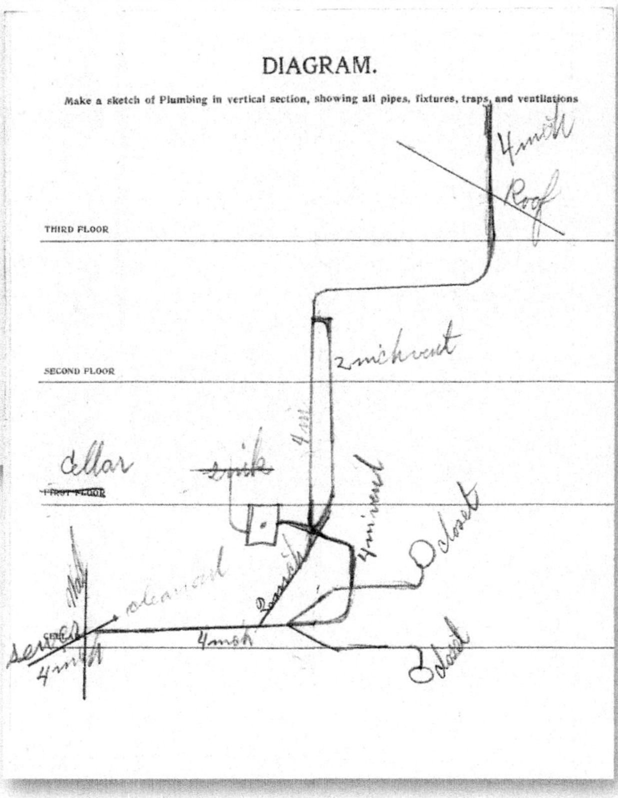

DIAGRAM.

Make a sketch of Plumbing in vertical section, showing all pipes, fixtures, traps, and ventilations

4 inch

Roof

THIRD FLOOR

2 inch vent

SECOND FLOOR

Cellar

~~FIRST FLOOR~~

4 in vent

closet

cleanout

4 inch

sewer

4 inch

closet

13. Registry of Deeds, Book 3705, pages 79-82, 26 June 1912

3705
79

in any event. To Have and To Hold the same to the said Mark Lewis and his heirs and assigns to their own use and behoof forever, subject nevertheless to the conditions therein contained and to redemption according to law. In Witness Whereof I hereto set my hand and seal this 24th day of June A.D. 1912. David Stern (seal) Commonwealth of Massachusetts. Suffolk ss. June 24, 1912. Then personally appeared the above named David Stern and acknowledged the foregoing instrument to be his free act and deed, before me, Joseph L. Klein Justice of the Peace.

Middlesex ss. June 26, 1912. 8 h. 45 m. A.M. Rec'd & Recorded.

Lewis to Charlestown Trust Co. Asst.

Know all Men by these Presents that I, Mark Lewis mortgagee named in and assignee and holder of three certain mortgages given by Wm. H. Clarke to me one dated December 5 A.D. 1911, and one other dated Jan 6, 1912, and another dated June 24th 1912, and recorded with Middlesex South District Deeds Book 3656 Page 141 and Book 3674 Page 323 respectively, the last one herewith, in consideration of one dollar and other valuable considerations paid by Charlestown Trust Company a Massachusetts Corporation the receipt whereof is hereby acknowledged do hereby assign, transfer and set over unto the said Charlestown Trust Company the said mortgage deed, the real estate thereby conveyed and the note and claim thereby secured. To Have and To Hold the same to the said Charlestown Trust Company and its successors and assigns to their own use and behoof forever, subject nevertheless to the conditions therein contained and to redemption according to law. In Witness Whereof I hereto set my hand and seal this 24th day of June A.D. 1912. Mark Lewis (seal) Commonwealth of Massachusetts. Suffolk ss. June 24, 1912. Then personally appeared the above named Mark Lewis and acknowledged the foregoing instrument to be his free act and deed before me, Stanley W. C. Downey Notary Public.

Middlesex ss. June 26, 1912. 8 h. 45 m. A.M. Rec'd & Recorded.

Congn. Agudas Achim Anshai Sfard of Newton to Watertown Savs. Bk.

Know all Men by these Presents that the Congregation Agudas Achim Anshai Sfard of Newton a religious corporation duly established under the laws of the Commonwealth of Massachusetts and located at Newton, in the County of Middlesex and Commonwealth aforesaid, in consideration of thirty five hundred (3500) dollars paid to it by the Watertown Savings Bank, a corporation established

3705
80

under the laws of said Commonwealth, the receipt of which sum is hereby acknowledged do hereby give, grant, bargain sell and convey to the said Watertown Savings Bank a certain parcel of land with the building to be erected thereon situated on the Northeasterly side of Adams Street in said Newton and bounded as follows: Beginning at a point on said northeasterly side of Adams Street at the southeasterly corner of lot numbered 21 (twenty-one) on a plan hereinafter referred to and thence running Northeasterly on said lot numbered 21 (twenty-one) one hundred (100) feet to land of S. Emma Stanton thence turning at a right angle and running Southeasterly on said land of S. Emma Stanton sixty (60) feet, thence turning at a right angle and running Southwesterly on a proposed court or private driveway one hundred (100) feet to Adams Street, thence turning and running Northwesterly on said Adams Street about sixty (60) feet to the point of beginning Containing six thousand (6000) square feet, more or less, and being a part of the lot numbered 19 (nineteen) on a plan recorded in Middlesex Southern District Registry of Deeds in Book of Plans No. 16 Plan 60, and being the same premises conveyed to grantor by Jacob Swartz by deed dated February 23, 1912, and recorded in said Registry in Book 3670 Page 55. To Have and To Hold the premises hereby granted with all the privileges and appurtenances thereto belonging, to the said Watertown Savings Bank and its assigns to its and their use and behoof forever. And the grantor hereby for itself and its successors and assigns covenants with the said Bank and its assigns that it is lawfully seized in fee simple of the granted premises, that they are free from incumbrances, that it has good right to sell and convey the same as aforesaid, and that it will and its successors and assigns shall forever Warrant and Defend the same to the said Bank and its assigns against the lawful claims and demands of all persons. Provided Nevertheless that if the grantor or its successors or assigns shall in three years from the date hereof pay to the said Bank or its assigns, the sum of thirty five hundred (3500) dollars with interest at the rate of five per cent per annum which interest shall be paid on the first days of April and October in each year, and at the maturity of the debt and until the full payment of the principal and interest aforesaid, shall pay all taxes and assessments (howsoever divided and to whomsoever assessed) upon the premises hereby conveyed, and upon the debt hereby secured, and shall, for the benefit of said Bank and its assigns, keep the buildings on said premises insured against loss by fire in a sum not less than thirty five hundred (3500) dollars, in such company or companies as it or they shall approve; (each and every policy to be held by the mortgagee or its assigns, and to be replaced with a satisfactory substitute at least three days before its expiration) and shall not commit or suffer any strip or waste of the premises hereby granted, or any breach of any covenant herein contained, then shall be void not only this deed but also a certain promissory note of even date herewith, which the grantor has signed, and in which it promises to pay to the said Bank or to its order, the said principal and interest at the times aforesaid. But upon default in the performance or observance of the foregoing condition the said Bank or its assigns having first published a notice of the time and place of sale once in each week for three consecutive weeks in some newspaper, if there be any published in said Newton, otherwise in any newspaper published in the County of Middlesex the first publication to be not less than twenty one days before the date of sale, may, by public auction in said Newton, sell the granted premises, or such portion thereof as may remain subject to this mortgage in case of any partial release of the same, with all the improvements appertaining thereto, and may, by proper deed or deeds, absolutely and in fee-simple, convey the same to the purchaser or purchasers. And such sale shall forever, both at law and in equity, bar the grantor and all persons claiming under it, from all right and interest in the premises thus conveyed. From the proceeds of such sale the said Bank or its assigns, shall be entitled to retain the full amount of the debt then secured by this deed, whether then or thereafter payable, and also all costs, charges and expenses to which the said Bank or its assigns, may have been subjected by reason of any default in the performance or observance of said condition, and shall render any surplus there may be to the grantor or to its successors or assigns. And it is agreed that, in case a sale shall be made as aforesaid, the grantor will, and its successors or assigns shall upon request, execute, acknowledge and deliver such further deeds or instruments as may be proper

3705
82

or necessary to confirm such sale, and to vest in the purchaser a perfect title to the premises sold, and the said Bank and its assigns are hereby appointed and constituted the attorney or attorneys irrevocable of the said grantor to execute and deliver to the said purchaser a full transfer of all policies of insurance on the buildings upon the land covered by this mortgage at the time of such sale, that the said Bank or its assigns or any person or persons in its or their behalf may purchase at such sale, and that any purchaser, other than the Bank or its assigns, shall not be responsible for the application of the purchase money and that until default in the performance or observance of the condition of this deed the grantor and its successors and assigns may hold and enjoy the premises hereby granted and receive the rents and profits thereof. In Witness Whereof the said Congregation Agudas Achim Anshai Sfard of Newton has caused its seal to be hereto affixed and these presents to be signed, acknowledged and delivered in its name and behalf by Jacob Swartz its treasurer this twenty fourth day of June A.D. 1912. Congregation Agudas Achim Anshai Sfard of Newton By Jacob Swartz Treasurer (seal) Commonwealth of Massachusetts. Middlesex ss. June 25, 1912. Then personally appeared the above named Jacob Swartz treasurer and acknowledged the foregoing instrument to be the free act and deed of the Congregation Agudas Achim Anshai Sfard of Newton before me, Reuben Forknall Justice of the Peace

Vote

At a special meeting of the Congregation Agudas Achim Anshai Sfard of Newton, duly called for the purpose and held at Newton, Mass., on the twenty fourth day of June 1912 the foregoing mortgage having been read and considered, the following vote was passed: Voted, that the treasurer Jacob Swartz is hereby authorized and instructed to execute, acknowledge and deliver in the name and behalf of the corporation, the mortgage which has just been read and to affix the corporate seal thereto. A true copy of vote. Attest: Joseph Kaplan Clerk of said corporation.

Middlesex ss. June 26, 1912. 9h. 20m. A.M. Rec'd & Recorded

Woburn Co-op. Bk to Johnson Disc

Know all Men by these Presents that the Woburn Co-operative Bank of Woburn Massachusetts the mortgagee named in a certain mortgage given by Thomas D. Johnson dated April 11, A.D. 1907 and recorded with Middlesex South District Deeds Lib 3293 Fol. 261 hereby acknowledge

14. Watertown Savings Bank, Original mortgage, 24 June 1912

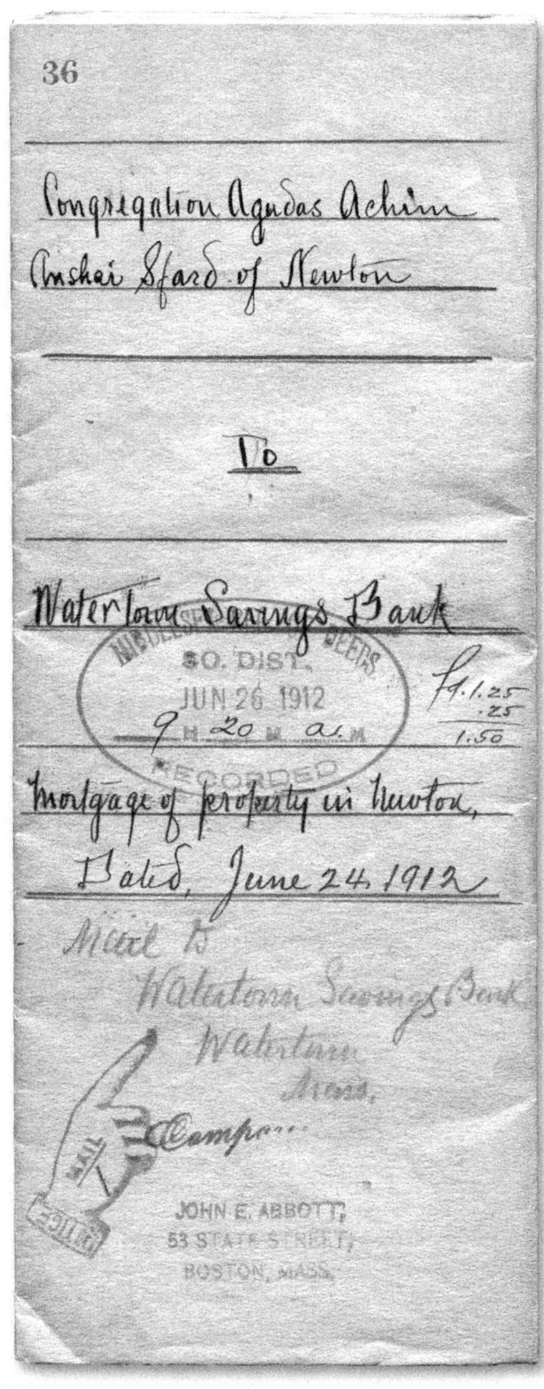

36

Congregation Agudas Achim
Anshai Sfard of Newton

To

Watertown Savings Bank

SO. DIST.
JUN 26 1912
9 H 20 M a. M
RECORDED

$1.25
.25
1.50

Mortgage of property in Newton,
Dated, June 24, 1912

Mail to
Watertown Savings Bank
Watertown
Mass.

JOHN E. ABBOTT,
53 STATE STREET,
BOSTON, MASS.

Document courtesy of Cynthia Spitzer

KNOW ALL MEN BY THESE PRESENTS That the Congregation Agudas Achim Anshai Sfard of Newton, a religious corporation, duly established under the laws of the Commonwealth of Massachusetts, and located at Newton, in the County of Middlesex and Commonwealth aforesaid, in consideration of thirty-five hundred (3500) dollars paid to it by the Watertown Savings Bank, a corporation established under the laws of said Commonwealth, the receipt of which sum is hereby acknowledged, do hereby give, grant, bargain, sell and convey to the said Watertown Savings Bank a certain parcel of land with the building to be erected thereon, situated on the Northeasterly side of Adams street, in said Newton, and bounded as follows:

Beginning at a point on said northeasterly side of Adams street at the southeasterly corner of lot numbered 21 (twenty-one) on a plan hereinafter referred to and thence running Northeasterly on said lot numbered 21 (twenty-one) one hundred (100) feet to land of S. Emma Stanton; thence turning at a right angle and running Southeasterly on said land of S. Emma Stanton sixty (60) feet; thence turning at a right angle and running Southwesterly on a proposed court or private driveway one hundred (100) feet to Adams street; thence turning and running Northwesterly on said Adams street about sixty (60) feet to the point of beginning. Containing six thousand (6000) square feet, more or less, and being a part of the lot numbered 19 (nineteen) on a plan recorded in Middlesex Southern District Registry of Deeds in Book of Plans No. 16, plan 60, and being the same premises conveyed to grantor by Jacob Swartz by deed dated February 23, 1912, and recorded in said Registry in Book 3670, page 557.

To have and to hold the premises hereby granted, with all the privileges and appurtenances thereto belonging, to the said Watertown Savings Bank and its assigns, to its and their use and behoof forever.

And the grantor hereby, for itself and its successors and assigns, covenants with the said Bank and its assigns that it is lawfully seized in fee simple of the granted premises; that they are free from incumbrances; that it has good right to sell and convey the same as aforesaid; and that it will, and its successors and assigns shall forever warrant and defend the same to the said Bank and its assigns against the lawful claims and demands of all persons.

Provided, nevertheless, that if the grantor or its successors or assigns, shall in three years from the date hereof, pay to the said Bank or its assigns, the sum of thirty-five hundred (3500) dollars, with interest at the rate of five per cent per annum; which interest shall be paid on the first days of April and October in each year, and at the maturity of the debt; and until the full payment of the principal and interest aforesaid, shall pay all taxes and assessments, (howsoever divided and to whomsoever assessed,) upon the premises hereby conveyed, and upon the debt hereby secured; and shall, for the benefit of said Bank and its assigns, keep the buildings on said premises insured against loss by fire in a sum not less than thirty-five hundred (3500) dollars, in such company or companies as it or they shall approve; (each and every policy to be held by the mortgagee or its assigns, and to be replaced with a satisfactory substitute at least three days before its expiration,) and shall not commit or suffer any strip or waste of the premises hereby granted, or any breach of any covenant herein contained;- then shall be void not only this deed, but also a certain promissory note of even date herewith, which the grantor has signed, and in which it promises to pay to the said Bank or to its order, the said principal and interest at the times aforesaid.

But upon default in the performance or observance of the foregoing condition, the said Bank or its assigns, having first published a notice of the time and place of sale, once in each week for three consecutive weeks, in some newspaper, if there be any, published in said Newton, otherwise in any newspaper published in the County of Middlesex, the first publication to be not less than twenty-one days before the date of sale, may, by public auction in said Newton, sell the granted premises, or such portion thereof as may remain subject to this mortgage in case of any partial release of the same, with all the improvements appertaining thereto; and may, by proper deed or deeds, absolutely and in fee-simple, convey the same to the purchaser or purchasers. And such sale shall forever, both at law and in equity, bar the grantor and all persons claiming under it, from all right and interest in the premises thus conveyed. From the proceeds of such sale the said Bank or its assigns, shall be entitled to retain the full amount of the debt then secured by this deed, whether then or thereafter payable, and also all costs, charges and expenses to which the said Bank or its assigns, may have been subjected by reason of any default in the performance or observance of said condition; and shall render any surplus there may be to the grantor or to its successors or assigns.

And it is agreed that, in case a sale shall be made as aforesaid, the grantor will, and its successors or assigns shall, upon request, execute, acknowledge and deliver such further deeds or instruments as may be proper or necessary to confirm such sale, and to vest in the purchaser a perfect title to the premises sold, and the said Bank and its assigns are hereby appointed and constituted the attorney or attorneys irrevocable of the said grantor to execute and deliver to the said purchaser a full transfer of all policies of insurance on the buildings upon the land covered by this mortgage at the time of such sale; that the said Bank or its assigns, or any person or persons in its or their behalf may purchase at such sale; and that any purchaser, other than the Bank or its assigns, shall not be responsible for the application of the purchase money; and that until default in the performance or observance of the condition of this deed the grantor and its successors and assigns may hold and enjoy the premises hereby granted and receive the rents and profits thereof.

IN WITNESS WHEREOF the said Congregation Agudas Achim Anshai Sfard of Newton has caused its corporate seal to be hereto affixed and these presents to be signed, acknowledged and delivered in its name and behalf by Jacob Swartz, its treasurer, this twenty-fourth day of June, A. D. 1912.

Congregation Agudas Achim Anshai
Sfard of Newton,
By Jacob Swartz
Treasurer.

COMMONWEALTH OF MASSACHUSETTS.

Middlesex, ss. June 26 1912.

Then personally appeared the above named Jacob Swartz, treasurer as aforesaid, and acknowledged the foregoing instrument to be the free act and deed of the Congregation Agudas Achim Anshai Sfard of Newton,

Before me, Reuben Forknall
Justice of the Peace.

At a special meeting of the Congregation Agudas Achim Anshai Sfard of Newton, duly called for the purpose and held at Newton, Mass., on the twenty-fourth day of June, 1912, the foregoing mortgage having been read and considered, the following vote was passed:-

VOTED, That the treasurer, Jacob Swartz, is hereby authorized and instructed to execute, acknowledge and deliver in the name and behalf of the corporation, the mortgage which has just been read, and to affix the corporate seal thereto.

A true copy of vote.

Attest:

Joseph Kaplan
Clerk of said corporation.

Cambridge, Mass. June 26 1912
9 o'clock and 20 minutes a M
Received and entered with Middlesex So. Dist. Deeds, Book 3705 Page 79 (Mtge + vote)
Attest: Edwin O. Childs
Register

FOOTNOTES

1. Newton City Directories
2. Wikipedia, Nonantum
3. Ekstein, Susan, page 831
4. Ekstein, Susan, page 839
5. Weingarten, page 11
6. Wikipedia, Jacob Schiff
7. Gilfix, Elliot, transcript, Historic Newton archives
8. Katz and Bayme, Continuity and Change, in Weingarten, page 38
9. Weingarten, page 40
10. Sherman. Moshe, in Weingarten, pages 34-36
11. Robinson, Ira, pp 503-504
12. Weingarten, page 84
13. Weingarten, page 82
14. Alpert, David, "The Man from Kovno"
15. American Jewish Year Book, 1915
16. Boston Landmarks Commission
17. Clingan, Carol, Database of all MA Synagogues, http://jgsgb.org/pdfs/MassSynagogues.pdf,
18. Zimiles, Murray, "Gilded Lions and Jeweled Horses" pp. 23-24. Professor Zimiles personally visited the Adams Street Shul to see our Ark in situ.
19. Wikipedia, Pale of Settlement
20. Petrovsky-Shtern, page 52
21. Antler, page 143, quoting Press, Fighting to Become American, pages 210-211
22. Dauber, page 112
23. Dauber page 131-132
24. Dauber page 16
25. Dauber page 289
26. Minter, page 9
27. Minter, page 38
28. Minter, page 31
29. Zimring, page 49
30. Zimring, page 28
31. Gilfix, Elliott, Historic Newton, interview, 1986
32. Newton Times, February 9, 1972

33. Ibid
34. Weingarten, page 3
35. Wikipedia, HIAS web site
36. Wikepedia, Galveston Movement
37. Zimring, page 44
38. Trentmann, page 598
39. Zimring, page 44
40. Wikipedia , 1924 Immigration Act
41. Zimring, page 44
42. Trentmann, page 598
43. Wikipedia, Immigration Act of 1924
44. Colletta, John, page 40
45. Swidey, Neil, pp 17-25
46. Durst, Dennis
47. Saada, web site
48. Prechtel-Kluskens, Claire, pp. 21-22
49. Holocaust Museum Holocaust Encyclopedia
50. Wikipedia, Breckenridge Long
51. Gilder Lehrman Institute of American History, Immigration Policy and World War II).
52. Wikipedia, US Naturalization Law
53. Belanger, Albert A.
54. Boston Globe, September 13, 2001
55. Wikipedia, Snuff
56. Touro Synagogue web site
57. Wieder, The Early Jewish Community of Boston's North End, ppg 50-51, in Weingarten, pages 47
58. Wieder, in Weingarten, page 48
59. Wieder, ppg 66-67, in Weingarten, page 49
60. Tablet magazine, (online) Tabletmag.com, Oct 29, 2012
61. The Forward, April 6, 2014
62. Newton Tab, April 3, 2013, page A8
63. Hal Leonard Corporation Web Site

BIBLIOGRAPHY

Alpert, David, "The Man From Kovno," americanjewisharchives.org/journal/PDF/1977

Antler, Joyce, *You Never Call, You Never Write*, Oxford University Press, 2007

Avoteynuonline.com, information about immigration

Belanger, Albert, *Les Franco-Américains et La Guerre Mondiale (The French Americans and the World War)*, Guide Franco-Americain, Fall-River Mass., 1921

Boston Daily Globe, November 21, 1904

Boston Landmarks Commission AREA FORM prepared as part of 1994 Survey of Dorchester, dated January, 1995 and recorded by Edward W. Gordon; C.G.Maguire Realty Co., owner. Samuel S. Levy, architect. 2 brick stores. Permit March 4, 1915. Completed Dec. 5, 1917. Jamaica Plain Historical Society by Richard Heath

Boyarin, Jonathan, *Mornings at the Stanton Street Shul*, Fordham University Press, 2011

Clingan, Carol, http://jgsgb.org/pdfs/MassSynagogues.pdf, a computer listing of every synagogue in MA, with dates and details, by city and neighborhood

Colletta, John P., *They Came in Ships*, Ancestry Publishing, Orem, Utah, 2002

Eckstein, Susan, "Community as Gift-Giving: Collectivist Roots of Volunteerism," American Sociological Review, Vol. 66, December 2001, ppgs 829-851

Dauber, Jeremy, *The Worlds of Sholem Aleichem*, Nextbook/Shocken, 2013

Durst, Dennis, "The Future in 1916; Madison Grant and the Passing of the Great Race," nomocracyinpolitics.com/Jan 21, 2016.

Fleishman, Thelma, "Agudas Achim Ashei Sfard,The Adams Street Synagogue, Newton, Massachusetts", an informal history based on an exhibition held at the Jackson Homestead, April-October 1986

Folk Art, Magazine of the American Folk Art Musuem, Fall 2007, pages 42-52

Gilfix, Beryl, "Adams Street Synagogue," Partners for Sacred Places, sacredplaces.org, 1995

Jewish Advocate, Boston, MA, Friday, August 2, 1912; Friday, December 6, 1912, page 7; Friday, December 20, 1912, page 2

"Kiddish, a Taste of Home," Tabletmag.org, October 29, 2012

Long, Breckenridge, Wikipedia

Minter, Adam, *Junkyard Planet*, Bloomsbury Publishing, 2013, pp 31-32

The Newton Tab, Apr 3, 2016, page A8

The Newton Times, July 31, 1912, page 1, The Newton Times, February 9, 1972, ppg 7, 8.

Petrovsky-Shtern, Yohanan, *The Golden Age: Shtetl—a New History of Jewish Life in East Europe*, Princeton University Press, page 165

Prechtel-Kluskens, Claire, "The Location of Naturalization Records," The Record, Vol 3, No.2, Nov 1996, pp 21-22

Robinson, Ira, "The First Hasidic Rabbis in North America," American Jewish Historical Society, American Jewish Archives.org/journal/1992, pp 503-504

Saada.org, [South Asian American Digital Archive], "Hindus too brunette to vote here," February 19, 2015

Sarna, Jonathan and Smith, Ellen, *The Jews of Boston*, The Combined Jewish Philanthropies of Greater Boston, Inc., Boston MA. 1995

Seixas and Washington letters, tourosynagogue.org

Shapiro, Laurie, "The syrupy tale of how Jews invited Kedem and modern America", the Forward, April 6, 2014

Sherman, Moshe, *Orthodox Judaism in America, A Biographical Dictionary and Sourcebook*, 1996

Smithsonian.com, "The US Government Turned Away Thousands of Jewish Refugees, Fearing That They Were Nazi Spies," Smithsonian.com, November 18, 2015

Solomon, Zachary, "Why Jews used to spit in shul," Jewniverse.com, Nov 19, 2015

Swidey, Neil, "Trump's Wall and Prescott Hall," Boston Sunday Globe Magazine, pp 17-25, February 5, 2017

Trentmann, Frank, *Empire of Things*, Harper/Collins Publishers, NY, 2016

Weingarten, Michael, *History of the Boston Synagogue, 1888-2013*, copyright 2013

Wilkes, Paul, *Excellent Catholic Parishes*, Paulist Press, New York, 2001

Zimiles, Murray, *Gilded Lions and Jeweled Horses: The Synagogue to the Carousel, Jewish Carving Traditions*, Brandeis University Press, 2007, pp 23-24

Zimiles, Murray, "The Synagogue to the Carousel, Folk Art" (Magazine of the American Folk Art Museum), Fall 2007, pp 43-50

Zimring, Carl, *Trash for Cash*, Rutgers University Press, 2005

Made in the USA
Middletown, DE
12 January 2021

31403604R10166